# ON THE WINGS OF THE DOVE

# On the Wings of the Dove

Noel Gibbard

BRYNTIRION PRESS

269·24

© Noel Gibbard 2002
First published 2002

ISBN 1 85049 186 0

*Cover design:* Jonathan Hurley Design Associates

Published by Bryntirion Press
Bryntirion, Bridgend CF31 4DX, Wales, UK
Printed by Gomer Press, Llandysul, Ceredigion, SA44 4QL

# Contents

# Acknowledgements

Many friends have helped with the preparation of this work, including Dr Phil Ellis, Dr Robert Newcombe, Lynda Newcombe, Catrin Lewis and Gill Burns, all of Cardiff; Mrs Jose and Mrs Dyer, Kenfig Hill, and Ronnie Perkins, Ty-croes, Ammanford. I am most grateful to them, and also to Pastor Desmond Cartwright for giving time to discussing aspects of the Pentecostal tradition and providing me with written material.

It was a pleasure to visit the Bruderhof in Donington, Kent. The Hindley family not only welcomed me but also set me on the track of relevant material relating to Germany.

The staff of the following libraries were of great help: The British Library, School of Oriental and African Studies, London; Angus Library and the Keston Centre, Oxford; New College, Edinburgh; the National Library of Wales, Aberystwyth, especially Dafydd Ifans; the Salisbury Library and the Central Library, Cardiff. I appreciate the co-operation of the Historical Society of the Presbyterian Church of Wales.

Librarians, missionary societies, colleges and archives sent me material, especially Spurgeon's College, London; McMaster College, USA; Grace Baptist Mission; South Africa General Mission; Worldwide Evangelisation Crusade; Valley Forge, Pennsylvania (ABMU); The Presbyterian Historical Society, Philadelphia; Nogent Sur Marne Bible College, France; and Tegai Roberts sent copies of valuable material from the archives in the Gaiman, Patagonia. The editor of *The Overcomer* gave permission to use Peter Frazer's tune 'Wondrous Cross'.

I must refer to the late Gerallt Wyn Davies, Chief Executive of the Evangelical Movement of Wales. He was a person who was concerned with revival and had been influenced by one of the children of the 1904–05 Revival in Wales. He urged me to pursue the work, and showed continuing interest in its development. Immediately before his period of suffering, he read all the chapters and made valuable suggestions.

Dr Eifion Evans agreed to write the Foreword. I appreciate this kindness from a friend and a person who has written extensively on revival.

Lastly I must thank Huw Kinsey for his general oversight, Edmund Owen for compiling the index, and above all Brenda Lewis for her care and patience in editing the work for the press.

Cardiff                                                                Noel Gibbard
July 2002

*To*
*Alun*

# Foreword

One of the most intriguing aspects of the Welsh Religious Revival of 1904 is its global spread. Within a comparatively short time of its commencement people were flocking to this little-known country on the Celtic fringe of Europe from neighbouring countries and across oceans. A decade later and all five continents had experienced its influence. From it there stemmed new ideas and new movements, not all spiritually creative or biblically sound, but challenging to faith, worship and practice. Its effects are still with us.

For such reasons, a book that explores that revival's international legacy is to be welcomed. With the advantage of historical perspective and expertise, Dr Noel Gibbard here offers an evaluation of that work that seeks to be biblical and comprehensive. He is familiar with the sources and writes sympathetically and yet judiciously. Universal in its scope and systematic in its treatment, the book gives a readable overview of the worldwide impact of that work of God. It will inform your mind, warm your heart and stimulate your faith.

Revival came to Wales in 1904 at a time when the foundations were being shaken, some in positive and others in negative ways. The means of communication were expanding, travel was easier, newspapers and magazines crossed borders and continents. Social and political structures were in turmoil, Christian dogma and values were under attack. These worldwide changes were challenged by a movement of God's Spirit in an isolated Principality through an insignificant human instrument. This was a former coal miner, Evan Roberts, and to compound the mystery, he ministered in a minority language. The impression left by this book is nothing if not thought-provoking. It chronicles the power of the gospel to transcend cultures, difficulties and prejudices.

Nor is the reader left in doubt as to the nature of true religious revival. The twentieth century has seen the emergence of many phenomena that lay claim to a Christian origin and to being initiated by the Holy Spirit. Dr Gibbard suggests the criteria by which they are to be measured, drawing attention to the centrality of God's Son and conformity to God's Word as the two most prominent features. In public worship, personal experience and evangelistic enterprise, revival always promotes the glory of God.

The Christian gospel transcends and transforms human culture. If the singing of hymns was a notable feature of the Revival in 1904, it was because those hymns had biblical content that gave expression to the convictions of those who sang them. The fervency and repetition may have been excessive to some observers, but there could be no doubt as to the reality of the spiritual involvement of most of the congregation. They were singing, not by the 'measure' of the tune in an emotional orgy, but by the 'weight' of theology in the words. Other people in another place may have shown different manifestations of personal commitment, but it was the same gospel that stirred them. What mattered was not the expression, of concern, plea or joy, of the moment, but the life-changing effect of the truth for the rest of that person's lifetime. The essence of Christianity is not a particular culture, to be transposed to another continent and imposed on an unsuspecting and unwilling people, but divine faith planted in the heart by the Holy Spirit and influencing all aspects of personality for good and for God. That is how true revival spreads, and human society is changed.

What was achieved then may be achieved again. Decline in numbers attending places of worship, the erosion of a Christian capital of standards and values, the emergence of 'New Age' culture, and of Postmodernism with its abandonment of absolute truth and right: neither any one of these, nor all of them together, is an obstacle to revival. On the contrary, it is when human resources have dwindled that revival is usually given. It is right to say 'given', because, as Dr Gibbard has shown so convincingly, such widespread gospel success can only come from God.

The story the author tells is an exciting one that holds out a glorious prospect. As long as it is the day of grace, what God did then, in the days of Evan Roberts and others like him, he can do again now, in our day. For this reason I heartily commend it.

Eifion Evans

# Abbreviations

| | |
|---|---|
| ABMU | American Baptist Missionary Union |
| AIM | Africa Inland Mission |
| B | Baptist |
| BMS | Baptist Missionary Society |
| *CGG* | *Cymru a'r Gymdeithas Genhadol* |
| CIM | China Inland Mission |
| CM | Calvinistic Methodist |
| CMA | Calvinistic Methodist Archives |
| CMS | Church Missionary Society |
| CWM | Council for World Mission |
| *DWB* | *Dictionary of Welsh Biography* |
| FFMU | Friends Foreign Missionary Union |
| LMS | London Missionary Society |
| NLW | National Library of Wales |
| PMU | Pentecostal Missionary Union |
| *RRW* | *Religious Revival in Wales* |
| SOAS | School of Oriental and African Studies |
| SVM | Student Volunteer Mission |
| SVMU | Student Volunteer Mission Union |
| *SWDN* | *South Wales Daily News* |
| *TCHB* | *Trafodion Cymdeithas Hanes y Bedyddwyr* |
| (W)MMS | (Wesleyan) Methodist Missionary Society |
| YMCA | Young Men's Christian Association |
| YWCA | Young Women's Christian Association |

# 1
# Background

In 1900, Europe was comparatively peaceful. It was the beginning of a new year and a new century, and there was a good measure of optimism. Yet, on the other hand, there was much uncertainty. Changes that had taken place in the previous century were leaving their mark on the church. On the Continent, especially, it was facing the challenge of socialism from without, and was being unsettled from within by radical changes in theology and biblical criticism.

## A 'leaning tower'?

Within the church the radical views of Julius Wellhausen (1844–1918) and David Strauss (1808–74) were exerting an increasing influence, whilst outside it Karl Marx and others were forcing it to rethink its teaching and mission. Christianity, as Owen Chadwick vividly expresses it, 'was the tallest pillar among existing landmarks', but the soil about it had been shifted and 'made the pillar look like the leaning tower of Pisa'.[1] Church leaders were rethinking Christianity, and a movement like the Social Democratic Party was attacking it: 'The Christian religion itself became one of the principal targets of Social Democratic propaganda.'[2]

In Germany and France the people were leaving the church or becoming indifferent to it. Levels of church attendance in Germany were very low in urban areas, and before the end of the nineteenth century there were signs of the same trend in rural areas too.[3] Representatives of the British and Foreign Bible Society were keenly aware of these changes. In Germany they found themselves working in a country where the majority of working men were estranged from Christianity.[3]

## Unrest

A number of events during 1905 serve to illustrate the unrest in many countries. The year was a significant one for France and Russia. In the former country a separation was achieved between Church and State, while in the latter religious toleration was introduced. Protestants in Roman Catholic France and Orthodox Russia were

13

given a new lease of life and were hoping for further renewal. Within the Scandinavian countries, it was the year when Sweden and Norway were separated politically—a separation that contributed to the national pride of both countries.

Furthermore, in 1905 the Russo-Japanese War ended, with Japan as the victor and not the great power Russia. Such a result 'was to enhance the self-respect of every thinking Asiatic'.[5] For Korea, however, this meant humiliation; and yet in defeat the country responded positively, realising more than ever that her destiny was in the hands of God. Many in Korea expected the church to organise opposition to Japan, and some responded to the call; but the majority were convinced that the great need was for spiritual renewal, which would be for the good of the church and the country as a whole.

Other events could be interpreted in different ways. An earthquake could be 'an act of God', the result of natural causes, or the voice of God. There was no doubt in the minds of the church people of Norway that the earthquake of 1905 was being used by God to call the people to repentance. They regarded this as the first step to revival. Pentecostals of America cherished the same belief when an earthquake occurred in 1906, and they considered the coming of the Spirit in the light of what they regarded as an apocalyptic event.[6] A famine in Japan created a vigorous response in the Christians to help those in need, and 'Hundreds of Japanese impressed by such selfless service were received into the faith.'[7]

## Christian churches and organisations

In spite of the uncertainties, there were those who saw Christianity not as a leaning tower, but rather as a rock that would stand, even if the soil around it were disturbed. This was the conviction of many within the church, and it was shared by organisations that were church-based, and by interdenominational and non-denominational societies.

The Evangelical Alliance (1846) brought individual evangelical believers together on an inter-church basis. The National Council of Evangelical Free Churches in Britain had branches in Australia, New Zealand and America. The Christian Endeavour Movement formed societies in churches, and by 1906 had 45,000 societies in the USA, about 10,000 in Britain and Ireland, almost 600 in India, and 300 in Germany.[8]

Other movements of note were the Young Men's Christian Association (YMCA) and Young Women's Christian Association (YWCA). At the death of its founder George Williams in 1905, the men's movement numbered 7,773 Associations, with 722,000 members.[9] The women's movement was very close to the heart of Mrs Jessie Penn-Lewis (of Neath, Richmond and Leicester), who will be mentioned often in this work. These organisations were evangelical and lay-orientated.

In addition, many new 'faith missions' were coming into being. One of the outstanding examples was the China Inland Mission of Hudson Taylor (CIM). Supporters of these various movements, societies and organisations were able to meet together in conventions for the promotion of spiritual life—whether large-scale conventions like Keswick in England, or smaller conventions such as were held in Germany and India.

### A. T. Pierson

In the USA, one of the most prominent missionary leaders was A. T. Pierson.[10] His work is significant in the context both of missionary societies and of the student world. He was one of the first members of the YMCA in New York and was influenced by the Revival of 1857–58. Under his revival preaching in Fort Street, Detroit, Michigan, hundreds of people were converted.

Pierson spoke at Northfield in 1886, which was D. L. Moody's first YMCA conference. Having been asked by Robert Wilder to hold an extra missionary meeting, he spoke on 'the evangelisation of the world in this generation'. This phrase became the slogan of the Student Volunteer Movement (SVM) pioneered by Robert Wilder. John K. Fairbank considered the YMCA to be 'the matrix' of the SVM and said, 'In both its origin and its early development the SVM owed a great deal to the religious revivalism that flourished within evangelical Protestantism.'[11]

A. T. Pierson also spoke at the British equivalent of the SVM, the Student Volunteer Missionary Union (SVMU) formed in 1892. Other aspects of his work involved editing *The Missionary Review of the World* and speaking at Keswick. Though a denominational man, he was a staunch supporter of the CIM and helped to organise the Africa Inland Mission (AIM).[12]

### Student work

A Students' Foreign Mission Union had been established in Britain in 1889, but under the leadership of an Aberystwyth College student, O. O. Williams, it was brought into the SVMU.[13] Williams became a missionary with the Presbyterian Church and was in Assam, India, when revival broke out there in 1905. The speakers at the SVMU

Liverpool Conference in 1896 included A. T. Pierson, George Williams (YMCA) and Sherwood Eddy. Count Moltke of Sweden was a visitor at its Conference at Aberystwyth in 1899; he and his wife were friends of Mrs Jessie Penn-Lewis.[14]

In 1895 the World Student Christian Federation was established— the plans for this were drawn up at Keswick—and John R. Mott was appointed as its secretary. The development of student work in South Africa owed much to the influence of Andrew Murray, who was a leading figure in the holiness movement and also a revival leader.[15]

## The gospel, prayer and revival

The supporters of these different societies and organisations were concerned with the gospel. In opposition to the liberal changes taking place in the church, they affirmed that the gospel was the power of God to change men and women. Man's sinful nature needed to be changed before there could be a change in the unjust structures of society. The gospel must be preached.

While there were well-known evangelists like D. L. Moody, Gypsy Smith and R. A. Torrey, a great deal of evangelism was done by men and women who were unknown.[16] Evangelism called for a measure of co-operation, as the Evangelical Alliance and the Federal Council of Evangelical Churches realised. The Council, under the leadership of Thomas Law, made Gypsy Smith its missioner, while the Alliance supported the work of R. A. Torrey.

There was also unanimity within the evangelical groupings as to the need for divine enabling in Christian work and the two main sources for that enabling, prayer and the Holy Spirit. It was at Keswick in 1902 that the Circle of Prayer for Worldwide Revival was inaugurated, though its beginnings can be traced to Chicago.[17] The call was taken up in Australia and reported in Keswick, where A. T. Pierson, Albert Head, C. G. Moore and F. Paynter were made honorary secretaries.

Within a few years, thousands had joined the Circle, promising to pray daily for worldwide revival. There was no subscription, but gifts were received and a register of members kept by local groups. Missionaries were expected to introduce the Circle to the national churches, so that missionaries, the churches and the Circle in Britain could be united in their praying. In harmony with this movement was the Fellowship movement in Germany, calling evangelicals within the State Church to pray for revival.[18]

The Evangelical Alliance arranged a week of prayer at the beginning of each year, at which intercession was made not only for home churches but also for churches overseas. During the first decade of the twentieth century, this week of prayer was to be significant in many revivals in many countries.

An organisation like the YMCA also welcomed revival and promoted it whenever possible. As already implied, revival held an important place in A. T. Pierson's thinking, and he, Robert Wilder and R. A. Torrey argued for a baptism of the Spirit separate from regeneration. It was to the Holy Spirit that they looked for spiritual renewal and revival in the churches.

## Wales

The churches in Wales were aware of significant political and religious changes in their own country as well as in other countries. Keir Hardie was elected as Member of Parliament for Merthyr and Aberdare in 1900, and his Independent Labour Party (ILP) was based on Christian principles. The development of socialism, however, meant the 'politicisation of labour', which created tension between the ILP on the one hand and the Liberal Party and the church on the other. 'The Nonconformists, with their tradition of Liberal politics, became increasingly concerned that the estrangement of working-class men from the chapels often accompanied their adoption of socialism.'[19] There were signs that theological modernism was gaining ground, though not so quickly as in England and Scotland.

Evangelical movements like the Christian Endeavour, the Evangelical Alliance and the National Council of Evangelical Free Churches had forged links with Wales. And in the colleges a number of Welsh students were associated with the SVMU. Ever since 1896 a strong desire had been expressed for a 'Keswick' in Wales, and in 1903 the dream was realised at Llandrindod.[20]

In Wales, as in other countries, there was a longing for a spiritual awakening, and denominational and informal meetings were held to cry to God that he would visit the land in the power of the Holy Spirit.[21] There is evidence for such gatherings in South Wales, and in West Wales a group of Presbyterian ministers were holding meetings to deepen their own spiritual life and that of their people.[22]

### *The West Wales meetings*

These Presbyterian ministers were Calvinistic Methodists who valued their Calvinistic and revival background, and one of them was a child of the 1859 Revival. They were also sensitive to the influence of the holiness movement. One of them had read Andrew Murray's *With Christ in the School of Prayer*, while another was acquainted with

John McNeil's *Spirit-Filled Life*.[23] The first meeting that they arranged was addressed by W. W. Lewis (Carmarthen) and J. M. Saunders and his wife (Swansea), all three of whom had received 'fresh inspiration' at the first Welsh Keswick.[24] Five meetings were arranged during 1904, and at the one that was held in Newquay in February, the testimony of Florrie Evans transformed the whole meeting.[25]

In September of that year Seth Joshua was visiting West Wales. He was the Forward Movement missioner of the Presbyterian Church of Wales, and his ministry had already been used to the salvation of scores of people. When he arrived he found a 'remarkable revival spirit'. That was on 18 September, and on the following day he recorded in his diary:[26]

> The revival is breaking out here in greater power. Many souls are receiving full assurance of salvation. The spirit of prayer and testimony is falling in a marvellous manner. The young are receiving the greatest means of blessing. They break out into prayer, praise, testimony and exhortation in a wonderful way.

And again on 20 September he wrote, 'The revival goes on.'

### Evan Roberts

That same month, Sidney Evans of Gorseinon, Swansea, was returning to the Preparatory School in Newcastle Emlyn to prepare for the Christian ministry. He was joined by Evan Roberts from Loughor, a village adjoining Gorseinon. Both of them were led through a spiritual crisis in separate Seth Joshua meetings, Sidney Evans at Newcastle Emlyn and Evan Roberts at Blaenannerch.

At the close of an early morning meeting at Blaenannerch, Seth Joshua prayed using the words 'Bend us', and in the 9 o'clock meeting those words burned in the heart of Evan Roberts. He fell on his knees, with his arms on the seat in front, and his tears felt like blood gushing from his face. As he perspired a lady kindly wiped his face. After two terrible minutes he cried out, 'Bend me! Bend me! Bend us!' Peace ruled in his heart and the congregation sang, 'I am coming, Lord, coming now to Thee'.[27]

On the last day of October in 1904, the young ex-miner, having spent only a few weeks in the Preparatory School, was on his way home to Loughor, assured by the guidance of the Spirit, a vision, and the counsel of a minister, that this was the right path for him to take. At meetings held during his first week back at Loughor, Evan

Roberts made known the four things that he considered necessary for revival:

- Confession of known sin.
- Removal of everything doubtful.
- Entire commitment to the Spirit.
- Public confession of Christ.[28]

The meetings continued in the second week, and on Sunday 13 November Evan Roberts was in Trecynon, Aberdare. This marked the beginning of a lengthy first tour through Glamorgan.

During that same period in November, revival broke out in Ammanford.[29] And on 8 November, R. B. Jones of Porth, Rhondda, began a series of meetings in Rhos, near Wrexham, which led to revival in that area.[30]

Between November 1904 and January 1906 Evan Roberts made four prolonged journeys. Then, after holding a few further meetings, he retired exhausted to the home of Mr and Mrs Penn-Lewis in Leicester.

*The news spreads*

Newspaper reports of the Revival appeared at the end of the second week of November 1904 and continued to spread news of the awakening. For a few years, the kingdom of God was to have greater prominence than the British Empire, and the experience of ordinary people would be read more avidly than the speeches of well-known politicians! W. T. Stead reminded his readers that while the British Empire 'floats upon the British navy' and the 'British navy steams on Welsh coal', it was from the Welsh churches that the 'compelling force' would come to revitalise not only Wales but the whole world.[31]

Not only did the news go out from Wales, but before the end of that year visitors began coming in from other countries to see what was happening. Some of those who came had had previous connections with Wales.[32]

# Part I
# EUROPE

# 2

# France

The Rev. Alfred Tilly, retired minister of Tredegarville Baptist Church, Cardiff, died in August 1905,[1] having enjoyed ten months of the Revival that had broken out in November 1904. He had welcomed the breaking of the dawn in Wales, as did two of the mourners at his funeral, his daughter Harriett and her husband Pastor Cadot of Chauney, France. Both families were staunch Protestants and wholeheartedly supported the Revival of 1904–05, and so the close family link between Chauney and Cardiff was further cemented by a strong religious bond.

Early in 1905 Pastor Cadot attended a number of revival meetings in Cardiff and district. On Monday 7 January he was present at a meeting at Tabernacle, Cardiff, where the congregation included representatives from many countries:[2]

> There were almost as many nationalities as on the Day of Pentecost, English, Irish, Scotch, Welsh, Jews, French, Swedes, Greeks, Italians, negroes and mulattoes, soldiers in uniform, civic dignitaries, learned professors, ministers of the Gospel, wealthy merchants, noted journalists—surely St Peter himself hardly looked out on a stranger or more varied throng.

Some of the eminent men referred to in the above report occupied the platform: among them were the Pastor of the Church,[3] a Justice of the Peace,[4] the Pastor from Paris, a Member of Parliament,[5] the Principal of the Baptist College,[6] and a prominent literary-political figure.[7] Although the Revival was a people's movement, they valued the support of the professional class.

France and Pastor Cadot were again in the forefront when he visited the Neath district.[9] The meetings at Tonna on 12 January lasted all day. Before the arrival of Evan Roberts a number of people took part spontaneously, including the two sisters Annie and Maggie Davies from Maesteg, and Cadot himself, speaking half-English and half-French.[10] The following day at Aberdulais the Frenchman related his conversion experience and 'implored the prayers of the congregation for his beloved France, captured by the Priest and the Rationalist'.[11] The congregation sang 'O Happy Day', and a fellow countryman of Cadot responded in French. 'Having shaken hands with the missioner, both went on their knees hand in hand, and there they prayed quietly, but fervently, for a revival in France.'[12]

Alfred Tilly was not the only one in Cardiff with French connections. During a meeting at Tabernacle William Edwards, Principal of the Baptist College, read a letter from a friend in Paris. He believed that revival was beginning in that city because in one meeting sixty people had professed conversion.[13]

### Reuben Saillens

Another eminent French pastor to visit Wales was Reuben Saillens, a Baptist.[14] He was a former student at the East London Training Institute and became closely associated with Baptist and revival movements in Europe. The Pioneer Mission[15] had his full support, and when he and M. Blocher attended the British Auxiliary they would tour England, doing so in 1904 and 1905.[16] During February 1905 Pastor Saillens was in Wales with a threefold purpose: to witness revival scenes, to be quickened in spirit personally, and to become acquainted with the hymns of the Revival, which he wished to translate into French.[17]

The Saillens company included his daughter. She was chief soprano in the choir of Queen Wilhelmina of Holland and was thrilled with the revival singing.[18] However, she had doubts about the revival movement because of its emotionalism. But during her last meeting in Wales, a meeting that took place at Saron, Nant-y-moel, in the Ogmore Valley, these doubts were dispelled. Earlier meetings had seemed so strange to her that she felt as if she were in a Hindu or Roman Catholic festival; and yet that could not be so, as there were no idols, images or ritual, and the spirit was different.

The meeting at Saron was not due to start until 7 o'clock, but by 5.30 p.m. the chapel was full. The visitor from Paris and her hostess, Mrs Jones the butcher's wife, were unable to enter because of the crowd, and they failed to get in through the vestry either. Returning to the front of the chapel, Mrs Jones suggested to a friend, Mrs Adams, that they should ask a policeman for assistance, explaining that they had a visitor from France whose father was in the chapel already. The policeman offered to help the young lady climb over the railings, but she was reluctant to do this. Anxious to assist, he then had a word with the men crowding round the entrance, and one of them cried, 'Let the two ladies through.' The two were allowed in, while Mrs Adams left for Bethel, where another revival meeting was taking place.

Greatly relieved, the two women entered the porch. Here there was another policeman, helmet in hand, weeping, with his ear to the door in order to catch every word from inside. When they reached the gallery, two young lads gave up their seats for them. Evan Roberts was in the pulpit and Annie Davies at his side praying, her face hidden in her hands. Evan Roberts addressed the congregation expressing concern that those present were Christians; unbelievers should be brought in who needed to be saved. A young woman interrupted the speaker with her crying, but he bowed his head for a while, collected himself and continued.

Although she could not understand anything, the visitor from France felt an invisible power gripping her heart. The whole congregation was united in praise as seven to ten people took part at once, but there was communion, not confusion. Many professed conversion and the meeting ended with the enthusiastic singing of *'Diolch Iddo'* (Praise Him). She was convinced that it was a genuine work of the Spirit of God, and that that same Spirit had transformed her own heart. She also marvelled at the love of 'these poor ignorant people' for God and for their neighbours.[19]

A Swiss pastor had accompanied Pastor Saillens on his visit to Wales in February 1905, and during March of that year there was another party from France and Switzerland in the Pontypridd district. It included Mlle Merle d'Aubigné, daughter of the well-known historian of the Reformation. The company visited Sardis and Penuel in Pontypridd before moving on to Hebron, Ton Pentre. The highlight of their stay was a visit to Penrhiw Colliery, Pontypridd, where they took part in an underground service.[20] From the bowels of the earth prayer was offered to the throne of heaven, John chapter 17 was read, and hymns sung, including 'Crown Him' and the 'hymn of the miner'—*'Yn y dyfroedd mawr a'r tonnau'* (In the deep waters and the waves).[21]

*Paul Passy*
Reuben Saillens was pastor of a Baptist church in Paris, but there were two other Baptist churches in Paris and Paul Passy was a member in one of them. That church, like the one in which Saillens ministered, belonged to the southern section, while the third was in the northern section.[22] Paul Passy was a Professor in the Sorbonne; he, Dr Sweet of Oxford and Dr Viëtor of Marburg were regarded 'as the three greatest authorities on phonetics'.[23] In many ways Paul Passy

was different from most of the visitors, being a distinguished academic and 'an enthusiastic Christian Socialist'.[24] He had an earlier link with Wales through his father Frederick Passy, who was a friend of Henry Richard, the apostle of peace.[25]

Like the other leaders from France, Paul Passy was a staunch Protestant. He was convinced that the Revival would help the cause of Protestantism in his own country and suggested that Christian workers should go from Wales to Brittany to encourage the struggling Protestants in that land. When Taldir, an eminent editor and literary figure in Brittany, heard this suggestion, he was most unhappy and made it clear that while Welshmen were warmly welcomed in his country, they should not proselytise among Roman Catholics.[26]

Passy corresponded with Evan Roberts and his secretary Mardy Davies, and visited Wales in 1905 and 1906. In August 1905, he spoke on the Second Coming of Christ at Bethel, Pontycymer, and was also present in a meeting at Tabernacle, Pontycymer.[27]

*Henri Bois and Rogues de Fursac*
To the list of prominent visitors two more names must be added: those of Henri Bois and Rogues de Fursac. Bois was a committed Christian, while de Fursac was an atheist commissioned by the Minister of Home Affairs to research into the influence of mysticism on disorder of the mind. The latter did not arrive until 1906, but Bois was in Wales during Easter 1905.[28] He visited Cardiff, Aberdare and the Rhondda Valleys in South Wales, and went to Trevor and Rhos (Wrexham) in North Wales. He had been provided with an introduction to William Edwards, Principal of the Baptist College, but when Bois arrived, he was away on a revival tour. However, on 11 April the Frenchman went through driving rain to see him and found the Principal at home.[29] After that Bois kept in constant touch with him.

One of the visitor's cherished experiences was taking part in a service underground in Pontypridd. He was lowered in a cage with eight others, and as soon as they reached pit bottom they could hear singing in the distance which they recognised as 'Guide me, O Thou great Jehovah' to the tune 'Bryn Calfaria'. Seeing between sixty and a hundred miners crouching in worship, Bois was reminded of the Roman catacombs and felt grateful that there was no persecution. What struck him was the prayerfulness of the miners: they were praying while singing, and praying while listening to the reading of God's Word. In the light of the safety lamp one of the company read from John chapter 1. In the darkness of the underground, the lamps, the reading, and the singing of 'Lead, kindly light' held a special significance. The miners who prayed were conscious of this and thanked God for the light that had shone into their hearts.[30]

While in North Wales, Henri Bois heard the visionary, Mrs Jones (Egryn), speaking. Her visions, and those of Evan Roberts, were important for him in assessing the Revival. In South Wales he came into contact with several people who would influence his response to the awakening. These were William Edwards; Sidney Evans, the future brother-in-law of Evan Roberts; Dan Roberts, Evan's brother; the lady singers; and visitors from abroad, including two students from Holland.[31]

## Holland

Included in the parties from the Continent were a number of Dutchmen, some of them having no English at all. It is recorded that they were present in Briton Ferry and Cwmavon. One of them had an unusual meeting with Mardy Davies and Evan Roberts. The two men were picnicking near Pontycymer, when a Dutchman appeared and communicated with them by using a Dutch-English dictionary. Through sign language he asked Evan Roberts to pray for him. This is one of many examples of the Revival breaking down barriers. The Dutchman, of course, would value such an experience highly; on returning home he would be able to tell his people that he had met Evan Roberts personally. Such meetings had special significance for many people during the Revival.

This Dutchman may possibly have been Johannes de Heer (1866–1961), a businessman and evangelist. In 1903 a word from Scripture had come to de Heer's mind from I Kings 5:9, and the words 'by sea' pointed him to England. He crossed to London, and there he bought a copy of *Victory Songs* and was convinced that Holland needed such a hymn book. After returning home he started collecting hymns, but before he had finished he heard of the Revival in Wales. With five friends, two of them ministers, de Heer left for Wales in February 1905. The Dutchman met Evan Roberts and took part in a meeting in Briton Ferry. During that meeting he saw in flaming letters on the opposite wall the very words from I Kings 5:9 that had come to his mind in 1903. He now had no doubt that Holland needed not only a hymn book but also the message of revival.[32]

Johannes de Heer returned to Holland and dedicated himself to the task of spreading the revival message. He finished the hymn book and made good use of it in revival meetings. He and his wife would take part in these; they would sing together, the husband also playing the organ or piano. The three themes of the preacher's message were redemption, the filling of the Spirit and the Second Coming of the Lord Jesus Christ. There were many visible results in terms of conversions, and a deep concern for revival was created. But Holland did not experience such a powerful revival as the people of Wales had known.[33]

The parties that came to Wales were interdenominational. Of those who came from France, Saillens and Passy were Baptists, while Cadot belonged to the Reformed Church. Lenoir and Lortsch (of whom more will be said later in this chapter) represented the Free Church and the British and Foreign Bible Society respectively. Most of those who came were not merely observers but willing participants. Rogues de Fursac would have been more of an observer than the rest, since he studied the Revival as a psychiatrist.

## Progress in France

The French papers took up the matter of revival with unusual zeal. According to the *British Weekly*, 'Exceptional interest and sympathy seems to be evinced in France, where some papers are issuing Revival supplements giving the life story of Evan Roberts.'[34] The papers *Le Christianisme*,[35] *L'Eglise Libre*[36] (which included a photograph of Evan Roberts), and *Le Martin*[37] were supportive; also *La Cloche d'Alarme* edited by Paul Passy[38] and *L'Evangeliste*,[39] which included an article by Mlle d'Aubigné on her return from Wales. *L'Aube* was 'the modest organ of the friend of revival'.[40] The most surprising contribution was from W. T. Stead, as he himself explains: 'I have been asked by the most widely circulated French review, *La Revue*, formerly *La Revue des Revues*, of Paris, to write a long article for their next number, setting forth the whole story of the revival.'[41] He was writing in February 1905, and in March the Methodist George Whelpton referred to W. T. Stead's 'remarkable article' in *La Revue*.[42]

According to the reports, French people were returning from Wales during February and March 1905. Even Cannes, not exactly a holy city, could not avoid the influence of the awakening. When J. J. Lucas visited the place on a Sunday in February, he preached in the morning at Holy Trinity, where Delabilière, formerly of All Saints, Birmingham, was chaplain. At the end of the sermon there was a time of open worship, in keeping with the emphasis on the freedom of the Spirit so prominent in the meetings in Wales.[43] The person who led in prayer was Sir George Williams (YMCA). J. J. Lucas left Cannes to visit other districts in order to give accounts of the Welsh Revival.

Nîmes is mentioned as a place deeply influenced by revival. When Pastor Saillens and Lenoir went there, they were encouraged by the number of conversions and on one evening had to open three buildings to accommodate the people.[44] The representatives of the Pioneer Mission supported the meetings wholeheartedly and co-operated with R. Dubarry, pastor of the church at Nîmes.[45]

During another visit to Nîmes Pastor Saillens' wife accompanied him, and they also visited Cannes, Marseilles, Montpellier and Vergeze in the South of France. Crowds attended the meetings at Marseilles; Pastors Houter and Lenoir assisted the husband and wife at this venue, while at Nîmes they were welcomed by a Methodist minister.[46] The meetings at Marseilles were held in the established Church, and eight hundred people attended for seven successive nights. Most of the gatherings were turned into times of prayer. At Nîmes, all the evangelical ministers in the area joined together. The meetings were held in the Methodist chapel, 'a large, compact place, perfect in its acoustics';[47] most of the meetings were long, one lasting from eight o'clock until eleven thirty. The fervency of the worship reminded some of those present of revival meetings in Wales.[48]

### Revival?

But was there revival in France? One leader acknowledged, 'Indeed, it is not revival yet, but the preparation and first fruits, for a more extensive work of grace.'[49] Pastor Saillens was more optimistic: 'We begin to see in Paris, what had been seen in Wales, and we see it in Marseilles, in French Switzerland and in the north of France.'[50] One of the places that had created great expectancy in Pastor Saillens was Vevey:[51]

> But our greatest encouragement was at the Vevey, in the Canton de Vaud. For three nights in succession I held gospel meetings in the theatre, the audience growing larger every day, and the place holding 1,000 being too small on the last night. Scenes identical with those we had seen in Wales happened in the after-meetings— people breaking down in prayer, crying for mercy, and rejoicing in it.

The meetings were supported by all the denominations.

Some of the Swiss Baptist churches belonged to the southern section, and Pastor Saillens received good news from La Chaux-de-Fonds, where Pastor Oriol, who was a former Spurgeon's student, ministered:[52]

Hundreds of conversions have taken place lately in revival meetings. Only a week ago at a gathering of about 1,000 young people in the Swiss town of La Chaux-de-Fonds, over 400 decision cards were handed in, and in the evening the same day a great crowd of 2,500 assembled to hear the Word, after which a prayer meeting at which everyone remained was held for over half an hour, with many decisions for Christ.

Four features are evident from this account: there were large crowds; the preaching was central; it was confirmed by prayer, and they made use of decision cards.

Pastor Saillens was glad of support from Britain. He visited London quite often and reported to Spurgeon's College on what was happening in France. He was present at a Conference on Revival at the College in May 1905, in the company of Thomas Spurgeon (College Principal), the Rev. Archibald Brown, and evangelist R. A. Torrey.[53] The Frenchman gave an optimistic account of what was happening in France, while R. A. Torrey during his address praised God for Evan Roberts. Pastor Saillens not only addressed the Conference but also sang his own version of '*Dyma gariad*' (Here is love). The Welsh Quartette (four Welsh students) sang their favourite hymns, all four of them having been in revival meetings in Wales during the Christmas vacation.[54]

Professor Passy was also busy commending the Revival in Wales and exhorting the people to more earnest prayer for revival. He and M. Sainton were members of the Rue de Lille Church in Paris, and took an active part in itinerant evangelism. According to the Professor, the revival movement was in full force in Lens and Levin,[55] and there was no doubt that the work of Pastor Cadot had contributed significantly to the success. He was by this time general evangelist for the northern section.[56] Passy himself spent five days at Lens and Levin, and many of those present had been to meetings in Wales. These five days, he reported, 'were the happiest of my life . . . On Saturday the chief meeting lasted from 3.30 to 9 p.m.; enthusiasm was at a high pitch all the time.'[57] The visitor was sure, however, that there was no sensationalism. Initially, the blessing was confined to a small Baptist church, but now it was spreading. One main reason was the return of Pastors Lenoir and Parker from Wales, and they had brought the Protestant denominations together. Even the streets and the ships were now echoing with revival songs.[58]

The Baptist work in Lens and Bethune was presided over by M. Farelly, a cousin of Pastor Cadot. In those places, 1905 was a very fruitful year and 322 baptisms had been recorded. Farelly's report also confirmed the impact of the Welsh Revival on those two places.[59]

*Paris*

It was only natural for the missioners to turn to Paris, the French capital, and the place with the highest number of Protestants of different traditions. R. Tudur Jones refers to an 'unexpected' description of Passy in Paris by Sir Robert Bruce Lockhart:[60]

> When I first saw him he was under the influence of Evan Roberts, the Welsh evangelist, and for the only time in my varied career I had the strange experience of appearing on the platform and singing Welsh revivalist hymns in French before a Paris slum audience. Passy said the prayers and played the harmonium with three fingers, while I sang the solos supported by a chorus of three trembling English students.

Mrs Penn-Lewis, however, did not regard her visit to Paris as a 'strange experience'. She was very much at home there, and she commented approvingly on the way that Saillens and Bois had reported the Welsh Revival. Saillens held a meeting in the YMCA and gave an account of the Welsh Revival to a congregation of seven hundred.[61]

Bois also held a meeting on his return from Wales; it took place in L'Oratoire, the leading Presbyterian Church in Paris. Once he had finished speaking, the meeting was left open for worship; the *British Weekly* believed that this was something new in Paris.[62] Bois could not forget the singing in Wales of '*Dyma gariad*' (Here is love) and referred to it as 'the love song' of the Revival. He marvelled at how effective the singing of that hymn was at L'Oratoire, even in a French translation, to a Welsh tune ('Tôn y botel'), with a French soloist.[63]

One result of these reports by Bois, Saillens, Passy and others was the formation of a number of united prayer meetings. At least one church that had been without a prayer meeting established one after the pastor came home from Wales.

Mrs Penn-Lewis herself addressed a united meeting in Paris, chaired informally by Professor Passy.[64] When she finished speaking to the congregation of seventy there was an outburst of praise: 'After I had given a brief message on what I had seen in Keswick and Wales, there was a blessed outburst of prayer.'[65]

*Conferences and conventions*

Other meetings of an interdenominational nature were those held by the YMCA, and the conventions that took place from 1905. The International Conference of the YMCA was held in Paris in 1905 and attracted thousands of visitors; they filled the Trocadero Palace, which had a seating capacity of seven thousand. Meetings were held in a revival atmosphere.[66]

Ministers from all the Protestant denominations came together to inaugurate the Valentigny Convention: 'The wonderful way in which the grace of God has manifested itself in the Welsh Revival has caused them and other French Christians to have a share in the blessing.'[67] The invitation was sent out by Pastor Babut ('the eloquent preacher and pastor of Nîmes'), Houter (President of the Home Missions of the Reformed Church), Blocher (Free Church), Pastor Saillens (Baptist), and Ullern (the Methodist who had been holding revival meetings in the south).[68] The convention meetings concentrated on prayer and Bible study during the day and evangelism in the evening. The eleven o'clock meeting was of a more private nature, for the discussion of such questions as

- What are the causes of the delay of revival in our country?
- Can we obtain revival now?
- In what measure can we expect revival to spread in our country, and prepare our country for the coming crisis?

Two main reasons were given for the dire need of revival: 'The double opposition of Rome and of infidelity.'[69]

**Extending the boundaries**

In the north of France, Pastor Cadot was joined by his wife, who travelled extensively over a wide area, while Mlle d'Aubigné was concerned with revival and its social implications, especially the promotion of temperance.[70] In pursuing this work she crossed the border into Belgium. In Liège in that country the children had their own prayer meeting, while at Charleroi, Auchel and La Fère what was noticeable was the number of conversions and the open confession of sin. One correspondent claimed, 'It would fill a volume to recount the marvellous things we saw' (at Henin-Lietard).[71]

The Synod of the Belgian Christian Church took the revival so seriously that it altered the 1905 agenda in order to discuss the Revival in Wales.[72] The Baptists of the Franco-Belgian Association were greatly encouraged by the interest in revival, and especially by the hundred and ten conversions that were recorded for 1905.[73]

Pastor Saillens extended his interest into Holland, where there were signs of awakening in some of the churches and a further quickening when some of the Dutchmen returned from revival meetings in Wales. One pastor was determined to go to Wales alone. He wanted to avoid all influences that would force him to a premature judgement. He visited Cardiff, Pontycymer and Bridgend, and was favourably impressed with what he saw and heard. In spite of the fact that he had very little English, he was enabled to speak fluently in that language.[74] At the beginning of 1906 Pastor Wilde was rejoicing because of the marvellous revival of the 'past three months'.[75] Pastor Saillens was still visiting Holland during 1906 and 1907 in order to encourage 'the friends of revival'.[76] J. Edwin Orr summarises the main characteristics of the work in the Netherlands: 'The Awakening in the Netherlands took the form of an anticipated multiplication of prayer meetings and increased activity in evangelism in the cities and the country towns.'[77]

Pastor Saillens also kept an eye on revival stirrings in Switzerland and visited as often as possible. A visitor to the Oratoire heard Saillens, Dardier and Lenoir speaking 'with much enthusiasm and conviction'.[78] Another enthusiast was M. Ernst of Zurich, who welcomed the news of revival in Wales and was grateful for the many prayer meetings that had been set up in Switzerland.[79] Yet another (unnamed) was charmed by the Welsh language: after returning home from Wales he sent for a dictionary so that he could remember some phrases and their meaning, especially '*Diolch Iddo*' (Praise Him) and '*Bendigedig*' (Blessed).[80]

Another fruit of the revival besides the increase in prayer meetings was the formation of an Alliance movement in Switzerland, which was inaugurated at a meeting in the YMCA on 19 October 1905.[81] This established unity between denominations and evangelical movements, and also paved the way for the week of prayer at the beginning of January 1906. As in other countries in Europe, a convention was held in Switzerland, at Chexbres, under the presidency of Pastor Saillens.[82]

Though busy in Europe, Pastor Saillens managed to go further afield. His church released him for two years to itinerate, and so he arranged to visit Algeria.[83] The believers in Algeria had already heard of the Welsh Revival, and for a month before Saillens' visit they held prayer meetings seeking an awakening similar to that in Wales. It was to a prayer meeting that Saillens was taken on his arrival, and this prepared him for the preaching services. Considering the few Protestant believers in that country, the congregations were large. On

Monday 27 November 1905 between a thousand and twelve hundred people came together 'to hear the "Preacher of the gospel" speak of the religious revival in Wales'.[84] The people were hungry for Saillens' messages; it was said of them, 'They drink in the Word.'[85]

Of interest to him as a Frenchman, and also to the people of Wales, was a lady who attended a number of the meetings. She was none other than H. N. Ranavalona, the Queen of Madagascar, who had been dethroned by the French but had been a close friend of the Welsh missionaries in Madagascar.[86] At these meetings the Frenchman and the Malagasy lady were united, and shared together the news of the Welsh Revival. The British and Foreign Bible Society believed that the series of meetings had been successful in terms of spiritual blessing, and also in creating interest in the work of the colporteurs, who had sold a hundred and seventy items in Algiers.[87]

*Benefits*

Some centres benefited from the Revival more than others. There can be no doubt that the Protestant witness in Paris was greatly strengthened; it was estimated in 1907 that there were seven hundred Baptists in the city.[88] Nîmes continued to be an important centre; a new chapel was opened in the town, and conventions were held there in which Pastor Saillens played a leading part.[89] The chairman of the 1907 convention was Pastor Babut, President of the 'Comité Evangelique de l'Eglise Réformée de Nîmes'; he had prayed for revival for a long time and trusted that the present awakening would lead to more unity generally among Protestants in France.[90] During that same year an important step was taken to promote unity through the setting up of a Protestant Federation.[91]

The Pioneer Mission continued to support the Protestant witness in France and was in constant touch with Pastor Saillens. Particular families in sympathy with the Revival in Wales also supported the work of the Mission in France. These included the Cory family in Cardiff[92] and the Soltau family in London.[93] William Soltau was also associated with the McCall Mission. His sister was head of the Mildmay Training Home (CIM) and friendly with Mrs Penn-Lewis. The two of them had attended revival meetings together in Wales.

In a Roman Catholic country like France, a sign of Protestant advance was the establishing of Sunday schools centred on the teaching of the Bible. Professor Passy reported that five of these had been started in Lens and Levin, and that children were flocking to them.[94]

Writing to a Welsh-speaking Welshman living in Seacombe, Passy mentioned another interesting development. As one who had visited the Welsh Revival, he was to address a meeting of atheists on that subject. Passy would have the company of some friends of the Revival, and they were to sing a number of hymns, including '*Diolch Iddo*' (Praise Him) and '*Dyma gariad*' (Here is love). He commented that Welsh hymns were being translated into French.[95]

Just as a convention like that at Nîmes kept the children of the revival together in France, so the convention at Chexbres accomplished that work in Switzerland. The convention embraced other countries through its visiting speakers, which included Lortsch of the British and Foreign Bible Society and Pastor Appéré of Paris.[96]

# 3
# Germany

The evangelical tradition in Germany was stronger than it was in France. It was here that Martin Luther had discovered the message of justification by faith alone—the tenet of a standing or falling church. But by the middle of the nineteenth century Germany was being taken over theologically by Julius Wellhausen (1844–1914) and F. C. Baur (1792–1860), and a radical, destructive attitude to the Bible was being adopted.

A number of efforts were made to counteract this development. Prominent scholars championed the conservative approach to the Bible and the Christian faith, especially F. A. G. Tholuck (1797–1877), Frederick Bleek (1793–1859) and E. W. Hengstenburg (1802–1869).[1] A significant contribution to the conservative cause was the formation, at the Gnadau Conference in 1890, of the Committee for Promoting Evangelical Fellowship and Evangelism. This Committee operated within the Lutheran Church, but the Tent Mission that was set up in 1902 had support from other denominations as well. Its main emphasis was evangelism.

Other societies and individuals made their contribution to the evangelical cause. Societies mentioned are the London Jews Society, the China Inland Mission and the Christian Endeavour. Visits by Dr Baedeker of the Open Brethren[2] and representatives of the British Evangelical Alliance built bridges between Britain and the Continent, and many of these men were keen supporters of Keswick. The Welsh lady Mrs Jessie Penn-Lewis had visited Germany in 1897 and corresponded with her friends there before, during and after the revival period.[3]

## Visits to Wales
Within the different evangelical circles there was a desire to be more committed to evangelism and a longing for revival. When news of the Welsh Revival reached Germany, many individuals and groups arranged to visit Wales. By the beginning of 1905 interest was quite strong. Mrs Penn-Lewis had even received a letter asking for the meaning of the Welsh words '*Plyg ni, O Arglwydd*' (Bend us, O

Lord), which had been heard in Germany. The Rev. Thomas Francis of Loughor, Gorseinon, had replied, quoting scriptural passages to illustrate the meaning.[4] It is quite possible that someone in Germany had heard or read the story of Evan Roberts the Welsh revivalist, and of the prayer that humbled him at Blaenannerch.

Germans were among a group of visitors at Cardiff, Pontycymer and Nant-y-moel, and a large group was present at meetings in Anglesey.[5] Some of these were mentioned by name: Jacob Vetter,[6] Johannes Seitz,[7] Pastor Lohmann,[8] and two missionary students, George Kraemer and Karl Hummel. Kraemer visited Rhos (Wrexham) with a Mr Haeder, and he told the people there that Rhos was a topic of conversation in Germany.[9] Many Germans made visits between February and August 1905, and some of them would also visit Keswick, and the Keswick in Wales at Llandrindod. The group that attended Llandrindod in 1905 arranged with Seth Joshua, the Forward Movement evangelist, to hold a prayer meeting, at which Evan Roberts and Principal William Edwards of Cardiff were present.[10] Llandrindod was uniting Germany and Wales, Keswick and the Forward Movement, Welsh-speaking and English-speaking revivalists.

Included in the parties from Germany were a few prominent ladies, who had come expressly to see the Revival: ladies like Countess Schimmelmann and Eva von Tiele-Winckler. The Countess attended an underground service in a colliery in Pontypridd, and came again to Wales the following year. The daughter of a Danish nobleman, she was brought up in the Court of Berlin and appointed Maid of Honour to the Empress Augusta. But she grew tired of the gaieties at court and devoted her large fortune to helping the needy and to many religious enterprises.[11]

Eva von Tiele-Winckler was the daughter of a wealthy industrialist, but like Countess Schimmelmann she had committed herself to the service of the poor and was caring for homeless children in the Friedenshort (Refuge of Peace).[12] Leaving her comfortable world, she had built herself a wooden hut so as to live as poor among the poor. Yet, despite her commitment, Eva was dissatisfied with her spiritual life. She heard news of the Welsh Revival from the Malche Bible School, and although the meaning of 'revival' was not clear to her, it quickened her desire for a deeper spiritual life. She knew of Pentecost in the Book of Acts, but wondered if such an event was possible in her day. As she considered the matter, Eva became convinced that God was leading her to Wales. A friend of hers, Fraulein Wasserzug, was also interested in making the journey. Before deciding

finally, Eva visited Kristina Roy in Hungary, who had been awakened
spiritually under the ministry of Dr Baedeker. Being strongly advised
by her to go to Wales, Eva von Tiele-Winckler set out with Fraulein
Wasserzug in March 1905.

The ladies spent two days in London, where they met Elizabeth
Baxter and Mrs Penn-Lewis. Eva von Tiele-Winckler spoke of this as
'an encounter which was to mean much to me'. After attending large
meetings in Cardiff, the visitors moved on to Neath, to meetings in 'a
circus-like building' seating about two thousand, which was almost
full. No one presided, yet there was a 'holy order', the singing was
full of praise and the faces of many glowed with joy. Eva von Tiele-
Winckler felt ashamed that she had been serving others for fifteen
years while lacking a truly spiritual life herself, and as the meeting
proceeded she experienced an inward change. 'I was simply melting,
and it was as if the ice around my heart was gradually thawing under
the warm, spring sunshine of grace that streamed towards me out of
all those shining eyes.'[13] The German lady experienced a new joy and
received an assurance of her acceptance with God. The experience
was confirmed in a group prayer meeting, and in meeting personally
with some of the converts.

The visitors travelled back to London in the company of three girls
who had taken part in revival meetings and were on their way to a
Welsh chapel in Stratford, London, to hold services there. On arrival,
Eva and her friend decided to attend the Welsh meetings and, after
some difficulty, found the building. For a while Eva was unmoved,
but suddenly the power of God gripped her, and she reaffirmed her
promise to do the will of God, whatever the cost, even if it meant
being a fool for Christ's sake.

She returned to Germany, but in a few months' time received an
invitation to visit the Keswick Convention in England. Her brother
Hans Werner was to attend, but being lame he needed some help
on the way, and his wife was ill at the time. So Eva accompanied
her brother to Keswick. Here she heard A. T. Pierson, Charles
Inwood, Theodore Monod, Stockmeyer (from Germany), and H. W.
Webb-Peploe.

In Webb-Peploe's meeting, words that he spoke kept ringing in
her ears, 'Give what you have.' She looked at her gold ring and the
silver clasp of her Bible and was convinced that she should give
them to God's service, but this did not happen until she attended a
ladies' prayer meeting. In a subsequent meeting, which was led by
Miss Soltau (CIM), Eva received confirmation that she had done the
right thing.[14]

## Back in Germany

Eva von Tiele-Winckler and others who visited Wales returned to report on what they had seen and experienced. As Eva shared her experiences in Wales and Keswick, her friends were convinced of sin, and this led to confession. There was evident spiritual blessing during October 1905, and in one meeting when Pastor Dolman was present (a pastor who was helping spiritually) it was felt that God was filling the room. They regarded what was happening not only as the rebirth of individuals, but also as reviving the work in the Home.

Through the witness of those who returned from Wales, new prayer groups came into being and those already in existence were strengthened. Such was the interest in revival that little red cards were printed and distributed with the inscription, 'Lord, send us an awakening, and begin in me.'[15]

Eva von Tiele-Winckler also persuaded others to visit Wales, and under her influence a visiting party was formed. When they attended a meeting in Swansea, one of them, Baron von Engel, told the congregation that 'a big religious movement' had started in Germany among all ranks of society.[16] Others who were active as revival missionaries were Witts, Countess Schimmelmann and Jacob Vetter. The Countess led revival meetings herself.[17]

Jacob Vetter had been working with the Tent Mission in the Ruhr Valley before going to Wales, but when he returned he witnessed a marked change, especially in Müllheim, a mining centre near Oberhausen.[18] A Lutheran pastor had invited the congregation to the schoolroom for a prayer meeting. This meeting led to a series of meetings which lasted for three weeks, and during this period five hundred people made a profession of faith.

During March 1905 two other pastors, Martin Girkon and Ernst Modersohn, were also leading revival meetings. Characterised by spontaneous prayers, ardent singing and public confession of sin,[19] these meetings were described as 'according to the Welsh pattern' and were attended by members of the established Church, the fellowships and the free churches. The work was carried on and confirmed by Jacob Vetter and the Tent Mission. During a period of six weeks, three thousand conversions were recorded.[20] Another prominent speaker besides Vetter was General von Viebahn, a man well suited to speaking to soldiers.

## Conferences

The conference held at Frienwalde at the end of May 1905 heard Pastor Lohmann give an account of the awakening at Müllheim.[21] The story thrilled conference members, including Mrs Penn-Lewis. She had travelled there along a new route through the Hook of Holland and was staying in a private villa belonging to Frau von Hockstetter. On the one-and-a-half hour journey to the conference from Berlin the Welsh lady had called at a 'Bibelhouse', and many of the women Christian workers there went with her to the conference.

*Frienwalde*
The conference's founder and director was Pastor Lohmann, and he addressed the first meeting on the theme of Christ's power while he was on earth. Following this, Mrs Penn-Lewis described the work of the Holy Spirit, and especially his role in baptising the believer into the death of Christ.[22] The spirit of prayer was manifest during the first two days, but it was on the last day that the power of God was really experienced. Mrs Penn-Lewis was speaking on Calvary as the place of reconciliation between Jew and Gentile (Ephesians 2:14f):[23]

> The Spirit suddenly 'fell' as I was speaking on Thurs. morning. A devoted worker rose & spoke in German—a brother arose and then shook hands with another – people wept & rose from all parts of the Hall—all confessing to one another 'divisions', 'hard thoughts' etc. against one another and this went on until we had to separate.

In a letter to a friend, the speaker described the meeting as 'extra-ordinary—marvellous—it was Pentecost'.[24] In the afternoon Mrs Penn-Lewis concentrated on the theme of the freedom of the children of God; at the end she appealed for consecration, and many came forward to dedicate themselves to God anew.

Farewell meetings were held before departing. In the morning the 'Bibelhouse' sisters sang in German the Welsh '*Diolch Iddo*' (Praise Him), and the climax was the singing of 'Crown Him' immediately before leaving. During the days of conference the Spirit of God was allowed to preside. Usually, a hymn would be given out by a Christian worker or by Pastor Lohmann, and time would be spent in prayer, with periods of silence followed by outbursts of praise. Very often a meeting would close without a hymn. Mrs Penn-Lewis stayed on for a while, and a meeting she attended on the Sunday included joyous singing, especially of the hymns 'I worship Thy love' and 'Luther's Hymn'.[25]

Mrs Penn-Lewis met Dr Baedeker at Frienwalde, and Charles Inwood in Berlin.[26] Inwood had attended revival meetings in Wales, and he was soon to return to England, to stand on the Keswick platform with R. B. Jones of Porth, Rhondda, and urge all present to pray for a worldwide revival.[27]

## Wandsbeck

During Whitsun, Mrs Penn-Lewis was present at the Wandsbeck Convention (the fourth for her to attend).[28] Wandsbeck was the centre of the work amongst the Jews, set up by Pastor D. H. Dolman and supported by the London Jews Society. During a period of seven years, five hundred Jews had been instructed in the teaching that Jesus Christ is the Messiah.[29] Others present at the 1905 Convention were Pastor Lohmann (Frienwalde) and F. S. Webster of All Souls Church, London, a representative of Keswick. He had taken a prominent part in revival meetings in Skewen, near Swansea.[30]

The company at Wandsbeck included representatives from Germany, Denmark, Holland, Russia and England. There were encouragements during the early days, but all present were expecting a greater blessing. Frau Dolman had told Mrs Penn-Lewis, 'We Germans are heavy and slow; you must not expect us to be moved like the Welsh.'[31] But Germans, Welsh and others were moved and melted. At a meeting in which Pastor Paul had spoken, the chairman asked for silence, and immediately every single person went on his knees to pray.[32] All hearts were bowed too, as the cornfield bends before the breeze. Souls could not be restrained, and fervent prayers and confessions arose simultaneously from all over the room. Almost every heart was seeking relief in spoken prayer.

Other similar meetings took place. According to Mrs Penn-Lewis there was very little singing, no repetition of favourite choruses, 'nor was there the soft singing that I heard in Wales, so sweet and subdued'.[33] General von Viebahn was one of the speakers at Wandsbeck, as was F. Mascher, who was soon to visit Keswick—a visit that was to have a profound influence on his spiritual life.[34]

## Charlottenburg

Jonathan Paul, one of the speakers at Wandsbeck, devoted much of his time to the Tent Mission. From July to September 1905 the centre of activity was Charlottenburg. Weekly prayer meetings had been held there for a while, not only to prepare for a Tent Mission, but also for the Christian Endeavour European Conference in July. The main theme of the Conference was 'Full Obedience to the King of Kings', and in keeping with that title R. A. Torrey spoke on 'The Secret of Entire Sanctification'.[35] In one meeting in particular there was 'a wave of spiritual power', with signs of revival like that 'which had taken place in Wales'.[36]

During the Tent Mission, those who had been to Keswick and Wales gave their testimonies. The large congregations were united in prayer, praise and testimony. According to one person present, it was a spiritual awakening, and 'such an awakening as we have not witnessed during the twenty-five years of our labour here'.[37]

*Blankenburg*

A fourth convention was held before the end of August 1905. Evangelical leaders and friends of revival gathered together at Blankenburg for the Alliance Convention, which had been established by Fraulein Weling in 1885.[38] Pastor Lohmann had returned from Wales just in time to be present. Others who joined him were Modersohn of Hamburg, Dolman of Wandsbeck, General von Viebahn, Charles Inwood from England, Baron Uixküll from Russia and Prince and Princess Bernadotte of Sweden.

The meetings held were similar to those at Frienwalde and Wandsbeck, with a strong emphasis on the baptism of the Spirit. R. A. Torrey spoke on Acts 1:4-8 and explained the conditions for receiving a fullness of the Spirit. Many claimed that experience: 'Numerous visitors received the baptism of the Spirit in the conference or were enthusiastic about the nature and method of this new way of working'.[39] A typical meeting was the one led by General von Viebahn:[40]

> At last we came to prayer. One prayed and another. Suddenly the Spirit fell upon us and numbers were praying at once. There was no disorder. It was all harmonious, like the advance of a wave. I clasped the brother whom I had, unconsciously to him, wronged in thought. We were sobbing on one another's shoulders. Criticism and restraint had gone. General von Viebahn called for the Glory Song [When all my labours and trials are o'er]. Over and over again it was sung with streaming eyes and hearts full of a new joy. I have never been in a meeting like it. If it was like Wales it is because the same Holy Spirit was present.

The main characteristics of the week were the spirit of unity, humble prayer, searching addresses, many conversions, and the falling of the Spirit in the meeting led by General von Viebahn. The spirit of prayer was powerful: as many as a thousand would gather together for the early morning prayer meeting.[41]

A most significant event took place during the Blankenburg Conference. An Alliance Bible School was set up in Berlin for the instruction of Russians in Germany.[42] Now that there was more religious freedom in Russia (proclaimed in 1905), those trained would be able to return there and bear witness to the gospel. The Council of the Alliance in Britain committed itself to the support of two of the first group of students. The event was significant for many reasons: it meant bringing Germans and Russians together; an opportunity was given to the less privileged to receive some education, and it was happening at a time of spiritual renewal in Russia. And as one author commented, 'Those working there had recognised that sound biblical teaching is a decisive help in any revival movement.'[43]

The composition of the committee is of interest: Baron Nicolay and Baron Uixküll represented Russia; and Baron von Thuemmler (President of the Blankenburg Conference), General von Viebahn, Herr Karl Mascher and Herr von Tiele-Winckler were the German representatives. (Tiele-Winckler was the brother of Eva von Tiele-Winkler—the one she had accompanied to Keswick earlier in 1905.[44]) The British representative was Dr Baedeker. This meant that several denominations were represented—Lutheran, Open Brethren and Baptist. The Baptists were finding it difficult to make progress in Germany, and even more so in Russia. Mascher, their representative on the committee, had suffered for his faith, as there was a lack of religious liberty in Saxony where he was a pastor.[45]

### Eberhard and Emmy Arnold
Eberhard Arnold (1883–1935) could have been a lecturer at the Alliance Bible School, but because of his many commitments he found it impossible to accept the invitation.[46] He had been converted as a young lad, and considered this experience to be crucial for the whole of his life. 'This had given a completely new direction to his life; from then on he felt the burning love for Jesus and decided to follow him whatever the cost.'[47] During his student days at Halle, Breslau and Erlangen, he faced two major issues: the relationship between Church and State and the nature of baptism. He came to the conclusion that Church and State should be separate and that infant baptism was unscriptural. Consequently, he was bitterly opposed by his family. In the eyes of his parents, he was in rebellion against the Lutheran Church and was turning his back on a long family tradition. It caused difficulties with his course as well, forcing him to change from theology to philosophy.[48]

Eberhard Arnold became a vital 'link man' in Germany. He was an intellectual, and his doctoral thesis, 'Original Christian and Anti-Christian Elements in Frederick Nietzche's Development', was highly commended by the examiners.[49] Though an intellectual, he could communicate well with the less able. He was still a student in 1905, but worked in close association with mature pastors. He was well-read in early church history, but was attracted to the Anabaptists and the Salvation Army, whose meetings he attended.[50]

The student had a prominent part in the conferences of the period from 1905 to 1908. He was a speaker at Blankenburg, and he contributed to the *Evangelical Alliance News*, working closely with Bernard Kühn and other leading evangelicals like von Viebahn, Girkon and Mascher.[51] He was at home in the Student Christian Movement and attended the Wernigerode Conference of 1905.[52] Here he first met Karl Heim, who was to become a distinguished theologian at Tübingen.[53] The two men were on friendly terms, though their relationship could not be described as intimate.

The Student Christian Movement meetings brought Eberhard Arnold into renewed fellowship with Ludwig von Gerdtell, a person he had known since about 1902. Gerdtell's lectures in Halle during 1902 had 'inspired a small revival'[54] among the secondary students, and in 1905 he was the instrument of revival in Riga, Latvia, where the hall could not contain all those who wanted to hear the young German aristocrat.[55] According to reports he was 'a brilliant and powerful speaker'.[56] Eberhard Arnold and Karl Heim organised meetings for Gerdtell during 1906 and 1907. People flocked to these meetings, and during the second series as many as a thousand were turned away by the police.[57]

But Gerdtell was becoming more and more unorthodox in his methods and lifestyle. He appeared in one meeting dressed in an evening suit, top hat and kid gloves, and Eberhard Arnold realised they would have to work separately.[58] There was no need for Arnold to be alone; he could attend the fellowship meeting in Halle (or 'the revival circle' as it was called), and he believed he could detect 'an increasingly pure return to primitive Christianity'.[59]

It was in one of these meetings that Eberhard met Emmy Hollander and she mentioned her response to his preaching: 'I had never heard or experienced anything like it in my life, there was such power and conviction.'[60] The two were married in 1909, and they both spoke in conferences and revival meetings. Emmy Hollander took part, for example, with Miss Soltau (CIM), Frau Wasserzug, Frau Redern and Eva von Tiele-Winkler in a Women's Missionary Prayer Union, on which Mrs Penn-Lewis reported.[61] She also kept up a correspondence with the Rederns, the Wasserzugs and the Tiele-Winklers.[62]

## The 'tongues' movement

Emmy Hollander and Eberhard Arnold were happy in the fellowship meetings and accepted the evangelicalism represented by the Blankenburg Convention. But during 1906 and the early part of 1907, differences emerged that were to lead to major disagreements. In 1906 the Gnadau Union adopted a more critical attitude towards pentecostal developments, especially that of speaking in tongues. Jonathan Paul had also introduced his teaching on the pure heart, which further complicated relationships. Rappard criticised Paul, pointing out the danger of elevating experience at the expense of dogma. Julius Dammann believed that many in Germany were too ready to imitate the forms and methods of the Welsh Revival, while Haarbeck advocated moderation and argued for a balanced opinion on controversial matters.[63] Mrs Penn-Lewis was one of the outspoken critics of the tongues movement, and the translation of some of her works into German led to further alienation between the two parties.

Emmy Hollander and Eberhard Arnold were very sensitive to these developments. Writing at midnight on 4-5 April 1907, Emmy informed Eberhard that Pastor Paul had been to Christiania (Oslo) to witness 'the wonderful revival movement'.[64] The Holy Spirit had descended in power as on the day of Pentecost and many had spoken in tongues. Jonathan Paul returned from Christiania full of enthusiasm for speaking in tongues,[65] and he was supported by Emil Meyer, who went to Christiania in June 1907.[66]

Meyer, like Jonathan Paul, was a prominent figure in church life in Germany, being leader of the Hamburg Strand Mission. He invited two Norwegian speakers to Hamburg—Dagmar Gregersen and Agnes Thelle Beckdahl.[67] Heinrich Dallmeyer, a young evangelist, joined Meyer and the Norwegians for eight days of evangelism at the end of June 1907.[68] Then, in July, Emmy Hollander met four brothers and sisters from Norway, who claimed to have been sent to Halle by the Holy Spirit. They were convinced that the baptism of the Spirit is followed by speaking in tongues. Both Emmy and Eberhard were cautious in their response.[69]

Heinrich Dallmeyer and others arranged for all those who were interested to meet at Kassel. At that meeting Dallmeyer expressed his support for the tongues movement, the Norwegian sisters spoke in tongues, and Heinrich's brother August Dallmeyer was baptised with the Holy Spirit. The meeting was prolonged as a result of a prophecy, which directed those present to tarry until the promises of Joel chapter 3 were fulfilled. And a revelation was given to one man, who lay on the floor as if dead, in the sole company of H. Dallmeyer.[70]

Some defended the prophecy and the vision, while others denounced them as contrary to the teaching of 1 Corinthians chapter 14. There was uproar from outside, too, as Kassel residents tried to prevent conference members from entering one of their churches. The situation became so bad that the police had to be called in to keep the peace.[71] There is no doubt that Heinrich Dallmeyer took too much responsibility on his own shoulders and should have shared more with other leaders. It was also rather unwise to give so much credence to the visitors from Norway.

The tongues movement became divisive. D. H. Dolman refused permission to the Norwegian sisters to speak at Wandsbeck, though acknowledging that genuine spiritual gifts could be exercised in that generation. The Blankenburg Conference took a firm stand against the movement, and the leaders, together with others, were disturbed to see the movement spreading to Halle, Kassel and other places.[72] Even Dallmeyer changed his mind and made a declaration on 17 November 1907. Elias Shrenk led the meeting and gave him an opportunity to explain himself. But Jonathan Paul and Emil Meyer remained staunch supporters of the movement.

Because of the serious differences, Emil Haarbeck and Elias Shrenk invited representatives of the fellowship meetings to come together at Barmen on 19-20 December 1907 for Dallmeyer to explain his position. Holzapfel and Modersohn, who declared their solidarity with Jonathan Paul, opposed him. A hymn was given out, 'Heart and heart united together', but separated hearts were trying to sing the hymn, and at the end of the first verse Michaelis got up to say that he could not sing those words while Jonathan Paul was being accused of having an alien spirit. After some discussion Baron von Tiele-Winckler read out Dallmeyer's statement, and the result was the Barmen Declaration.[73]

The Declaration of Barmen asked for a period of six months to consider all the relevant matters peacefully and thoroughly. It was an attempt to calm the feelings of those who were concerned with the pentecostal developments. It could have been read as advocating a mediating position, but there were also criticisms of the tongues movement. A call was made for all to humble themselves before God, and a warning sounded against 'strange spirits'.

One of those present at the meeting was Emil Meyer, who reported on it to T. B. Barratt in Sweden. 'There were several brethren who were united in their condemnation, but the majority did not dare to pass judgement on the movement.'[74] T. B. Barratt gave Jonathan Paul, Emil Meyer and Emil Humburg his full support.[75] This link strengthened the tongues movement in Germany, making co-operation between those of differing opinions even more difficult. The leaders of Blankenburg and Wandsbeck withdrew from the tongues movement; they and their supporters looked to Keswick and the champions of the Welsh Revival. This was true of Dolman, the Tiele-Wincklers, the Wasserzugs, Emmy Hollander and Eberhard Arnold, though some of them took a different path later. By the end of 1908 there were no signs of reconciliation.[76]

**Further afield**
The Welsh Revival had a marked influence on France and Germany, but with other countries like Hungary, Bulgaria, Spain and Italy it is difficult to know what happened during 1905–8. In Hungary, Professor Szabo had the oversight of 80,000 members of the Reformed Church, and was described as a man full of the Holy Spirit and in full sympathy with revival movements. A Pentecost happened in his country, but in 'a small measure'.[77] In Bulgaria, the awakenings during 1905 are described as 'widespread'.[78] In Spain there were meetings resembling those in Wales, and in Portugal three columns in one of the Portuguese papers were devoted to the Revival in Wales.[79] Visitors from Italy were present in Treharris and Neath, South Wales, during April 1905, and groups in Italy itself were praying for revival.[80]

# 4
# Scandinavian Countries

Towards the end of the nineteenth century there was a reaction in the Scandinavian countries against the liberalism in the churches. The reaction was strengthened by Anglo-American influences; it was reported that 129,000 copies of Sankey's Hymnal had been sold during 1899.[1] There was a return to the Bible, and a greater emphasis on prayer.[2] Even a London paper drew attention to this return to the Word of God, and mentioned the week of prayer in Stockholm that had brought a 'rich harvest' to the churches.[3]

## Norway
A marked impetus was given to the evangelical witness in Norway by the setting up of the City Mission in 1902, with T. B. Barratt as city missioner,[4] a man who had a burden for evangelism and revival. The Mission had the following three aims:[5]

- to awaken and maintain a deep religious life amongst the population
- to help forward its moral and social state
- to promote the general culture of the people on a Christian foundation.

T. B. Barratt had a desire to be baptised by the Holy Spirit, which he explained in the same way as R. A. Torrey—that is, as power for service.[6]

Barratt was a Methodist, but the man who joined him in the work, Albert Lunde, was a Lutheran.[7] He had been converted in Chicago when he was a sailor, and came under the influence of D. L. Moody. Returning to Norway, Lunde worked with Barratt for the spiritual renewal of the country. As a Lutheran, he succeeded in establishing a good relationship with the state church.[8] Hundreds of people flocked to the meetings held by the two missioners, and reports appeared in *Byposten*, edited by Barratt. R. Silyn Roberts, from Wales, visited some of the Scandinavian countries during 1904 and refers to revival meetings held during Christmas of that year. He was most impressed with Lunde's work, marvelling at his having to move from a small schoolroom in Farsund to a theatre and, when that also became too small, to a church with a seating capacity of five thousand.[9]

In *Byposten*, Barratt reported events in Wales as well as Norway. Special attention was given to Evan Roberts himself, and 'The account of "How Evan Roberts received the Holy Ghost" began to make the people long to obtain the same blessing.'[10] These articles must have appeared soon after the revival started in Wales, for in a letter to Evan Roberts on 2 January 1905 Barratt wrote: 'The accounts I have given of the revival in Wales, have been and are still a means of inspiration to us all.'[11] Mrs Penn-Lewis also received word from Norway:[12]

> The meetings are very similar to the Revival meetings in Wales. The hall is packed long before the time of the service. A hymn is started by some one, and the people sing until the preacher arrives. During prayer there is a low murmur throughout the building: 'Lord, we are powerless; help us, Lord Jesus'; and the people are bowed with a sense of the presence of God. The side rooms are used for the inquirers, and are filled with people, the Christians dealing with the unsaved.

Nowhere outside of Wales was the revival more powerful than in Norway, and Albert Lunde was regarded as the Evan Roberts of that country.

Another visitor, J. B. Smith from England, had travelled to Christiana in the company of emigrants from the United States of America. They all sang hymns together, and on arrival were joined by steamer passengers from New York. Some left by boat for a near-by island singing 'The Glory Song' and 'Never Lose Sight of Jesus'.[13] According to the visitor, many people had seen the words 'Behold, I come quickly' written in the sky in large letters, and this stirred a good number to seek after God. Thirty of those who were converted left for America to bear witness to the gospel. Like other reporters, Smith commented that the meetings were like those in Wales.[14]

Mrs Penn-Lewis continued to inform her readers of what was happening in Norway, doing so well into 1906. The revival was bearing fruit in the Sunday schools; families were being united in the faith, and all classes of people were being reached with the gospel. Prince Bernadotte gave his support to the revival, which reached the prison as well as the palace:[15]

The result of the revival in the prison so far is, that 30 prisoners have given themselves to God. They take hold of free grace & have peace & joy. There is a great longing to spread the Gospel, & when they have opportunity to write, they seek to bring their relations & friends to Christ. It is just the same with the jailers and warders. Those who have come to Christ are standing true & resisting temptation.

A prison was just the place to test the quality of the lives of the converted.

The sensational events of the revival attracted the attention of journalists, and they, like Barratt in *Byposten*, spread the news of revival. Barratt and Lunde visited other countries, and propaganda literature was also sent out from Norway. In these ways, Norway played an important role in the spread of revival over a large area.[16]

## Sweden

Pastor Richard Edhelberg believed that there were tokens of revival in Sweden at the end of 1904 and the beginning of 1905.[17] The Swedes knew of what was happening in Wales and Norway, and during February 1905 visitors from Sweden were present at meetings in Cardiff and Nant-y-moel.[18] Before May 1905, the people of Nerike, for example, were rejoicing because 'We have Wales in Nerike.'[19] The spiritual upsurge started amongst the Methodists, and people thronged to the meetings, where 'Hundreds were converted.'[20] During May 1905 Albert Lunde visited Sweden and 'was welcomed by nobility and gentry, bishops and clergy, as well as vast throngs of the common people'.[21]

Many Welshmen advertised what was happening in Sweden and Wales. The Rev. H. Elfed Lewis of King's Cross, London, received letters from a friend in Sweden, who was so impressed with what he had seen in Wales that he was determined to return and bring some friends with him.[22] Another Welshman, R. Williams, gave an account of Ephraim Sandblom's visit to Wales during August 1905.[23] He was in Llanwrtyd, a popular holiday resort in mid-Wales, and attended a prayer meeting for visitors, during which Evan Roberts spoke. Emotions were stirred so deeply that there were bursts of praise, and Annie Davies, one of the soloists of the Revival, broke out into the singing of '*Dyma gariad*' (Here is love). Sandblom felt he had to take part in prayer and interceded on behalf of Sweden. He was followed immediately by Evan Roberts, urging further prayer for the visitor and his country. Sandblom was able to spend some time with

Evan Roberts, Sidney Evans and soloist Sam Jenkins. The Swede and others also joined together for a picnic on a nearby hill, their singing of 'Bringing in the sheaves' echoing through the countryside.[24] During his visit to Wales, Sandblom had asked for prayer for a conference at Soderlege in early October. After returning, he wrote to Sidney Evans informing him that had he been present at Soderlege he would have thought he was in Wales.

Many people in the meetings at Soderlege were filled with the Holy Spirit and praised God fervently for such an experience. It was a wonderful sight to see nobility, a son of the king, army officers, rich and poor from all denominations—'all kneeling together in prayer and praise in one spirit. Oh! It was marvellous. We could scarcely go to bed for joy.'[25] The Swede had an opportunity to speak of the revival in Wales, 'to tell of the Lord's mighty works among you'.[26] The Sunday before writing he had known the power of God in preaching in a way unprecedented in his ministry. The experience had humbled him, and made him much more careful to trust God at all times.

A month later (in November), revival scenes were witnessed at Philadelphia Chapel, Stockholm. The person who sent the report to *The Christian* was Pastor Richard Edhelberg, the man who had discerned tokens of blessing at the beginning of the year.[27] In the north of Stockholm, on the Sunday before Christmas, the preaching of a pastor had a tremendous impact on the congregation. Hundreds were crying to God for mercy. Some of the meetings lasted for as long as four or five hours. As in other countries, the evangelistic zeal was evident: forty-five from the Bible School attached to Philadelphia Chapel left for different parts of Sweden to proclaim the good news of salvation.[28]

Mrs Penn-Lewis had her contacts in Sweden, as in so many other countries. Her main contact was Madam Kurke [Kurck], whom she had first met in 1896. She informed Mrs Penn-Lewis that a group of ladies were meeting for prayer, and that three of the group intended visiting Norway.[29] The week of prayer in January 1906 was fuel for the fire, and one marked result was the conversion of families. Both Mrs Penn-Lewis and Madam Kurke were being opposed for taking such a prominent part in revival, because they were females. They were not discouraged and, writing to her friend, Madam Kurke reminded her that they were suffering together: 'You and I are in the mill being grinded into fine white flour.'[30]

As the revival spread it affected the Swedish part of Finland. In many of the meetings men and women fell to the floor crying for

mercy, and 'outstanding results were recorded' at Knopio. The ministry of Frans Hannula drew the young people to the meetings.[31] Baron
Nicolay rejoiced at the interdenominational character of the meetings—a spirit that was especially evident in Helsingfors, where
Lutherans, Baptists, Methodists and Salvationists worshipped together
on neutral ground in the YMCA.[32] The Baron was convinced that the
Evangelical Alliance had prepared the way for greater unity. He also
believed that the revival would quicken and strengthen that process.

## Denmark

As in Norway, the Inner City Mission paved the way for revival in
Denmark.[33] The work of the Mission bore fruit around 1902, and by
1905 there was generally a renewed interest in spiritual matters, and
even examples of local awakenings. There was a hunger for revival
and, in the opinion of J. Edwin Orr, 'With the news of the Welsh
Revival the Danish movement reached full force.'[34] When they heard
of the Revival in Wales a number of pastors wrote a letter to the
churches in Wales. One of them, P. M. S. Jensin, wrote a covering
letter to Evan Roberts, expressing the conviction that they were
one—the Danes, Evan Roberts, and 'the crowd of praying, singing
and blessed children of God with you'.[35] Jensin hoped very much that
Evan Roberts would respond.

Jensin and the other signatories represented the Baptists, Congregationalists, Methodists and Salvation Army. They asked for the
letter to be read in the Welsh churches so that prayer could be offered
for Denmark. They had already known encouragement, both in the
week of prayer at the beginning of January, and in a series of meetings that had attracted large crowds.[36]

Both letters were dated 7 April 1905, and by June a number of
groups were meeting to pray for revival.[37] A Welshman, R. Silyn
Roberts, was in Denmark during July and met Miss Wentler, a
Lutheran, and headmistress of the first girls' school in the country.
The Danish lady was thrilled to hear of revival events in Wales, and
she in turn informed R. Silyn Roberts of the revival groups meeting
in Denmark. Though a Lutheran, she was one with members of the
Free Churches in her longing for revival.[38]

Pastor Mollerup was another Lutheran committed to revival, and
one who appreciated all the help Denmark was receiving from the
Evangelical Alliance in Britain. He gladly welcomed representatives
of the Alliance to a series of meetings in Copenhagen from 31
October to 7 November 1905. The representatives were also glad to
meet Mollerup and give him more information about revival in

Britain.[39] This would encourage the Dane, who 'had been greatly stirred by reading of the work in Wales and Norway and Sweden, and had for some time been leading his people into earnest prayer for definite Revival in Copenhagen'.[40]

As a Lutheran, Mollerup knew that he would face opposition from the State Church, and many within that Church frowned on his co-operation with Nonconformists. He found a friend, however, in his fellow Lutheran, Pastor Finiger, and with the support of others the two of them held meetings in the Concert Hall on the Bredgarde. Five to six thousand people tried to enter a hall seating two thousand, and other halls and a church had to be opened. Night after night the people gathered:[41]

> All restraints vanished before the full tide of blessing, and tears of penitents and rejoicings of the new converts made all men see that God was indeed working in their midst. Indeed, so mightily did God's Spirit work that many cases occurred of people being awakened and brought to decision for Jesus Christ on their way to the hall. The streets were filled with echoes of the Revival hymns, the chief favourites being 'The Glory Song' (*'Det bliver Himlen ja Himlen for mig'*), 'Like a river glorious' (*'Fred som kan bevare'*) and 'There is sunshine in my soul' (*'Der er i min Sigel i Deg'*).

The Alliance representatives joined in the meetings wholeheartedly, and believed that 'The story of this glad work in Copenhagen reads like New Testament history, and forms part of the unwritten Acts of the Holy Spirit.'[42]

Influential laymen, including Count and Countess Moltke and Oscar Oxholm, joined the pastors. The Count and Countess had long been active Christian workers, and Mrs Penn-Lewis had attended a meeting in their home in 1898.[43] The Countess had attended one of the student conferences at Aberystwyth with her husband (see page 16), and the Count was a revival speaker, especially in the overflow meetings. All three laymen were staunch supporters of the Evangelical Alliance;[44] in their thinking and experience they combined the Lutheran tradition, the teaching of Keswick, and the spirit of revival.

All three of them took an active part in arranging the first Danish Alliance Conference in 1906. It had been Countess Moltke's custom to attend the Wandsbeck Convention, but now they had their own convention in Denmark—'Wandsbeck has now a little child.'[45] Thousands were present for that first convention in Copenhagen; it was held in a beautiful wood, where the King of Denmark resided.

The speakers included Oxholm and Fuller Gooch from London (Alliance), whose address was followed by 'prayers, sobs and confession to God'.[46]

As in other countries, the Alliance arranged a week of prayer at the beginning of January each year. Countess Moltke was much pleased with the meetings at the beginning of 1907. As co-Secretary with Pastor Mollerup, she informed *Evangelical Christendom* that during the first three days the different denominations had prayers in their own churches, though the leaders and a few others did meet jointly for intercession.[47] The next three days were spent together in the YMCA, and the Sunday evening meeting was in the 'Concert Palast', when all the seats were taken up half an hour before the service. In Countess Moltke's opinion, 'It was the most blessed meeting the Alliance has ever had.'[48]

The revival continued into 1907, but the Danish Clergy Association did not respond to it positively. J. Edwin Orr expresses surprise at the lack of response. The clergy allotted time to discussing finance, liturgy and farming for priests, but none to the revival that was taking place in so many parts of Denmark.[49]

It is difficult to assess what was happening in Iceland. There are references to revival in June 1905, but the British press did not continue to investigate events in that land.[50]

### Change of course

The course of the revival in the Scandinavian countries was radically changed, mainly because of outside influences. Pentecostalism was introduced from Los Angeles, USA, but what was happening there was related to developments in Wales.

Holiness movements had emerged in Los Angeles before 1906. As Synan says, 'The reputation of Los Angeles as a congenial home for new religious ideas was already founded in 1906.'[51] By that time C. F. Parham had presented his teaching on the baptism of the Spirit, with 'glossolalia' as evidence of that experience.[52] The acceptance of his teaching led to the Azusa Street Pentecostal revival in April 1906. One of the leaders was W. J. Seymour,[53] one of Parham's pupils; he had held meetings at Bonnie Bray on the sixth of that month, and it was he who led the people to Azusa Street, where 'a monumental revival began'.[54] The whole area around Azusa Street was in a frenzy, as hundreds to begin with, and then thousands, gathered together. They spoke and sang in tongues, shouted, cried and danced. W. J. Seymour preached very little, and when he did, he would threaten with evil consequences all who did not accept his teaching.

## Joseph Smale

Another centre of attraction in Los Angeles was the First Baptist Church, where Joseph Smale was pastor. He had been educated at Spurgeon's College, London,[55] and he believed that revival was the great need of the day. It was said of him and his people, 'They were praying for a revival like they had in Wales.'[56] Joseph Smale had visited Wales during the Revival, and what he experienced convinced him more than ever of the need for a similar work in Los Angeles. Frank Bartleman says of Joseph Smale's return from Wales:[57]

> For some weeks special services have been held in the First Baptist Church, Los Angeles. Pastor Smale has returned from Wales, where he was in touch with Evan Roberts, and the revival. He registers his conviction that Los Angeles will soon be shaken by the mighty power of God.

Joseph Smale had returned in May 1905, and immediately after his return he arranged the first meeting, which was on 28 May. He read from Acts 2, verses 14 to 18, and then[58]

> I simply told them the story, as I knew it, of the Welsh Revival, and the Spirit used the message mightily, so that at the close of the service, some two hundred people bowed in penitence before the Lord.

This led to further meetings:[59]

> I have not seen so fervent meetings anywhere outside of Wales. One Lord's Day, quite two-thirds of the congregation remained to pray, and were in contrition before the Lord. We are looking now for a greater awakening and for Los Angeles to be shaken by the Holy Ghost.

Not all his people agreed with the pastor, and he left the First Baptist Church to form a New Testament Church. Revival meetings continued in the new centre, but it was not until the Azusa Street meetings that Joseph Smale spoke in tongues.[60]

## Frank Bartleman

Frank Bartleman, who had referred to Smale's return from Wales, visited W. J. Seymour's prayer meetings prior to the Azusa Street revival. After supporting Joseph Smale for a brief period, he then

established another mission in Los Angeles. He also was busy advocating the baptism of the Spirit with signs following. Synan is of the
opinion that 'His journalism not only informed the world about the
Pentecostal movement but in a large measure also helped to form it.'[61]
Like Smale and Seymour, Bartleman was thrilled with the news of
revival in Wales. He had heard F. B. Meyer speaking of his visit to
Wales, and 'My soul was stirred to its depths.'[62] Bartleman also distributed reports and pamphlets dealing with revival, including works
by Campbell Morgan and S. B. Shaw. Someone sent the journalist
five thousand copies of a pamphlet on the Revival in Wales, and
Bartleman distributed every one of them in no time.

Although he could not visit Wales, Frank Bartleman was determined to contact Evan Roberts. He wrote to him on three occasions,
and each time received an answer. The burden in all the letters was
the request for prayer. Responding to the first letter, Evan Roberts
urged Bartleman and the people to pray, wait and believe in God's
promises.[63] In his second reply the Welsh revivalist rejoiced with
Frank Bartleman because he was beginning to experience 'wonderful
things'.[64] The main thrust of his last response was the need to be
aware of the terrible spiritual conflict that was going on. But the
Welshman was also optimistic: 'We had a mighty down pouring of
the Holy Spirit last Saturday night.'[65] Frank Bartleman not only welcomed the Revival in Wales, but he also welcomed what was happening in Azusa Street, including the speaking with tongues.

*T. B. Barratt*
As well as Joseph Smale and Frank Bartleman, one other must be
mentioned. He is T. B. Barratt, the city missioner from Norway and
editor of *Byposten*. He left for the USA to raise money for the City
Mission, but was also anxious to know what was happening in the
religious scene in that country. He heard Torrey and Alexander and
met the 'evangelist Jones', who had taken part in revival meetings
with Evan Roberts.[66] T. B. Barratt continued to make use of *Byposten*,
and it was the means of telling his people at home what was happening in Azusa Street. 'This account gave, no doubt, many a mighty
shock in Norway when they read it in *Byposten*.'[67]

T. B. Barratt entered into the Pentecostal experience in stages. He
received 'full cleansing' on the last day of September 1906, baptism
of the Spirit on 8 October, and full blessing with speaking in tongues
on 15 November, greatly helped by advice from Azusa Street.[68] On
his return to Norway, he was the means of spreading the Pentecostal
message: 'It caught like fire in dry grass.'[69] A. A. Boddy, one of the

chief pioneers of Pentecostalism in Britain, bears witness to what he experienced when he visited Christiana: 'My four days in Christiana can never be forgotten. I stood with Evan Roberts in Tonypandy, but have never witnessed such scenes as those in Norway.'[70] Pentecostalism eventually spread to fifty-one centres in Norway.[71]

The events in Norway were reported in Sweden, and when Lewi Pethrus read them he decided to visit Norway. During his visit he was baptised with the Holy Spirit. 'Returning to Sweden with a transformed ministry he commenced what was destined to become one of the most outstanding ministries not only of his own country but of the world.'[72] Lewi Pethrus was a Baptist, and with another Baptist minister he promoted the Pentecostal movement. When T. B. Barratt visited Uppsala, a hundred students came to hear him and received help from him and his friend Pastor Ahgren.[73]

From Sweden T. B Barratt visited Denmark. His most enthusiastic supporter in that country was Pastor Christensen of the Methodist Episcopal Church.[74] A 'remarkable incident' during T. B. Barratt's visit was the conversion of the Danish actress Anna Larssen, who became the wife of Bjorner, one of the leaders of the Apostolic Church.[75]

The tongues movement spread to Finland, Holland, Switzerland, Germany and France. This meant that the Scandinavian countries, and most countries in Europe, were influenced by this movement to a greater or lesser degree.

# 5
# Russia

The evangelical faith made very little headway in Russia until the second half of the nineteenth century. The spiritual progress that was then achieved can be traced to at least four specific factors.

## Spiritual influences
First of all, there was a *spiritual renewal from within*. This happened especially in the south of the country, with its roots among the German peasants in the Russian Ukraine. A good number found a new, vital and biblical Christianity which they contrasted with the more formal, liturgical religion of the Orthodox Church.

The movement spread within the Church and had a wide impact: 'The irruption of the biblical, reformed gospel into that part of the Ukraine which belonged to the Tsarist Empire took place with such dynamism that it seemed to many a miracle.'[1] The Stundists, as they were called, were members of the Orthodox Church but had real misgivings about the religious-political system in Russia, where 'The Church had become a bailiff of the state and state police were the executive organ of the Church.'[2] A clash with State and Church was inevitable. Like the leaders of the Protestant Reformation, the Stundists with their Bible-based study and worship groups were regarded as schismatics.

A further significant development for them was their acceptance of believer's baptism. Slowly they realised that they would have to leave the State Church. They formed themselves into congregations according to the pattern in the Book of Acts. A radical change in conversion became central to their thinking and experience, and the outward act of baptism took the place of the liturgy of the Orthodox Church, which they regarded as empty. The result of these changes was bitter persecution from State and Church, taking the form of legal reprisals and illegal persecution by priests and police.

*Baptist work*
The Baptist work in Russia, the second of the four features, was pioneered by the German, Johann Oncken (1800–84), and confirmed

by Julius Köbner (1806–84) and Vasili Pavlov (1854–1924), who emerged as an effective leader in sympathy with the Stundists.[3] Pavlov was twice exiled and, when threatened the third time, escaped to Romania, where he ministered to Stundist refugees.[4]

*Lord Radstock*

The third influence was the ministry of Lord Radstock,[5] confirmed by the work of Dr Baedeker.[6] Lord Radstock was in contact with a group of men and women in St. Petersburg. They belonged to the aristocracy and included Count Korff and Baron Wrede.[7] Meetings were held in the homes of Princess Lieven, Princess Galitsin and Colonel Paschkoff.[8] According to Princess Lieven, Radstock 'could not be called a brilliant speaker',[9] but he had a winning way with people, and 'He had a simple way of developing the main Christian concepts by using the bible, to which he constantly referred his hearers.'[10]

Most of the leading believers in St. Petersburg were influenced by him. Count Korff, chamberlain to the Tsar, was probably a believer before he met Radstock, but 'The decisive impetus in Count Korff's life came through him.'[11] Princess Lieven's mother and the two sisters Kozlianoff responded positively to Radstock's message, as did the Princess's aunt, Princess Gagarin. The latter is described as 'young, beautiful, very happily married and extremely rich', but she did not find satisfaction until she joined the Radstock group.[12] Madam Paschkoff was another convert; her husband was initially opposed to Radstock's teaching, but a prayer of Radstock reached his heart and he too became a zealous believer. Madam Tchertkoff, Madam Paschkoff's sister, also belonged to the company.[13]

This group met together to help each other spiritually and to work socially. They helped one another by sharing together personally and by holding more formal meetings. The work in the area was twofold: giving material help to the needy and distributing Bibles. Some of them, especially Baroness Wrede, did tremendous work in the prisons. Their numbers increased so markedly that it was reported that 'There were no less than forty homes opened to Radstockist meetings', and in 1891 twenty-eight out of forty-one dioceses were 'infected' by 'heresies'.[14]

In 1866, Lord Radstock had been the instrument used by God to the salvation of Dr Baedeker. The doctor and his wife visited Russia and stayed with Princess Lieven, joining in fellowship with the Lieven family, Kargel, Baron and Baroness Wrede, and 'my dear friend' Colonel Paschkoff.[15] Kargel[16] travelled with Dr Baedeker, and they were joined by Davidson of the British and Foreign Bible

Society.[17] Kargel and Davidson not only provided Dr Baedeker with company, but they had contacts in Russia, and Davidson was able to secure a supply of Bibles. Baroness von Wrede opened up prison doors for Baedeker to visit the prisoners. Like Radstock, the doctor was not a brilliant speaker; yet he, too, could communicate effectively with the Russians.

*Student work*

One of the members of the St. Petersburg circle was Baron Paul Nicolay.[18] Coming from Finland, he was a strong link in the chain of events in Finland, Germany and Russia. Besides belonging to the St. Petersburg group, Baron Nicolay commenced work among students —and this is the fourth feature of the spiritual background. He met John R. Mott in 1899, and on 18 November of that year the Russian Student Christian Movement came into being (RSCM).[19] During the first few years progress was slow, but there was some growth in 1903, despite the fact that a high percentage of students regarded themselves as atheists. Baron Nicolay had the support of Kargel and Miss Peucker.[20] When Karl Heim, secretary of the German Student Movement, visited Russia in 1903, he could see signs of real interest among many of the students. Even so, he found his visit to Princess Lieven's home much more encouraging, for there he experienced 'a quite unexpected encounter with a piece of New Testament Christian life'.[21]

One of Baron Nicolay's main aims was to create an interest in reading the Bible. Indeed, in all the features mentioned the Bible was central—as the means of preaching, understanding a personal experience of God, and comprehending the doctrine of the church and the nature of revival. Baron Waldemar Uixküll,[22] a prominent figure in Russian evangelicalism, believed that there were three main reasons for the spiritual changes in Russia. These were the work of the British and Foreign Bible Society in providing Scriptures for the people, the brave suffering of believers, and the teaching of the Orthodox Church (because its strong emphasis on law showed the people the need for grace).[23]

**Mrs Jessie Penn-Lewis**

Before the end of the nineteenth century another person emerges on the stage, the enigmatic Welsh lady, Mrs Jessie Penn-Lewis. During her visits to Russia she became friendly with the aristocratic circle in St. Petersburg, including Princess Lieven, Madam Tchertkoff, Madam Korff and Baron Paul Nicolay.[24] Two other persons—the sisters Olga and Sophie Wolkoff—cared for Mrs Penn-Lewis during her third visit when she was very ill.[25] There is no doubt that she felt at home in the comfort of the Russian palaces. She describes her visit to Princess Lieven with pleasure:

> I then went to Princess Lieven where I dined, then was driven in their private sledge, under magnificent furs, behind a pair of beautiful black horses, to another house where we had a very large meeting in a dining room.[26]

The visitor also attended services in what used to be the Lieven ball-room but had become a place of meeting for Russian believers. Princess Lieven acknowledged the debt of the group to Mrs Penn-Lewis. After referring to the visits of Commissioner Duff of the Salvation Army and Grattan Guinness, the Princess added her tribute to the Welsh visitor: 'Mrs Penn-Lewis came several times and awakened new aspirations in our midst.'[27]

Mrs Penn-Lewis appreciated the fellowship meetings and, like Karl Heim, believed that they resembled New Testament Christianity. Her desire was to see the spiritual lives of the believers deepened, and that this should lead on to revival. On one occasion she herself says, 'I pinned them all to Dr Andrew Murray's seven steps to blessing.'[28] When revival broke out in Wales her concern for Russia became more intense: 'No other land is so *deep* in my heart. Wales is my Country after the flesh and Russia my Country after the Spirit—you know God has said so.'[29] The Holy Spirit was working in Wales and other countries. He was ready to bring Pentecost to Russia:[30]

> He is ready to do so in Russia also—if His people will set themselves unto prayer. God has put Russia very deeply in my heart since He sent me to you in 1897 & it has been with many tears & anguish of heart that I have pleaded for the land this last year.

Mrs Penn-Lewis corresponded with her friends in Russia, and met some of them during her visit to Germany in 1905. That same year Madam Tchertkoff was staying with her in England.[31] The believers in Russia welcomed translations of the Welsh lady's works.

### William Fetler

Mrs Penn-Lewis made known to the Christian world what was happening in Wales. Russians were visiting Wales, and in an account of a meeting in Neath, South Wales, she referred to a Russian gentleman who took part.[32] Many of the scenes she reported she had witnessed herself, while other accounts were received from friends,[33] including William Fetler from Latvia, who was at that time in London. He was the son of a Baptist minister who was expected to do his work and keep his family on £20 a year. Following his conversion at the age of fifteen, William Fetler had a desire to preach the gospel and, with the help of a dictionary (as he had very little English), he applied to Spurgeon's College, London. He was accepted and entered the college in 1903.[34]

During his stay at the college William Fetler attended revival meetings in Wales, doing so in the company of fellow students, and of Dr McCaig (the Principal), the Rev. Thomas Spurgeon and two deacons from the Metropolitan Tabernacle.[35] Some of the Welsh students there, home for the Christmas holidays, had already attended many of the revival meetings. When the party from London arrived, they went to the Welsh Baptist chapel on the Hayes in Cardiff. William Fetler took part in the meeting, and Charles Davies, minister of the church, was amazed at what he heard.[36] Fetler revelled in the open worship of revival times and acknowledged that God's hand was upon Evan Roberts. One author is of the opinion that 'Fetler's involvement in the revival was total. He became a personal friend of Evan Roberts.'[37]

Early in 1905, scenes similar to those in Wales were witnessed at Spurgeon's College and the Metropolitan Tabernacle, with Fetler and the Welsh students taking a prominent part in them.[38] By this time the foreign student was burning with revival fire, and anxious to see it spreading to Russia. There were hopeful signs in that land already, and William Fetler sent Mrs Penn-Lewis reports of what was happening in Riga, Latvia, St. Petersburg and other places.

**Events in Russia**
In the reports (most of them from Fetler), Mrs Penn-Lewis pinpointed events in some of the centres, especially a week of prayer for Russia, the establishing of a convention, and the success of Christian literature distribution. At Windau, the terminus of the Moscow–Windau railway, earnest prayer meetings had been held from the autumn of 1905. On one Sunday in the middle of 1906, the morning was devoted to prayer and the afternoon to dealing with those who wanted to consecrate their lives to God:[39]

> First of all we knelt and cried before God! It was a prayer such as never known before. At least 50 persons prayed at a time. It was

like the sound of a rushing mighty wind, and yet, also—as a brother remarked—like to the music of a harp. At first one lost sheep came forward, testifying that she had found peace. A young sailor followed. We fell on our knees and thanked God. And thus came young men and women by twos and threes, aged men too, and such who had known the Lord, but had turned their backs to the Father's home.

There was continuing blessing during August, when Fetler also reported a spiritual quickening among many in the city of Kieff.[40]

The young Russian must have been delighted to hear from his uncle in Melitopol, with the news that[41]

Some 600 were present in the morning service; in the second 800, and during the third we could not easily number them, for the hall was quite packed and over a 1,000 souls were outside in the court.

The uncle was also encouraged because a great number, including acknowledged atheists, were reading their Bibles.

The same enthusiasm for reading the Scriptures was found in Riga, where one service was turned into a large Bible class, with young and old diligently searching the Word of God, and the Spirit of God moving many to pray 'like at Windau'.[42] Siberia was not only a place for the Government's unwanted persons but also a centre for God's favoured people. Young and old were being powerfully transformed:

One is breathless with joy, seeing the zeal of our young men and maidens, devoting themselves, and the best of their lives to the Lord's service, like Joshua, son of Nun.[43]

A call for prayer was initiated by the *Christian* (Russian), supported by Baron Paul Nicolay from the St. Petersburg group, and a word of encouragement was received from F. B. Meyer in England. Prayer circles were formed, and meetings also continued in the homes of Princess Lieven and a Princess in Livland.[44] There were encouraging reports of the week for prayer from Riga, Omsk, South Crimea, Yalta, Armenia, Berlin, Finland, and the Russian believers in Paris. In one place (unnamed), 'There was a powerful outpouring of the Holy Ghost, and the characteristics were much the same as they had been in Wales.'[45]

Those involved in the week of prayer were also involved in establishing a convention at Estland in Estonia. Baron Uixküll inaugurated
it, supported by Baron Paul Nicolay, Pastor Kargel and Baron von
Glehn. On the last day of the meetings, Pastor Kargel spoke for an
hour and a half on the suffering of Christ and the crucifixion of the
old life for the Christian. All were humbled before God. 'It was',
according to one present, 'as if the Lord Himself was walking in our
midst, touching our hearts.'[46]

Another way to stimulate interest in the Scriptures and spiritual
matters was to obtain good literature for the people. The works of
J. C. Ryle and C. H. Spurgeon were popular in Russia. Several
thousands of tracts were distributed—a work made possible by the
support of the Religious Tract Society, the Children's Special
Service Mission and the Drummond Tract Society, Stirling.[47] The
believers in Russia were still asking for Mrs Penn-Lewis's works,
and many of them were translated into Russian. She lost one of her
supporters, however, when one of two sisters died in 1906 (probably
one of the Wolkoff sisters who had cared for her during her third
visit to Russia).[48]

## Fetler's return

William Fetler was glad of these developments in Russia, but
realised that large areas of the country had not been touched by the
spiritual revival: 'The great bulk is yet untouched.'[49] In 1907 he
returned to Russia with great anticipation. He had worked for a
while with Russians in London and was uncertain as to his future,
thinking that possibly he would be called to China; but E. A. Carter,
founder of the Pioneer Mission, urged him to go back to Russia. He
responded positively and was accompanied to the East London
Docks by his friend, the Welshman Caradoc Jones, who sang the
Welsh hymn 'We'll view from the mountains of Canaan' to the tune
'Crugybar'.[50] On his arrival in St. Petersburg [Leningrad] William
Fetler was welcomed by Princess Lieven, Madam Tchertkoff and
other believers.

Meetings were held in many places, including the palace of
Princess Lieven, and William Fetler himself took care of a small congregation in St. Petersburg. After a few months he and his people
were looking for a larger hall to accommodate all that were coming
to worship. The programme for a typical Sunday was as follows.
After worship at 10 o'clock, there would be a meeting with candidates for baptism. After lunch, a Sunday school was held in Princess
Lieven's Hall. At 5.15 p.m. they met for prayer, then held a Lettish

(Latvian) service at 6, a Lettish church meeting at 7.15, and a Russian service at 8 o'clock.

One journalist referred to William Fetler as the most conspicuous leader in Russia and marvelled at what had been accomplished in a short time. In addition to the Sunday services there was much activity during the week:[51]

> Soon he had a preacher's training class, and out of that came a Wednesday evening Bible lecture class, to which five to seven hundred people come of every grade, from peasant to artisan to nobility, even to royalty. He uses the blackboard in the style of Campbell Morgan. He also has a Thursday night lecture for the students of St. Petersburg University and high schools, with large attendances and converts who at once become active workers.

Accounts of Fetler's preaching speak of his 'impassioned sermons' and the 'infectious enthusiasm that easily moved his audience'.[52]

*Growth and unity*

There was rapid progress in the work. Six hundred people were baptised during a period of two months, and twenty-five had been baptised each week in the river Don in Rostoff.[53] By June 1908 it was possible for eight Sunday schools to come together for a joint meeting, with Fetler, Kargel and Prokhanoff taking part.[54] The work attracted attention in many countries of the world, including Wales, England, Australia and America.

It was a great help for William Fetler and others that the Russian Evangelical Alliance had been established in 1906. This was an alliance that he himself had helped to form, together with Baron Paul Nicolay and J. S. Prokhanoff.[55] It brought some unity to the evangelical witness, although there was division later on. The Alliance's main aim was to bring individual believers, not churches, together, so that they would be aware of one another and be able to help each other in facing the opposition from State and Church that was continuing even after 1905.

An American reporter expressed the expectations that people had of William Fetler:[56]

> Twenty-eight years of age, speaking four languages, consumed with Pauline passion for the salvation of his countrymen, Wilhelm Fetler bids fair, if his life is spared, to be one of the moulding influences in a new Russia.

Many in Britain would echo that opinion, and the link between them and Russia was further strengthened when a centre called 'Slavanka' was opened in Southbourne, Hampshire.[57] This centre was visited occasionally by Fetler himself.

# Part II
# The AMERICAs
# and the
# WEST INDIES

# 6
# The United States
# of America

Like Wales, the United States of America has a long history of revival. The awakenings in the States, however, were more varied in character than the awakenings in Wales. By 1900 the classical teaching of Jonathan Edwards, the camp meeting tradition, the innovations of Charles Finney, the Revival of 1858–59 and the evangelism of D. L. Moody had contributed substantially to the life of the churches. Sometimes one tradition was the key factor in a revival, while at other times two or more traditions would be evident.[1]

Churches were therefore no strangers to revival. D. L. Moody acknowledged that though evangelism was important, the real need of the States was for revival, and J. Wilbur Chapman and R. A. Torrey agreed with him. The desire for revival was fed by the growth of holiness movements, and by the emergence in 1901, at Topeka, Kansas, of the 'pentecostal' phenomenon of speaking in tongues.[2]

## A common emphasis

Although differing on points of doctrine, the evangelical churches and the fragmented holiness movement were one in their emphasis on spiritual renewal. They were also of one mind in opposing what they regarded as a common enemy—the growth of liberal theology. There were many leaders and authors who were critical of traditional Protestantism: in their view it overemphasised individualism and neglected social problems. This critical trend culminated in the work of Washington Gladden and Walter Rauschenbusch, the main exponents of the 'Social Gospel'.[3] Evangelical churches of all kinds, however, whether holiness churches that had seceded from historical denominations or evangelical churches within the denominations, were one in their emphasis on personal salvation and revival.

It is no surprise, then, that evangelical churches in the States welcomed news of revival in other countries. And there can be no doubt that the Welsh Revival of 1904–05 had a significant influence on the Revival of 1905 in the States. This is evident from the words of a New York minister: 'You have no conception how the revival in

Wales has appealed to the American people, and how it has led to the quickening of churches throughout the states.'[4] Letters and visitors arrived giving reports of events in Wales; journalists gave attention to the Revival in various newspapers, and some journalists visited Wales to experience the awakening for themselves.

The newspapers played a crucial part. Given that two-fifths of the population were living in towns of over 4,000 people, they could be easily reached by the press.[5] What the people read not only created interest but also moved many to action, as at Indiana and Michigan, where a number of extra prayer meetings were arranged.[6]

## The press

The front page of the *Michigan Christian Herald* had a photograph of Evan Roberts, with an article 'Story of Evan Roberts, the Welsh Evangelist'.[7] Another contributor to that paper rejoiced that 'The Revival Spirit is Widespread and Growing', but urged its readers to learn from what was happening in Wales.[8] There the revival was dealing with lukewarmness and a materialistic spirit, and as these factors were also evident in America there should be concentrated prayer for revival.

In general, readers were given an accurate account of what was happening in Wales, but there was the occasional slip. For example, 'Methodism' was equated with 'Wesleyanism', and Evan Roberts was said to have spent twelve months in Newcastle Emlyn, whereas he was only there for about six weeks.

The newspapers introduced Evan Roberts to America as a young man hardly ever without a Bible near him, committed to his work, and thrust into prominence 'for which', according to one report, 'there seemed no adequate antecedent preparation'.[9] He was raised up to lead 'the people's awakening', when it was possible for all to take part in a service. The correspondent believed that if the power of the revival passed away there would be lasting effects.[10]

Campbell Morgan depicted the revival leader as 'hardly more than a boy, simple and natural, no orator, no leader of men', and aptly described the revival as one of song and prayer.[11] He was of the opinion that the revival did not originate with Evan Roberts, but that he was a product of the revival.

Another correspondent was astounded to read, in an English daily paper, 'The greatest revival in the history of the world has just begun in Wales.'[12] He had read the words 'some five weeks ago', and since then he had made enquiries and was assured that scenes like those at Pentecost were being repeated in Wales seven days a week.[13]

One address that was influential in spreading news of the Welsh Revival was Campbell Morgan's 'Lessons Drawn from the Welsh Revival'. This address was included in the *Michigan Christian Herald* in February 1905,[14] and also in S. D. Shaw's *The Great Revival in Wales*, together with items from *The Times* and other newspapers.[15] Another author who included Campbell Morgan's address in one of his works was Arthur Goodrich, in *The Story of the Welsh Revival*.[16] Two large editions of the address were distributed free of charge, and the demand for them was such that the publishers decided to sell them at four dollars per thousand. Another of the contributors to Shaw's book was A. T. Pierson, and to Goodrich's book, W. T. Stead.

## Prominent journalists

Like Shaw, Pierson and Stead were prominent journalists. Both men visited Wales during the Revival, Stead doing so in the company of Gypsy Smith and Thomas Law of the Free Church Federation.[17] Like Mrs Penn-Lewis, Stead was an interpreter of the Welsh Revival to the world at large, and in his *Review of Reviews* he covered news from many countries.

A. T. Pierson, as editor of *The Missionary Review,* also included news of Wales and other countries.[18] During his visit to Wales he met Mrs Penn-Lewis and attended revival meetings in her company.[19] He traced the beginning of the Welsh Revival to Cardiganshire, but it was after Evan Roberts returned to his home in Loughor that the revival spread.[20] The visitor and F. B. Meyer spoke at the Revival convention at Pontypridd in South Wales in March 1905. When F. B. Meyer himself went to America, he addressed a 'rapt congregation in Los Angeles on the Welsh Revival'.[21]

George T. B. Davies was another journalist in full sympathy with the Welsh Revival. He travelled extensively and included Wales in his journeys. When visiting Swansea in South Wales, he arrived at a revival meeting at 10.45 p.m.[22] Even at that hour, scores of people were seeking admission to the chapel, and the visitor was only allowed in when he explained to a policeman that he was a journalist from Chicago. The place was 'crowded to suffocation'; there were 1,500 present in a building made to hold 700. Although he could not understand the Welsh language, George T. B. Davies experienced a 'strange thrill' when Evan Roberts prayed.[23]

The journalist was able to meet the revivalist and share a meal on two occasions; he believed that the religious leader showed signs of tiredness. When asked for a message for America, Evan Roberts replied by giving the four points he had drawn up during the first week of revival in Loughor—confession of sin, the removal of everything doubtful, obedience, and public confession of Christ.[24] The Welshman addressed America in two other ways: he wrote an article to the *Homiletical Review*[25] and sent a personal letter to someone in Ione, Oregon.[26]

## The spreading flame

It is difficult, if not impossible, to pinpoint when and where the revival broke out in America. When it did, it spread quickly. By April 1905 revivals were reported in Pittsburg, Atlanta, Binghampton, Colorado Springs, Pueblo, Fort Collins and Cripple Creek.[27] The revival was more intense in some places than others, notably in Schenectady district and Denver.

Schenectady was a populous place, thriving economically because of the plant of the General Electric Company; but material well-being did not prevent a ready response to a spiritual message.[28] A Mr Adams was named as one of the leaders, and he stated that they had not received any outside help (meaning, probably, no help from outside evangelists). There had been, however, a spirit of expectancy for some time, 'the great revival in Wales, already lasting nine months, having stirred up all denominations to hold union services'.[29] The whole city was moved, saloons and theatres were emptied and churches filled. Interdenominational rallies were held, and 'By Sunday, 22 January, all the evangelical churches in town had been moved, with packed congregations in each, and the movement continued for months on end.'[30]

In Upper New York State the January week of prayer inspired the churches, and the revival spirit was experienced in twenty-six of them.[31] And Denver, five hundred miles from New York, was profoundly influenced by revival. Seven evangelists were involved in preaching, including Wilbur Chapman.[32] As a result of prayer at the beginning of January 1905 it was decided to close the shops on 20 January from 12.30 to 2 p.m.[33] Five hundred shops were closed, prayer meetings were arranged, and altogether ten thousand people gathered in three places—Tabor Opera House, the Cnotis Theatre and the Coliseum. Processions were also arranged, in which as many as two thousand would take part.[34]

## Canada

Over the border in Canada, revival was experienced in Manitoba, Winnipeg and Toronto, where there was a Welsh pastor, Ivor

Pritchard, who corresponded with Evan Roberts.[35] In British Columbia, missioners of the Church Missionary Society and the Methodist Missionary Society were instruments of revival. The Methodists worked along the Skeena River, 'Where bands of converted Indians visit villages and settlements of the tribes; they have their own "Glory Song" and march through the villages with the Bible in one hand and their snowshoes in the other.'[36]

# 7
# The Welsh communities in the USA

B y the end of the nineteenth century, the Welsh communities in the United States were facing a number of difficulties, linguistically, socially and religiously. The communities reflected the areas in Wales from which the settlers had come: colliers from the Rhondda were found in Scranton; descendants of Llŷn farmers in Remsen –Steuben; steelworkers from Llanelli in Pittsburgh, and men from the slate quarries of North Wales in New York–Vermont.

As long as the Welsh occupied a particular area, their identity could be safeguarded; but as time went on this became increasingly difficult. Lack of employment would force members of a community to leave, breaking up the close-knit fellowship. The slate quarries of New York–Vermont, for example, had 'a history of boom and bust', and many of the Welsh from Granville had to move to Utica.[1] Moving from one place to another, however, was only one aspect of the process of assimilation. When the quarrymen from Granville moved to Utica they found a greater ethnic diversity in that county.[2] In an area known as the Welsh Hills, Pittston, the Welsh had to give way to the Italians. A little later, during the second decade of the twentieth century, the Poles arrived in the stable Welsh community of Steuben.[3]

But there was a greater danger of losing their identity through becoming absorbed into the American way of life, as lived out through the medium of the English language. As in Wales, many ministers believed that English should be used in the services to attract the people, especially the youngsters. Even as early as 1877, J. Edryd Jones, pastor at Oliphant, had introduced English services on Sunday evenings.[4] When Jermyn, Rushdale, had a new minister in 1891, they decided to have some English services,[5] and in 1901 Bethel (Congregational) decided to have an English service in the morning.[6]

Churches that kept solely to the Welsh language retained the language but suffered numerically. People who had emigrated from Wales would naturally find it more difficult to change their language than those born of Welsh parents in America. One thing common to both bilingual and Welsh churches was the 'eisteddfod', and they regarded this as an important aspect of their identity.

### News from Wales
News of the revival in Wales quickened the hopes of the Welsh communities in the States. It was a possible source of renewal spiritually, and such a renewal could create a renewed interest in the Welsh language. Letters arrived giving details of events in Wales, but even more precious was the company of visiting ministers, men like L. Ton Evans[7] and T. Gwernogle Evans.[8] They were welcomed as preachers, as representatives of Wales, and even of a particular district, as their names suggest. Any sign of spiritual renewal would be fanned by prayer by the churches themselves, and reported by the press in Wales.

As early as November 1904, Emmanuel, Newcastle, experienced a stirring of the Spirit of God. From November 1904 to July 1905 a total of 53 persons were admitted into membership—a fact reported by the Welsh press in Wales.[9]

*Seren Cymru* also drew its readers' attention to Parish Street, Wilkesbarre (Pa.).[10] It related how J. D. Roberts of Wilkesbarre, having read an account of revival in *Seren Cymru,* had decided to set aside his prepared sermon for the following Sunday, desiring to depend completely on the guidance of the Holy Spirit.[11] When the minister read his text that Sunday morning, he was so aware of the presence of God that he broke down completely. Deeply moved, he urged his people to open their hearts to the Spirit of God, and the effect was described as 'direct and overwhelming'. The sound of wailing and crying spread through the congregation, and a number of people openly confessed their sins. The same kind of meeting took place in the afternoon and evening, and these meetings continued for weeks. Between 8 January and 16 February 1905, 104 people had been baptised on profession of their faith in Christ.[12]

The year 1904–05 proved very difficult for John Thomas Griffith, Baptist minister at Edwardsdale.[13] The most trying experience for him was the death of his wife; but he was sustained by his own personal faith, by the church, and by revival experiences. He read the accounts of revival in Wales written by 'Spinther' in *Seren Cymru* and informed the author that God had not forgotten them in Edwardsdale.[14] He had thought of leaving the church, but felt that he had to stay to care for 'the spiritual babes'. Between December 1904 and April 1905 the minister received 73 into membership, and 100 during a whole year. In spite of tribulation, John Thomas Griffith could say that 1904 and 1905 'were among my most prosperous years in a spiritual sense'.[15]

## Vermont and New York State

In Fair Haven, Vermont, a prayer meeting was held every Friday in the Welsh Calvinistic Methodist chapel, followed by a young people's meeting. At the beginning of December 1904 the young people's leader decided to read accounts of the Welsh Revival from *Y Goleuad*. The young people responded enthusiastically and arranged a prayer meeting 'to plead with God for a spiritual awakening'.[16] The leader and his fellow officers attended other meetings in the church in order to tell the story of the Welsh Revival.

Joint meetings were held between the Calvinistic Methodists and the Congregationalists. Great freedom in prayer was experienced, especially on Tuesday 10 January 1905, when a number of young men and women prayed for family and friends by name.[17] Meetings could last for a long time: one held in the Congregational church started at 6.30 and continued until 11 o'clock. By March 1905 the fruit of these joint meetings was evident, as 40 people had professed conversion.

The week of prayer at the beginning of January 1905 led to more fervent prayer and an increase in the number of prayer meetings. The young people of Fair Haven were especially active. Whatever meeting was held in the churches, a young people's prayer meeting would follow.[18] A Sunday afternoon meeting was held in the two Welsh chapels alternately, and occasionally in some of the American chapels as well—though it was generally felt that the Americans had not caught the revival fire like the Welsh. Another aspect of the young people's ministry was their social concern, evidenced by their readiness to visit the sick and the poor and to help them materially and spiritually. Thirteen converted Welshmen held services on different streets, venturing even to areas that were not considered respectable.[19]

Between Fair Haven and West Pawlett there were eleven Welsh churches, three of them Congregational and eight Calvinistic Methodist. All these experienced a spiritual quickening, but Fair Haven, West Pawlett and Castleton are mentioned as centres profoundly influenced by the power of God's Spirit. All the churches were keen to invite Evan Roberts to America, and the May Assembly (Calvinistic Methodist) actually sent him an invitation; but he had 'no light from the Lord to make any promise to come over'.[20] The churches were bitterly disappointed; they believed that a visit from the revivalist would have confirmed what had been accomplished during 1905.

*Granville*

Only twelve miles from Fair Haven was Granville, another centre that enjoyed spiritual refreshment during 1905. The two Welsh churches here (Congregational and Calvinistic Methodist) joined together for prayer during the first week of January and, as in Fair Haven, the young people took a prominent part in the meetings. One Friday evening over twenty of them were eagerly awaiting their opportunity to pray; they had to be quick, as one followed another without a break. By March 1905 between seventy and eighty had professed conversion in the two churches. When the report was sent to *Y Cyfaill*, the united prayer meetings had lasted seven weeks, and the ladies had also started a united afternoon prayer meeting.[21]

Fair Haven contributed to the success of the work at Granville. A visitor from Fair Haven attended a Saturday night prayer meeting there. Considering it was pay night for the quarrymen, a surprisingly high number of people had gathered together.[22] The young man from Fair Haven led a lively meeting, and such was the freedom experienced that it was decided to hold extra meetings on the Sunday. Five meetings were held, the last of them being a ladies' prayer meeting at ten o'clock in the evening. The presence of God was very real in these meetings, so much so that in one of them all present were on their knees in the pews. A strange silence fell upon the congregation, occasionally broken by sobbing prayers. The Granville people responded by visiting Fair Haven. The churches joined together for two days during Easter 1905, and even the six o'clock Sunday morning prayer meeting was well attended, with the prayers of the Granville women 'like perfume to anoint the Saviour'.[23]

As there was visible fruit in Vermont, it was possible to find more people there to visit other areas. There was no lack of workers; as many as eighty-four persons could take part in a meeting.[24] Many of them not only visited other areas but presented the need for revival in denominational meetings. Believers of the Calvinistic Methodist Church carried the fire with them to the May Assembly in Rome, New York State. Although the Welsh church there acknowledged the need for revival, it had not actually experienced it. On the Saturday afternoon, after dealing with the business items, Mr Solomon Griffiths, who was presiding, suggested holding a society or fellowship meeting.[25] This proposal was accepted, and opportunity was given for the Vermont believers to tell the story of revival in their district. The account humbled those present, and brought them together on Sunday believing that God would bless them. Such was the convicting power of the Spirit and the reality of God's presence that Joseph Roberts, one of the ministers in New York State, was convinced that revival had broken out in Rome.[26]

Another opportunity for revivalists to come together was at preaching festivals, such as the one held at Granville in October 1905. When at Rome, Joseph Roberts[27] had suggested that they should concentrate on prayer even at the expense of preaching. At Granville, however, with Joseph Roberts present, the preaching was central. He himself took part, as did D. M. Richards (Utica)[28] and John W. Morris (South Poultney).[29] But the sermon that made the deepest impression was delivered by J. C. Jones (Chicago),[30] who developed his sermon on the days of the week. Before he had finished, the congregation broke out into praise and rejoicing. Many of those present believed that this meeting was the 'crown of the Revival'.[31]

**Pennsylvania**

News of revival in Wales fell on good ground in Scranton (Pa.), and David Jones (Congregational) zealously led revival meetings. He could 'lift the congregation to such a pitch of religious enthusiasm' that, on at least one occasion, the other invited preacher refused to preach.[32] David Jones received sixty into membership on a communion Sunday in February 1905, while another minister, Thomas C. Edwards (Cynonfardd), received a hundred and twenty 'in recent weeks'.[33] The same encouraging news was reported from Johnston, New Castle and Ebensburg, where J. Twyson Jones was possessed by the spirit of revival.[34]

The revival led to changes in many churches and denominational gatherings; these were born of a desire to follow the leading of the Spirit rather than keeping slavishly to traditional methods. The Quarterly Meeting of the Congregationalists, 11-12 March 1905, gave little attention to business matters and concentrated on prayer and the sharing of religious experiences. A group of ministers met in the home of J. Vinson Stephens, Pittston, for study and prayer, but as the revival progressed, prayer became their main concern.[35] The people at Tabernacle, Scranton, had been celebrating St David's Day by arranging a supper, the proceeds of which went into church funds. In 1905, however, a religious concert was held to mark the day, as this was felt to be more in keeping with the spirit of revival and more appropriate to a place of worship.[36]

The Tabernacle had experienced a spiritual explosion, but an explosion of a different kind took place in May 1905. The building was seriously damaged when a group of men attempted to destroy it using dynamite.[37] The Tabernacle people believed it to be the work of those connected with the drink trade. The chapel's location was a visible illustration of the conflict between the chapels and the brewers, for in the road where it was situated (covering a distance of four hundred yards), every other building was a public house. As in Wales, chapel-goers regarded ale as harmful, and the brewers as enemies of religion.[38]

The Baptists at Hyde Park (Scranton), under the leadership of their minister J. Cromwell Hughes from Swansea (Wales), met regularly for prayer. They were clearly inspired by the week of prayer at the beginning of January 1905, because it led to persevering prayer every night except Saturday, and by the middle of February twenty-three people had professed conversion. The practice here reflected the linguistic changes taking place: on Sunday morning the service was in Welsh, and on Sunday evening in English.[39]

**Other areas**

Although there was concentrated activity in Pennsylvania, New York State and Vermont, many other areas felt the influence of revival. To the south, in Ocean City, New Jersey, a hundred people professed conversion, and the Calvinistic Methodists had to build a bigger chapel.[40] On 12 March 1905, Youngstown (to the west in Ohio) received forty candidates into church membership.[41] Further west, the wind of revival was blowing 'even in this Babylon'—that is, Chicago.[42]

Hebron chapel in Chicago had been praying for revival for some time. They were greatly encouraged by the week of prayer at the beginning of January 1905, and by April the prayer meetings had already continued for nine weeks. One meeting on 17 February was remembered because J. C. Jones, minister of Hebron, publicly consecrated himself anew to the work of the Christian ministry. In the same meeting twelve new converts asked for membership. The following Sunday, J. C. Jones baptised three people, gave the right hand of fellowship to eleven adults and received thirteen of the church's young people into membership. Children of about fifteen years of age were holding prayer meetings, and in the Ladies' Aid Society the main topic of conversation was that of revival.[43]

In Emerson (Iowa), R. H. Jones read *Y Goleuad* to keep himself informed of events in Wales, and after the week of prayer in January he was convinced that the prophecy of Joel, chapter 2, would be

fulfilled in Emerson.[44] To the north of Iowa was Minnesota, where
H. P. Morgan (Wesleyan) ministered; he had been an assistant to John
Evans, Eglwysbach, in Pontypridd, Wales. In Minnesota, 'A sudden
and powerful awakening was experienced in the life of the churches
and desire was expressed for a united mission.'[45] Forty missioners
took part in the crusade, in which O. F. Pugh, originally from
Machynlleth, North Wales, 'rendered excellent service as a singing
evangelist'.[46]

There were fewer Welsh people to the west than on the East Coast.
One person concerned with revival was J. Lewis Jones of Ione,
Oregon, who had been brought up in Wales. He was delighted to
receive a letter from Evan Roberts himself, in which he explained
how 'self' was the hindrance to revival blessing.[47] According to Evan
Roberts, the path to blessing was prayer, daily reading of the Bible
and a total surrender to God. In his own words, 'If we want to suc-
ceed and possess full joy, we must not think of our success and our
joy, because it is self; but let God's will be our only and sufficient
joy.'[48] So Evan Roberts' experience and method of revival were being
presented on the west side of America.

**Visitors from Wales**
Many Welsh ministers, together with others, contributed substantially
to the progress of the revival in the USA. A group left Wales early in
1905: they included W. Rees (at that time in London), W. B. Jones,
Pen-y-cae (North Wales), and T. Teifion Richards from Swansea
(South Wales).[49] Rees and Richards concentrated on reporting the
revival, while Jones explained the issues involved in the Education
Bill and their implications for Wales. At Randolph, when William
Rees gave an account of the Welsh revival, he was asked to lead a
prayer meeting according to the pattern followed in his home country.
In Dawn he spoke again for an hour on 'The Revival in Wales', and
kept to the same theme at Emporia, the Welsh and English churches
at Denver.[50]

*Ellinor Williams*
Ellinor Williams had arrived in America before the beginning of the
revival. She had been a member at Castle Street Baptist Church in
Llangollen and was for a while a temperance worker in North Wales.[51]
Writing from Philadelphia on 9 January 1905 she rejoiced in the fact
that the breezes of revival in Wales were felt in America and
informed her friends that revival was spreading in the Welsh churches
and in others as well.[52] The Welsh lady had met President Roosevelt,

who was 'highly pleased with the success of the Welsh Revival'.[53] Ellinor Williams was convinced that the answer to the need of the churches was revival—an awakening that would bring men, women and children to a saving knowledge of the Lord Jesus Christ.

The lady from Wales combined temperance work and preaching. During her preaching tours she visited churches that were enjoying revival and encouraged prayer in other areas. She visited Wilkesbarre and Plymouth, where D. Rhoslyn Davies had received scores of people into membership in a matter of months.[54] During the month of May 1905 she spoke once a day for most of the month, and three times every Sunday. After meeting with many Welsh people in Shenandoah, she moved on to Providence, where she met the minister W. F. Davies and 'dear Llinos Haf'. The latter was an evangelist from South Wales who helped Miss Williams with the singing; her musical items included '*Dychweliad yr Amen*' (The return of the Amen), which was also sung in Wales.[55]

Language barriers were broken down. Ellinor Williams spoke in English at Hyde Park and York, where the Dutch people also came into the Welsh church to relate their experiences of revival. Denominational barriers were also removed. In Philadelphia, the Welsh sang Welsh songs in the English Methodist Episcopal Church, while the minister gave an account of the revival in Wales. Ellinor Williams was a Baptist but was happy to visit churches of all denominations. She was encouraged by the meetings in the Wesleyan churches at Bangor and Utica, and admired those who attended the meetings in the Congregational Church in Edwardsville, coming there straight from work.[56] When she travelled along the Suzueharina river she was accompanied by a Congregational minister and Dr J. Wynne Jones, a Presbyterian, who invited her to his home town of Baltimore. Dr Jones had left Beaufort (Gwent) as a young man, and had taken part in the Civil War. He was ordained and became pastor of a Welsh church, but soon an English cause was added to the pastorate. He was regarded as 'one of the most influential Welshmen in America'.[57]

During 1906 Ellinor Williams spent much time in New York and Granville, two areas that had known revival during the previous year. She left Johnstown for New York on 9 January 1906, and after a meeting on 11th Street visited the Rescue Settlement for Girls in the slums of China Town. One of the workers at the Settlement was Ruth Price, a Welsh girl whose parents had emigrated from Aberdare, South Wales. At midnight the preacher addressed hundreds of people in the Mission Hall: some of them were in rags, and many of them the worse for wear through drinking and fighting. The following night, she took part in a very intense revival meeting on 13th Street, and was assured that the Spirit of God was still at work. The Welsh lady felt that the alabaster box had been broken and the incense was filling the place.[58]

Three meetings had been arranged for Miss Williams at Granville.[59] There was a good spirit in the Sunday morning meeting in the Congregational chapel, and also in the united prayer meeting in the afternoon. At 5 o'clock a goodly number gathered at the Welsh Calvinistic Methodist Church. For an hour they sang, praised and prayed, and by 6 o'clock the chapel was overflowing, as people were coming in all the time. It was decided to continue the meetings the following week. Three nights were taken up with singing and addresses, one night devoted to a fellowship meeting in order to share experiences, and on the last night Ellinor Williams addressed the meeting on temperance.[60] She commended the ministers of Granville for their wisdom in arranging reading/study classes in the churches. She was glad also that the ministers intended calling all the Welsh preachers together to a preaching festival. Ellinor Williams described the area as being 'bathed' in the Spirit of God.[61]

Characteristic of many of the meetings was the note of praise for what God had accomplished during 1905. Rows of men and women would be on their knees, and Ellinor Williams described the presence of God as the bush burning without being consumed.[62] The fire was still burning in West Pawlett when Miss Williams visited early in 1906. She was told that almost all the Welsh people were church members, many of them converted or restored during the revival. At one meeting she attended, every single person was broken in spirit and weeping.

At Coke Memorial, Utica, D. D. Davies was holding the fort until the arrival of the new minister, Arthur Harris, a child of the Welsh revival, converted in the Rhondda. Ellinor Williams attended the first meeting in the church after he arrived, happy that another Welsh revivalist had settled in America.[63] At Tabernacle, Utica, the Welsh lady heard an unusual announcement. The minister of the church, William Wallace, had been to the Baptist World Congress in London and had visited Wales during the revival. It was his intention to show pictures of events in Wales with appropriate music.[64]

Even in 1907 Ellinor Williams could testify to revival meetings. She mentions specifically Columbus in Ohio, Johnstown in Pittsburgh, and Canonsbury. In the last place, however, a strike had created a division among the Welsh people and affected the spirit of the meetings.[65]

*Other visitors*

Ellinor Williams was in America for an extended period, while other preachers and evangelists paid brief visits. A group of three left early in 1906.[66] They were J. Tudor Rees, a lawyer working in London, Gwilym O. Griffiths (Baptist), who was from Caernarvonshire but ministering in England, and the tenor singer Dewi Michael, who had taken part in revival meetings in Wales.[67] They toured Canada and America. Their last meeting was held at Oakland, America, and it lasted three hours. Gwilym O. Griffiths spoke on the parable of the Prodigal Son, and Dewi Michael sang and also summarised the main events of the Welsh Revival. The meeting closed with the singing of '*Dyma gariad*' (Here is love).[68]

These visitors were followed by Gypsy Smith, who was sponsored by the Free Church Council, London. One person who heard him at Portland was Howell Davies; he was impressed with the evangelist's mastery of Scripture and delighted with the references to revival experiences in Pontypridd, Merthyr Tydfil and Wrexham. The evangelist also told the congregation how the singing in Wales had impressed him.[69]

*Seth Joshua and Sam Jenkins*

The Forward Movement of the Presbyterian Church of Wales was also interested in the revival in America and sent Seth Joshua and the soloist Sam Jenkins on a preaching tour.[70] Seth Joshua received a letter of commendation from the Quarterly Association at Cardigan. Both men were given a send-off at Liverpool before sailing on 26 September 1906.[71] The day after his arrival in America, Seth Joshua visited A. B. Simpson at the Tabernacle Christian Alliance and the Welsh Church in New York. Meetings were held in many revival centres, including Middle Granville, Pawlett and Wilkesbarre.[72]

Seth Joshua returned after a few months, but Sam Jenkins remained, and was joined by T. C. Thomas and his wife, who were from Bedlinog (South Wales).[73] The three of them travelled through Wisconsin, Ohio, New York State and Vermont. They would preach and give an account of the Welsh Revival, and Sam Jenkins would sing, though when the group visited Racine (Wisconsin) his voice was rather strained.[74]

Utica was throbbing with activity. Wilbur Chapman was holding revival meetings there, assisted in song by Edward Lloyd (originally from Blaenau Ffestiniog, Merionethshire), who moved the congregation with a rendering of 'The Light of the World'.[75] In the east of the city Dr Toy was the preacher in English, while the Welsh group held

meetings in Moriah (CM). T. C. Thomas based his messages on
Psalm 87, Matthew 19:30 and John 12:32. From Utica the revivalists
travelled to Ramsen and Rome before returning home.[76]

### R. B. Jones

Before Sam Jenkins and T.C. Thomas and his wife had finished their
tour in March 1907, R. B. Jones had arrived in America. He was the
Baptist minister at Ynys-hir, Rhondda, and a prominent revival
leader, having been the means of igniting the revival fire at Rhos,
Wrexham.[77] He combined revival work with a faithful ministry in the
Rhondda. The Welsh preacher had connections in America. One of
these was the son of Dr Morris of Treorchy (Rhondda) and secretary
of the Association that had invited R. B. Jones to America. A member
in Edwardsville had been in Dr Morris's church in Treorchy. L. Ton
Evans ('Junius') had ministered in Edwardsville, but was in Wales
during part of 1905.[78] Hyde Park, Scranton, was interested in R. B.
Jones personally and had extended an invitation to him to be their
pastor.[79] Had he accepted, Wales would have lost a most able revival
teacher.

Before leaving, R. B. Jones received a letter from Evan Roberts, in
which he prayerfully desired God's blessing on the evangelist.[80] Evan
Roberts had opened his Bible and his eye caught a verse that inspired
him to turn to poetry. He composed eleven verses to express his good
wishes to R. B. Jones, making use of the metaphor of the sea and
developing it in terms of the storm, shelter and rudder. Two of the
revivalist's favourite themes emerge in the verses—Christ's blood
shed on the cross, and Christ's victory over Satan—two themes that
were dear to R. B. Jones as well. Prayerfully commended to God by
Evan Roberts, other friends, and the church at Ainon, Ynys-hir, R. B.
Jones crossed to America and was warmly welcomed in
Pennsylvania.

This 'strange and dear man' began his ministry at Edwardsville on
Monday 23 February and continued until 3 March.[81] The Baptist
chapel was too small to accommodate the crowd, and they had to
move to the Welsh Congregational chapel. In that chapel they
enjoyed the company of the ministers T. C. Edwards, J. T. Griffith,
and J. W. Norris (an American who, in spite of the fact that he did
not understand Welsh, attended a number of revival meetings).[82] John
Morgan had a special reason for welcoming the evangelist, as he and
R. B. Jones had been brought up together in Dowlais, Merthyr Tydfil.
The missioner spent a week at Edwardsville and the same length of
time in two different chapels in Wilkesbarre, Parsons and Pittston.

In Parish Street, Wilkesbarre, five hundred of the congregation formed a procession, singing hymns as they marched through the streets and inviting many people to the meetings.[83] They held an open-air service, which was something new in that area. R. B. Jones was at home in the procession and in the open-air service, being used to both forms of witness in Wales. Soon after his visit to Parsons, the chapel was set on fire. The assumption was that this had something to do with the Welshman's visit;[84] the brewers were not suspected, as in the explosion in Scranton. When R. B. Jones visited Scranton, *he* was the dynamite, and his ministry was described as 'powerful and cutting'.[85] There were varying responses to his appearance and ministry: a lady in West Side thought he resembled Evan Roberts,[86] while the press thought of the missioner as another Billy Sunday—'a very strange comparison', as Brynmor Pierce Jones aptly commented.[87] During his stay at Scranton, the preacher expounded Romans chapter 8, verse 12, and his message on 'The Kingdom' was 'striking'.[88]

Throughout the tour there was a good response. The experience of a member in Edwardsville is typical of many. She attended a number of the meetings and felt 'broken and made over entirely':[89]

What I have experienced has also been the experience of scores, very many in our own church, and many in all the churches he has laboured in so far; not only churches but communities. Talk of Revival; it was not as exciting as in Wales, but the change of life is just as intense and as real, I am sure.

The church at Edwardsville supported R. B. Jones wholeheartedly. A letter sent to him by Wm. J. Nicholas after his return to Wales clearly expresses this support.[90] The writer had no doubt that the church had greatly benefited from the ministry, but the greatest impact was made on the young people. The older folk tended to be traditional and formal. Nicholas also reported continuing encouragements in many areas: one minister had received thirty-two candidates into membership as a result of the Welshman's visit. The main burden of the letter was to invite R. B. Jones to the pastorate of Edwardsville. He had to refuse this invitation too, but it is evident that they esteemed him highly in that church.

The letter from America hinted at criticism of R. B. Jones, especially from the older folk. But some of the ministers were not too happy with the preaching either, Cromwell Hughes of Hyde Park being the most outspoken. This was ironic, because he had welcomed the revival and now ministered in the church that had previously

extended to R. B Jones an invitation to the pastorate. The minister of
Hyde Park believed that 'the apostle of Keswick' was too demanding
in his preaching, and that he neglected themes of grace, peace and
liberty.[91] Others, not named, agreed with Cromwell Hughes, and
some churches had decided not to have such services again. The
critics, however, were outnumbered by the supporters, and Wm. J.
Nicholas assured R. B. Jones that the young people of Hyde Park
would welcome him, 'regardless of difficulties'.[92]

R. B. Jones returned to Wales to a welcome described as 'a big
emotional affair', at which his friend W. S. Jones presided. Dr
Morris, Treorchy, believed that the mission was the 'most effective
ever conducted by a Welshman in America'.[93]

# 8
# South America: Patagonia

The Welsh people in Patagonia were further removed from Wales than their brothers and sisters in the United States of America. Welsh chapels and ministers were few indeed in Patagonia, and rarely did the people have occasion to welcome someone from Wales.

The Welshmen did not, however, hang up their harps; they sang songs to the Lord in an alien land, and this helped them to make it their home. Those songs often had a tinge of *hiraeth*—a *hiraeth* that would take on an added hue when newspapers and magazines arrived from Wales. Journals often mentioned were *Y Faner*, *Yr Herald Cymraeg*, *Y Glorian* (Blaenau Ffestiniog), *Cymru* and *Y Goleuad*, and popular reading in English included the *South Wales Daily News* and W. T. Stead's *Review of Reviews*.[1] Among the avid readers were Griffith Griffith (Gutyn Ebrill),[2] Eluned Morgan the author,[3] and W. M. Hughes, Gaiman[4]—three people who witnessed and experienced the revival when it reached Patagonia.

W. M. Hughes, Gaiman, had visited Cwm Hyfryd in the shadow of the Andes in January 1905, and discovered that the revival in Wales was already a topic of conversation. When he returned to the Gaiman, prayer meetings had been arranged there, and by the middle of February some of these went on for several successive nights.[5] By the end of February the revival spirit had spread to Bryngwyn:

27 Monday. *Clywed fod y cyrddau Adfywiadol yn fywiog yn y Bryngwyn cystal â'r Gaiman. Llwydded yr Iôr y pur a'r gonest.*[6]

The meetings continued through March and April.

In addition to the praying itself, accounts of revival in Wales would be read out in the chapels. 'H. G.' did this on Sunday evening, 26 March, reading to the congregation Elfed Lewis's article in *Y Faner*.[7] Griffith Griffith referred to an aged, able minister with a newspaper in his hand reading 'an account of the fiery revival in Wales'.[8] This, according to the reporter, was a 'new thing'. By reading and listening, therefore, the Welsh of Patagonia would have

quite a clear picture of what was happening in Wales. Much of the
information was included in *Y Drafod*, the Patagonia paper that was
published in Welsh with a page or two of Spanish, to act as a bridge
between the Welsh and the Spaniards.[9] So readers were able to
assess the Welsh Revival,[10] learn about Evan Roberts personally,[11]
and know what the popular hymns were, some of which were
included in *Y Drafod*.[12]

A quiet prayer meeting could suddenly be transformed. In a meeting that was held some time during April, an intense spirit of prayer
fell like lightning upon the congregation. The whole congregation
was humbled, all praying and most of them crying. W. M. Hughes
was convinced that it was a true work of the Spirit of God, and that
no external circumstances could account for the dramatic change.[13]
To confirm the work, Robert Jones the minister urged the people to
pray for revival every day at one o'clock in the afternoon.[14]

### The May meetings

It was during the following month that the most powerful work of the
Spirit of God was experienced, especially on Tuesday and Wednesday 16 and 17 May.[15] A united prayer meeting was held on Tuesday
attended by all ages. There were fears that the inclement weather and
muddy roads would prevent many from coming, but a good number
turned up, and those present felt freedom in praying and a new spirit
in the singing. Some of the original sayings that emerge in a revival
were heard in the meeting. One man was rejoicing because he was at
the throne of grace and not at the counter of the *fonda* (public house).
Another likewise deplored his time in the *fonda*; he had regarded
Zion as a myrtle tree in the valley, while the *fonda* was thriving at the
expense of the workers, but now matters had been reversed.[16]

Griffith Griffith gives a general account of the May meetings:[17]

17 WEDNESDAY. *Cwrdd Gweddi i'r ieuengtyd yn y Gaiman—cynul-
liadau lluosog ar hyd y dydd. Effeithiau grymus yn dilyn. Amryw
yn listio â'r fyddin—yn eu plith Morgan Rhenwlad, Harry Garfield
a Willie Jones, Caerfyrddin, ac eraill.*

   *Gobeithio y bydd yr effeithiau yn dilyn ac i barhau o dan
ddylanwad 'yr ysbryd'. Mr. Humphreys (wedi dychwelyd o'r
Andes) gyda hwy yn y Gaiman, yn y cyrddau y ddeuddydd hyn.*

Another person bears witness in greater detail.[18] The young people
came together on Wednesday morning at 9 o'clock. The hymn
'*Arglwydd Iesu, dysg i'm gerdded*' (Lord Jesus, teach me to walk)

was sung heartily, and a young man besought God to meet with them on that occasion, followed by another young man who invited all present to go on their knees to pray. According to Sarah Morgans de Roberts, all the youngsters were overwhelmed emotionally, hardly able to speak. It was in a very broken and humble spirit that they joined the other worshippers at 10 o'clock. This meeting continued until 12.30 p.m., with many taking part spontaneously, including some of the young ladies.[19]

The revivalists were back in the chapel at 2 o'clock and, as in the morning, many ladies took part, including Eluned Morgan.[20] Deep conviction of sin was felt, leading to bursts of joy when forgiveness of sin was experienced. Specific prayers for individuals were offered, portions of Scripture quoted, and hymns given out at intervals, including '*Dyma gariad*' (Here is love), '*Hapus Awr*' (Happy day) and '*Taflwch Raff Bywyd*' (Throw out the lifeline)—hymns which were also popular in the Welsh Revival. The eyewitness continued her description of the meeting:[21]

> Sisters were weeping and kissing brothers, fathers shaking hands with their sons, boys kissing each other—I saw Herber and Cynddelw. Some fled. Strong men weeping like children. Some were waving their handkerchiefs, while others were bending their hats and waving them and others again with arms raised. Enoch Harries was on the platform shouting. The large congregation was singing '*Diolch Iddo*' [Praise Him], with most of them weeping. After announcing that the converts should go to the vestry by 5.30 p.m. for their names to be recorded, prayer was offered and they went for a good tea.

As in revival meetings in Wales, the minister tested the meeting, but one young man felt that he could improve on the invitation. He rushed to the front and started naming his friends, imploring them to receive Jesus Christ as Saviour.[22] Another meeting was held after tea when, once again, many took part in prayer, some doing so for the first time.[23]

Another person present on that Wednesday mentions further characteristics of the revival meetings.[24] While singing '*Diolch Iddo*' (Praise Him), the congregation would improvise, and instead of '*Diolch Iddo*' would sing '*Ar ei ben bo'r goron*' (Crown Him), followed by '*Fyth am gofio llwch y llawr*' (For ever remembering the dust of the earth). The children were very prominent and would even arrange their own prayer meetings. A few believers saw a sign appearing in the sky. On one occasion, as the worshippers were approaching Dinam, they could see a ball of fire above the chapel, which they took as a sign of God's presence, ready to bless, but by purifying.[25]

## Continuing prayer

The united prayer meetings continued to be the mainstay of the revival. Work on the farm was organised in such a way that family and servants could attend in turn. The young people were more than ready to take part. They figured prominently in a farewell meeting to Tudur Evans, son of the minister J. C. Evans, who was leaving for Wales to prepare for the Christian ministry.[26] There was sorrow in parting with him, but joy as well, because Tudur Evans was one of the revival's converts.

Lewis Humphreys, a child of the 1859 Revival in Wales, welcomed the revival in Patagonia.[27] He had visited the Andes, and returned with verses composed by Owen Williams, the schoolmaster at Cwm Hyfryd. The theme was a desire for worldwide revival.[28] Lewis Humphreys had written to Evan Roberts in March and received a reply in June 1905. Unable to read it at a united prayer meeting as he was prevented from attending, he sent the letter to *Y Drafod* so that it could be read by as many as possible.[29]

Prayer meetings, usually united, continued for some months. In many places they were held regularly every night. Occasionally, only one or two meetings were held during a week, in order to bring as many as possible together in one place.[30] In addition to prayer, attention was given to Bible study in Welsh and Spanish. Before the end of July 1905 a Spanish Bible study was held in the Welsh chapel, Tabernacle.[31] In this way Spanish speakers were reached, and some of them started to attend revival meetings too. Crowds gathered together at Bethesda on a Monday and Tuesday, and one of the features of the meetings was the prayers of young people asking God to forgive their parents for not urging them to attend a place of worship. The most striking feature, however, was the singing of '*Dyma gariad*' (Here is love) by a young Spanish soldier. The reporter was convinced that more room should be given to the Spanish language.[32]

United prayer meetings were held for two days in November 1905, but by this time they were quieter than in May. Those who had only just started to pray in public could, without any difficulty, quote from Scripture and the hymn book. More variety was introduced into the meetings: besides prayer sessions, there were addresses on topics such as 'Temperance', 'The freedom of the slaves' and 'Christian liberty', and items like recitations and solos. Missionary interest was revived, and the churches were urged to hold a missionary prayer meeting on the first Monday of every month, as was happening in Wales. The churches in the Gaiman were already collecting in order to support a home missioner, and all the churches in Patagonia were expecting Wales to send a minister to them.[33]

## Colonia Sarmiento

The revival reached Colonia Sarmiento, where a small group of Welsh people had settled, far removed from one another. Hungering for spiritual provision, they began to meet on 26 March 1905, and this led to other meetings. They sang hymns together, and decided to start a Sunday school. News of revival arrived from Chubut, and they had visits from Tudur Evans and Esau Evans. The spirit of revival was soon felt in their midst. Mrs Owen Jones recalls the 'good meetings' of that time:[34]

*Daeth llawer o'r Bechgyn ymlaen i gymryd rhan heb eu cymell, rhai heb wybod beth oedd cyrddau o'r blaen. Nid oedd yno Weinidogion na swyddogion yr adeg yma, ychydig o boblogaeth a rheini yn bell oddi wrth ei gilydd. Roedd y ffyrdd yn ddrwg, ffosydd naturiol a rheini yn llawn dwr ac wedi rhewi yn aml, ac yn beryglus i'r ceffylau syrthio. Ond er y cwbl lle yr oedd Ewyllys nid oedd troi nôl. Mynd ar gefn y sgribliad tenau yn y nos, yn aml lig a hanner a dwy lig i'r tai i gadw cwrdd gweddi.*

Fervent prayers were offered for friends and family, mentioned by name. For Sunday and weeknight meetings the people were welcomed in different homes.

Although Welsh was usually the language of worship, other languages were used occasionally. One service was held in the home of Fernando Mirando, who had married a Welsh girl, and there were examples of Welsh, English and Spanish people coming together:[35]

*Nid oedd gennym gapel y pryd hwnnw, ond daeth y Cymry at ei gilydd a rhai o genhedloedd eraill. Byddem yn canu mewn tair iaith, Saesneg a spanish. Byddem yn mynd i'w tai trwy ganiatâd, ac yn cael ein gwawdio weithiau. Roedd fel adeg Twr Babel.*

Representatives of all nations enjoyed much freedom in worship, and many professed conversion.

One of the regulars at the prayer meeting was Owen Jones, and his prayer would always be 'The grace of our Lord Jesus Christ be with you always.' In one meeting, however, he was sitting by the fire, dozing, when suddenly he got up and started to pray with words flowing from his heart. This was typical of what happened to many during this time. As a result of these meetings the Welsh believers in Colonia Sarmiento were drawn closer together, and they established a day school and a literary society.[36]

## Eluned Morgan

Most of the Welsh people in Patagonia had never visited the mother country, but a small minority did venture to make the long crossing. One of them was Eluned Morgan, who had visited Wales in 1903 and worked with Ifano Jones in the Public Library in Cardiff.[37] She had returned to Patagonia and was present at the revival meetings during May 1905. On the last day of May a farewell meeting was held for her, as she was going to visit Wales once again. During this stay in Wales she was able to assess the development of the revival, send news to Patagonia and receive news of revival in that land.[38]

Eluned Morgan met Evan Roberts on at least two occasions. Writing on 1 December 1905 she told J. C. Evans in Patagonia that at last she had met the revivalist, heard him speak, and shaken hands with him. The meeting took place at Trecynon, Aberdare, on 27 November 1905, and Eluned Morgan believed that the door of heaven had been opened when Evan Roberts himself arrived. As usual, he had a message to pass on. His word for Patagonia was that they should persevere in spite of all obstacles and disappointments; he assured the Welsh in that land that the prayer of faith and a holy life would always prevail. Evan Roberts himself believed that the Tuesday morning meeting in Trecynon was the best of the whole revival, and for Eluned Morgan it was a foretaste of the perfect fellowship of the people of God in heaven. It would not have surprised her if Jesus Christ had appeared on the clouds of heaven to descend upon them in blessing; the place was well prepared for him by the tears of his people.[39]

The second occasion of meeting him was at Swansea, when Eluned Morgan was reminded of 'that morning in the Vestry in Gaiman—that old, sacred Vestry'.[40] She concluded from talking to Evan Roberts that he would consider returning with her to Patagonia. She also visited his home in Loughor, meeting his father and mother, his brother Dan and his sisters. During her stay Eluned Morgan shared with the people of Wales some of the events in Patagonia. For example, on 19 March 1906 she spoke at Crwbin, Carmarthenshire, on 'Patagonia before and after the Revival'.[41] On the following day, D. D. Walters of the Congregational church in Crwbin was set apart to be a minister in Patagonia.[42] Included in the news from Patagonia (which pleased Eluned Morgan very much) was the fact that the Spanish-speaking people were 'coming into the light', but she was not surprised that the Roman Catholic Church was 'beginning to roar'. Its way of expressing its displeasure was to prohibit its people from reading the Scriptures.[43]

Eluned Morgan returned to Patagonia in June 1906 and expressed surprise at the high spiritual temperature evident in the land. There was a welcome emphasis on holy living and 'on doing something for Jesus'.[44] She was still optimistic during 1907, and could not understand the critics of the revival who were claiming that the influences had passed away. She acknowledged that the flames were not burning so brightly as in 1905, but there were a substantial number of people who could contradict the critics. Eluned Morgan's own spirit was refreshed early in 1908 through reading *With Christ among the Miners* by Elvet Lewis. This book had been a real means of grace to her.[45]

### Criticism

In her account of what was happening in Patagonia, Eluned Morgan refers to criticism of the revival. The most outspoken critic was 'Rhidyllydd' in *Y Drafod*.[46] The criticisms he made were relevant: he pointed out the ill effects of too many late nights and, while acknowledging that it was wrong to quench the Spirit of God, reminded his readers that the Spirit could be grieved by irreverent worship. But 'Rhidyllydd' was not only afraid of enthusiasm; he was also critical of the traditional doctrines accepted by the church. He was answered by 'Vox', who reminded 'Rhidyllydd' of David dancing before the ark, and of the accusation on the Day of Pentecost that the believers were full of new wine. The manifest presence of God removes formality and enables believers to be themselves.[47] Yet, whilst there was criticism of the work in Patagonia, it was never so severe as in some parts of Wales.

*Y Drafod* included some criticisms of the Revival in Wales too. In April it drew attention to the opinion of 'Cymro Llundain' regarding the controversy started by Peter Price, Congregational minister in Dowlais, in *The Western Mail*.[48] The Patagonian paper also included more sympathetic assessments, but pointed out some dangers of the revival. The most helpful was by Elvet Lewis in his articles, 'Y

Diwygiad: Rhybuddion' from *Y Cymro*, and 'Cenedl i Grist' from *The British Weekly* and translated in *Y Cymro*.[49] In the first article Elvet Lewis underlined two main dangers seen in Wales that could serve as a warning to Patagonia. First, the Welsh minister was afraid of imitation, and he knew of some leaders in Wales who were imitating the methods of Evan Roberts. The second danger was a rift between young and old. There was a tendency for older people to be impatient with the enthusiasm of the younger generation, while the youngsters lacked respect for those who were more experienced than they in the Christian life. There was need for care, patience and love.

# 9
# The West Indies

The revival in the West Indies spread from island to island, but the main centre was Jamaica. Miss King, a correspondent of Mrs Penn-Lewis, kept *The Life of Faith* informed of events in that country. 'On January 24 (1905), moved by reports of what was going on in Wales, our correspondent sent out an invitation to a number of Christian friends to unite in prayer once a week for Jamaica.'[1] Interest was created in a number of places. At Salem there was 'a remarkable service' led by John Burnham, formerly one of C. H. Spurgeon's evangelists.[2] A lady got up in tears to ask for prayer, and by the end of the service the number of seekers had reached fifty.

News of awakening was received from Spanish Town and Kingston, where *The Revival News* was published. A general conviction was being created that the need of the hour was for the Holy Spirit to come in renewing power. People needed to experience the indwelling of the Holy Spirit, and 'in this we recognize the prominent teaching of the Revival in Wales'.[3]

## Intercession

A 'Revival League of Intercession' was formed, and it made *The Revival News* its official organ. According to the accounts, the characteristics of the meetings were the powerful working of the Holy Spirit (but without traces of fanaticism), numerous conversions, the strengthening of Christians, and prayer. The children arranged a prayer meeting of their own.[4] Considerable numbers gathered together for meetings, and large numbers professed conversion. The church at Bethnal was full every night, while at St. Andrew's Church, within a brief period of time, six hundred confessed Christ as Saviour and Lord.[5]

The 'triumphant work of the Holy Spirit' was manifested at Clarendon, where George Turner ministered. But the 'triumph' came after weeks of agonising prayer.[6] In June 1906 two weeks were set aside for prayer, during which time many more ministers became convinced of the need for revival. Knowing what had happened in Wales when ministers were changed and became involved in revival,

George Turner and his wife saw this as a most encouraging development. Raglan Phillips was invited to hold meetings at Clarendon to
further the work of renewal. The first meeting was held on 26
August, followed by a week of three services each day. It was a time
of serious heart-searching: a number of reconciliations took place,
backsliders were restored, and many from outside the church attended
regularly.[7] Between August and December 1906, three thousand
people had been 'deeply affected by this movement'.[8]

Public confession of faith was evident in the meetings, but on one
occasion it happened in an unusual way. G. E. Henderson arranged a
baptismal service at 6.30 in the morning, when seventy candidates
were to be baptised in the sea. Many travelled great distances to be
present, some of them camping out overnight. People came in carts
or on mules or horses, and the procession was seen for miles. It was
estimated that the crowd numbered three thousand.[9]

Believers on the island of St. Kitts were very much aware of what
was happening in Wales. The heading in one newspaper read, 'Wales
repeated in the West Indies'.[10] In a short period of time, five hundred
men, women and children declared their commitment to the Lord
Jesus Christ.

Believers in Wales were also conscious that help was needed in the
West Indies. Knowing the need for leaders there during the revival,
the Llanfyllin Circuit of the Wesleyan Methodists was moved to send
out F. W. Vaughan.[11] He joined others already working there, including F. Ellis, Grenada Bag, Wilfred Wright and John Price (St. Kitts).
They welcomed the newcomer and commented on the similarity
between the work in Wales and the West Indies. Progress was particularly evident at Sandypoint, where, during a ten-day period, five
hundred and thirteen converts were recorded.[12]

**Difficulties**
The revival had to face a number of difficulties. Not all the ministers
were sympathetic to such a movement, and when a leading minister
spoke out against the awakening, many accepted his opinion because
of his position. Others criticised the emotionalism and disorder of
the meetings. The revivalists responded by pointing to the changed
lives of hundreds of people. They acknowledged that there was
emotion, but believed that it furthered the spiritual growth of
believers. Generally, they claimed, there was no confusion. In its
editorial, *The Revival News* acknowledged that great care was called
for, because spurious forms of revival had been welcomed in
Jamaica.[13]

Opposition came also from the rum-shop keepers, who claimed that the revival songs were making people mad. Because of this serious development, 'his Excellency the Governor had given orders that the meetings were to be stopped as the Lunatic Asylum was full'.[14]

Miss King of Newport, who had already written to Mrs Penn-Lewis, was prompted to write again. She had been greatly helped by reading Mrs Penn-Lewis's *Living Waters* and had also seen a photograph of the Welsh lady that had been a means of inspiration to her.[15] According to Miss King, most of the blame for the misunderstanding and confusion in Jamaica rested with the ministers. Their disapproval meant that the leadership was in the hands of 'some hot-headed enthusiasts devoid of judgement'.[16] She expressed gratitude to Mrs Penn-Lewis for her articles in *The Life of Faith*, from which many were benefiting.

### Earthquake

It was not only revival that was shaking Jamaica. Suddenly, in 1907, an earthquake struck Kingston.[17] Many said it was the result of natural causes, while others could see the hand of God in it. As one coolie woman said, 'Kinston too much rude—plenty cuss. Massa God bex blige fe lick him.'[18] There is no doubt that it had an impact on the people and turned large numbers to the church.

At Linstead, for example, on one Sunday evening, four thousand people came together to worship. In this meeting (and in others too) a collection was made to help those who had suffered loss because of the earthquake.[19] Its impact was felt at Kingston, Redwood, Ewerton and Jericho. Even though the chapel at Redwood had been rent in three places, the members still held meetings on the Sunday. At Jericho, a series of services started the day before the earthquake (although the pastor was ill in bed). But such difficulties did not deter the worshippers from meeting in the church, and during one half-night of prayer the leaders had to deal with a hundred and ten enquirers. At Mount Hermon a meeting started on the night of the earthquake, and, as in Jericho, the believers continued to meet in the church building.[20]

### Continuing work

Raglan Phillips, who was one of the instruments of revival during 1906 and 1907, continued to lead services during 1908. Under his ministry, the work already begun was confirmed, and he was also the means of spreading the revival into new areas. At Richmond Park, fifty professed conversion on the same evening, while W. B. Esson, a Congregational minister, reported hundreds of conversions in his area.[21] By this time, however, the revival was not so widespread as it had been in the previous two years.

# Part III
# AFRICA
# and
# MADAGASCAR

# 10
# South Africa

Discussing what he called a 'spiritual uplift' in South Africa, J. Edwin Orr mentions two main reasons for its emergence. They were the Peace Mission of Gypsy Smith, and the impact of the Welsh Revival 1904–05 on Afrikaan- and English-speaking churches.[1]

Gypsy Smith visited the country in 1904 and, after a rather cold reception, was accepted by the different denominations. Aggregate attendance at the meetings exceeding three thousand. He returned to Britain to take part in the Welsh Revival, so had an understanding of what was happening in South Africa and in Wales.

News of the Welsh Revival had 'an electrifying effect' upon Christians in South Africa, even in remote parts of the country.[2] One source of information was *The Life of Faith*. As a missionary informed Mrs Penn-Lewis, 'We make straight for the article on Revival week by week as *The Life of Faith* comes, for it is such a linking with the "host of the Lord" in all lands.'[3] Bessie Porter, a friend of Mrs Penn-Lewis, was a missionary with the South Africa General Mission (SAGM) and kept her informed of events in that country.[4]

The SAGM was founded by Spencer Walton, and Andrew Murray was its first president.[5] In 1895, Andrew Murray had spoken at Keswick, and during his stay in Britain had addressed a YWCA meeting at Richmond organised by Mrs Penn-Lewis.[6] Albert Head, chairman of Keswick and Keswick in Wales, kept in close touch with South Africa and with revival leaders in Wales.[7] In 1905 he visited South Africa with SAGM worker A. G. Mercer. The latter had spent some time in Wales during the Revival,[8] and both men were anxious to share the means of revival with Christians in that land. They stayed with Andrew Murray, who was recovering from a slight stroke but was full of enthusiasm for their visit. In one of the early meetings in Johannesburg, 'we told them about the Revival in Wales'.[9]

## Conventions
The most important event of the tour was attending the Wellington Convention, which was organised on the Keswick pattern.[10] Believers

in that area could recognise 'signs of change in at least two neigh-bouring villages'. They were optimistic that the Convention would fan the spirit of hope.[11] Albert Head shared the ministry with Methodist evangelist W. M. Douglas. There was much freedom in prayer, and on one occasion 'A couple of hundred people engaged in prayer from 10 p.m. until 1 a.m., when half those retired, but the remainder continued with a fresh intensity.'[12] W. M. Douglas had travelled extensively, and revival had accompanied his ministry. When he attended revival meetings in South Africa, he could hear 'an echo of the Revival in Wales'.[13]

Further encouragements came from outside—a letter from Evan Roberts the revivalist,[14] and the visit of Charles Inwood in 1906.[15] The latter ministered at conventions in Pretoria, Bloemfontein, East London and Port Elizabeth. East London is mentioned in particular, because in a few days the congregation grew from 300 to 1,000, while Port Elizabeth was notable for the manifestation of God's presence:[16]

> From the first night God began to work mightily. The Word was with power. In some of the later meetings the congregation was swept by the Spirit as a field of corn bowed by a strong wind; and the closing service surpassed in power any we have held hitherto. The Holy Spirit was supreme. I have no hesitation in placing the Port Elizabeth Convention as first in spiritual power.

During the same period, Stuart Holden and his wife were also minis-tering in South Africa, both of them, like Albert Head and Charles Inwood, in the Keswick tradition.

### Across denominations

Revival was experienced within denominations and across denomina-tional boundaries. While the Baptists of South Africa benefited from revival, they also rejoiced that others, all over South Africa, were sharing in spiritual renewal.[17] In the Dutch Reformed Church in Villiersdorp an outstanding revival was experienced. Ten days of prayer during Whitsun was supported for the first time by all the evangelical groupings.[18] The Dutch Reformed, Methodist and Presbyterian papers gave news of revival in Wales and other parts of the world. R. O. Wynne Roberts, a Presbyterian minister from Wales, was struck by the numerous references to the Welsh Revival in the General Assembly of the Presbyterian Church of South Africa.[19] As he listened to the proceedings, the Welshman longed for help from Wales. He would like young men, gifted speakers in Welsh and

English, to come and tell them more about the Revival in Wales. Further help was received by John R. Mott's visit in 1906; he was able to draw together ministers from different denominations. A bonus of his visit was the opportunity it gave him to meet Andrew Murray, who had wielded much influence on the student leader.[20]

The same pattern can be discerned during 1907 and 1908, as traffic between Britain and South Africa continued.In 1907, Bessie Porter was present at the Keswick in Wales, Llandrindod, and surveyed the work of the YWCA worldwide.[21] In 1908 it was F. B. Meyer's turn to visit South Africa. The Christians were looking forward to his coming to Grahamstown because they were aware of much superficiality in the churches there. Francis Chalmers, writing to Mrs Penn-Lewis about the visit, added a postscript: 'I hope that Evan Roberts is better: I was so interested in all I read re the Welsh Revival.'[22]

Further west, some areas believed that revival was on the way, but though there was a warming of the spiritual climate, no great harvest was realised. In one of these areas A. J. Wookey, an LMS missionary from Llanelli, Powys, faithfully persevered.[23] He lived at Vryburg and had oversight of the important station at Kuruman. Generally speaking, the churches that had been established were large and unruly, but slow progress was being made, and a new church had just been built in one place in the Barolong district. 'At Morokweng, in the same district, a marked revival of spiritual life has gladdened the missionary's heart.'[24] The revival was localised; had it spread, it would have been difficult for A. J. Wookey, occupied as he was as chief reviser of the Sechwana Scriptures. That work was duly completed and was of long-term benefit to Kuruman.

## Central and East Africa
Govan Roberts, one of the LMS missionaries in Central Africa, believed that many areas were 'catching the fire'.[25] A week of prayer was held in August 1905, followed by a visit of some boys from the Training Institute of the United Free Church of Scotland in Nyasaland. Considering their age, they were spiritually mature; each one took care of a district and held classes for enquirers in seven villages. In a short time the number of enquirers increased from twenty-three to a hundred and sixty-three. As a result of this work, crowds came together for meetings, and the giving of believers increased dramatically. The gifts included money, bracelets, rings and beads. One of the teachers could not find time to cook, 'so constant is the demand for the Word of Life'.[26] The missionary never imagined that he would see ninety-six hearers meeting at 6.30 a.m., all eager to study the

Word of God. An hour later he would join the congregation for worship, and this was followed by a meeting for church members to
study the Apostles' Creed.[27]

To the east, David John Rees from South Wales was Secretary of
the CMS Ussagara Mission.[28] As he visited the different areas, he was
pleased with the calibre of the teachers at Ukaguru and with the fact
that so many were attending the meetings. He was more than pleased
with what was happening at Bindo: 'Here, and in a few other centres,
we see the signs of an awakening for which we thank God. The people are coming in large numbers.'[29] Clear steps were to be followed in
dealing with people personally. Hearers would become enquirers, and
when they professed conversion they would become catechumens.
After six months, they would usually be accepted into church membership.[30]

The Congo (Zaire) has particular interest for Wales. One of the
prominent missionaries there was Henry Richards, a member of
Tredegarville Baptist Church, Cardiff, and a local colporteur.[31] It was
his minister Alfred Tilly who had recommended him for overseas
mission work[32] with the Livingstone Inland Mission, of which Tilly
was secretary. This was the first society to open up the Congo after
the time of David Livingstone, and it was a mission staunchly supported by the brothers Richard and John Cory.[33] Henry Richards was
sent out in 1879 and was one of the leaders of the revival that took
place in 1889.[34] He joined other men who had gained experience in
Christian work in Cardiff, including Storm (also from Tredegarville),
Telford and Johnson. The first mission station was named 'Cardiff',
and for a while the second was called 'Cory'.[35]

By 1905, therefore, Henry Richards was a mature senior missionary. On the basis of his personal faith and his work in the Congo he
looked for revival, of which he had had a taste twenty years earlier.
There were signs of revival during 1905, and one area actually experienced an awakening. Many answers to prayer were received, and
dreams and visions were evident too.[36] According to a missionary of
the Regions Beyond Missionary Union (which took over the
Livingstone Inland Mission), the revival 'was powerfully stimulated'
by those manifestations.[37] The missionary acknowledged that the
people were naturally superstitious, but despite this believed that in
many lives a genuine work of grace was evident. Lives were changed,
prayer was more fervent, and there was a much greater zeal to take the
gospel to others.

One means of promoting revival was the United Protestant
Conference. The conference for 1906 gave prominence to the subject

of revival, and there were at least three Welshmen present: Henry Richards, Thomas Hope Morgan of the Congo Balolo Mission, and Thomas Lewis of the BMS. Some of the conference members had been on furlough and had visited revival meetings in Wales. Their reports inspired prayer for revival in Africa. In one of the meetings, Thomas Lewis read a paper on the Welsh Revival prepared by William Edwards, Principal of the Baptist College, Cardiff, 'and the spirit of revival seemed to grip us'.[38] Those present could return to their stations and continue to pray for revival. The Regions Beyond Missionary Union was greatly encouraged; it could report before the end of 1906 that eight hundred people had been baptised on profession of their faith.[39]

# 11
# Madagascar

The pioneers of the Protestant Mission in Madagascar were four men from Wales: David Jones, Thomas Bevan, David Griffiths and David Johns. The Welshmen were joined by John Jeffreys, Edward Baker and J. J. Freeman.[1] By 1835 the Bible had been translated and churches established, and between 1831 and 1835 the churches enjoyed a remarkable spiritual awakening. The period from 1835 to 1861 was one of severe persecution for the Christians, but their faith was strengthened through suffering. The mission made steady progress until about 1890, and in 1891 another awakening spread over parts of Madagascar.[2] It strengthened the believers to face a further crisis in 1895, when the French arrived. The new government adopted an anti-Protestant policy, though it was more tolerant in its dealings with the Paris Mission. The coming of the French, however, brought gain as well as loss, for it drew the missionary societies closer together and drove them to utter dependence upon God.

Apart from the difficulties caused by French government policy, early in the twentieth century many of the missionaries were facing troubles of their own. J. E. Thorne's wife was taken ill, and they also lost the financial aid for their children. Robert Griffith's wife was disabled, and Thomas Rowlands' house and schoolroom were partly destroyed by fire.[3] There was also a shortage of food, as floods had covered the rice fields.[4] As they sought to cope with these discouragements, the missionaries received the heartening news of revival in Wales. This moved the Welshmen D. D. Green, Robert Griffith and Thomas Rowlands[5] to pray for revival in Madagascar, and they were joined by other LMS missionaries.

Robert Griffith, J. E. Thorne and the Sharmans worked in the north of the Island. The Welshman noticed renewed zeal for Bible study, while the Sharmans witnessed the changed lives of the boys in their school and reported on the deepening of the spiritual lives of believers. Christian Endeavour meetings had just been established in some churches, and they were experiencing a quickening of interest in study and worship. News of these spiritual encouragements was carried to Friends' school, and within a brief period a hundred pupils professed conversion.

Down in the south, D. D. Green noted the spirit of humility and praise that marked many of the meetings. Thomas Rowlands, also in the south, marvelled at the reconciliations taking place, even in the quarrelling church at Ambohimandroso. In one meeting a lady suddenly rose and appealed for reconciliation, a sense of guilt came over the congregation and confession was made. Then, as a visible proof of peace, the quarrelling groups were photographed together.[6]

Thomas Rowlands felt like Barnabas when he visited Antioch and 'saw the grace of God' (Acts 11:23).[7] During the month of May 1905 these works of grace became more evident in the south. Thomas and Elizabeth Rowlands received accounts of the Revival in Wales and read them to the Christians. They were so impressed that they came together to pray for revival: 'Not only did the news, which every mail from home brought, intensify the longing until it glowed into prayer, but it became the current topic of conversation with many.'[8]

Thomas Rowlands described the meeting held on the first Friday in May. In that Christian Endeavour service the sermon, based on Mark 10:46-52, moved the whole congregation:[9]

> May 6th, at the close of a meeting a few of the most earnest came back to pray and confess sin. In confession they broke down one after another. Suddenly there was a scene of wildest confusion, some sobbing, some praying or singing scraps of penitential hymns. The head teacher (conspicuous from the first for his holy zeal) was on his face on the floor weeping and praying. There was not a dry eye there. This went on for half an hour or more, then as we feared for physical results, we sang a hymn or two, and that calmed then down. It was getting dark, so we broke up; but they got together again, and late at night continued to praise and pray. Thus, we had the earnest of more to follow, and no one doubted that we had our Pentecost.

There was a danger that that meeting might get out of hand, but the missionaries handled it wisely. The following Sunday eighty-three converts were baptised, and prayer was made for them and also for the annual May meetings.

## The May meetings

The first day of the meetings (21 May) was grey and wet. But that did not prevent eight hundred worshippers from coming to join the believers at Fianarantsoa, making a total of over a thousand.[10] To the delight of Thomas and Elizabeth Rowlands and Arthur Huckett, the two chapels in the town were crowded. It was a quiet first day, the main encouragement being a prayer meeting attended by six hundred women. In the meeting held early next morning, many got up to confess their sin, and some fell on their faces on the floor. But when the reports from the districts were received, the atmosphere changed and the whole congregation broke out in praise and rejoicing. In the afternoon the church members met in one chapel, and the non-members in the other building, where forty-six people responded to the call of the gospel. They continued to praise God as they left these meetings, and they also visited homes in the area. In the home of Thomas and Elizabeth Rowlands every room was crowded with rejoicing believers and anxious enquirers.[11]

Elizabeth Rowlands refers to many who were broken in spirit as they confessed their sin, 'actually shaking as if in an ague', and describes what happened on the last day of the meetings:[12]

> Especially was this true on the morning of the last day. Never was such a thing known to such a degree here before. In the afternoon of the last day, the Christians all joined in one church to partake of the communion and consecrate themselves to God, in solemn league and covenant, and in singing a beautiful translation of 'Take my life and let it be'. In the night from every Protestant house and hamlet 'songs of praises' ascended to Heaven from a grateful, happy people; and next morning they returned to their homes and work, in the power of the Holy Ghost. It is still going on. From several villages and towns we hear that people are deeply convicted of sin and are giving themselves to God.

Visions and dreams also featured in some of the meetings.

The missionaries believed they were enjoying Pentecost, but realised they must be careful to make the right use of this new-found power. They needed such power not only to grow in the Christian faith but also to withstand evil forces that were at work in the island. The Christian workers could see many men and women influenced and possessed by alien spirits, so the presence of evil spirits was very real to them. Elizabeth Rowlands cites an example of 'a young man who seemed as if a veritable demon was tearing him before finally departing'.[13] The evil spirits were always injurious, causing sadness and confusion and making human beings less than human. The Holy Spirit, after the demon was cast out, would bring cleansing and harmony. The missionaries, like Paul in Ephesians chapter 6, regarded this evil presence as a spiritual problem, not as something merely psychological or physiological.

Elizabeth Rowlands and Rakotovao, the headmaster mentioned in the meetings on 6 May, were constrained to evangelise in the villages and arranged a preaching tour. They would announce their coming beforehand so that the local believers would have time to pray. The willing response to the gospel convinced the two evangelists that the revival was a genuine work of God.[14]

Charles Collins and some of his people were present at the May meetings. Even on their way home many of them were moved to pray that God would work mightily in their home district.[15] On the first Sunday at home, a prayer meeting was held before the morning service. In the service itself a young man, a freed slave, got up and related vividly what had taken place in Fianarantsoa. Spiritual forces were released throughout the congregation and the meeting was turned into a time of prayer, praise and searching the Scriptures. The same spirit was felt in the afternoon Sunday school, when one class of girls was weeping so loudly that they had to be counselled by a minister and his wife. So loud was the weeping that people were hurrying from the streets to know what was happening.[16]

Charles Collins and his wife returned late from the May meetings, and when they arrived they were amazed at what they saw. The church had been transformed. The Sunday was different; many more were coming to the services, there was more freedom in worship, and the day was highly respected. One father had reimbursed his daughter for the loss she had suffered by not working on the Sunday. Whole families were getting rid of their idols and making it known publicly that they belonged to the Lord Jesus Christ. During a brief unspecified period, over 140 persons professed conversion:[17] 41 from the Sunday school, 23 preparing to be teachers, 22 who were already in the church, and 56 rededicating themselves to the service of God.

**Steady progress**

The missionaries and their co-workers continued to go out from the stations to the villages. Charles Collins described a meeting at Ambohinamboarina where there was simultaneous prayer, confession of sin and healing of quarrels. They saw a marked increase in baptisms, the missionary baptising fifty-one in one meeting. At home, Collins received a sack full of idols; the converts preferred this open witness to getting rid of them secretly.[18] According to Thomas Rowlands, membership in some churches had doubled, and in others trebled.[19]

Nothing could dampen the zeal of Elizabeth Rowlands, who itiner-
ated untiringly over a large area. The object of one of her journeys
was to open a new chapel, which meant being away from the station
for four days. On a Saturday during her journey she attended a service in which the message, on Luke 9:51-56, led the congregation to
a time of self-examination. On reaching her destination the missionary had time only for a cup of tea before the start of the service.
Under the ministry of the Word of God many fell to the floor, while
others were striving in prayer on behalf of friends and family: 'It was
a typical Welsh Revival.'[20]

After the meeting, refreshments were taken before returning again
to the chapel. During two of the meetings a hundred people made an
open stand for the Lord Jesus Christ. The meetings continued the following day: nobody presided, yet there was order; each person taking
part was wise and gracious. The meetings, however, had to be drawn
to a close because some of them had a long journey home. Elizabeth
Rowlands returned to the same place two months later, and in one of
the meetings three stood up to confess Christ as Saviour. She also
noted the ministry of the women as an important feature; they were
praying, visiting and preaching, and she regarded this as the dawn of
a new era in Madagascar.[21]

Most LMS stations were affected by the revival. With reference to
a recent journey, Elizabeth Rowlands could say at the end of her
report: 'I will only add, that in the seven divisions of our district we
have had evangelistic and revival services during the past months,
and many hundreds have decided for Christ.'[22] Charles Collins confirmed the Welsh missionary's optimistic view, adding, 'The good
work still continues in this district.'[23]

It was not only the LMS missionaries who were rejoicing at the
progress of the revival. Missionaries of the Friends Foreign Mission
Union (FFMU) had been faithfully sowing and were now reaping a
harvest. In Mandridrano, West Ankarat, 'we have had Revival in
many of our congregations', and it was the topic of conversation in
the markets of the district.[24] In one area there was a severe fever,
causing one district to lose a hundred and nine members and two
pastors. However, the work of grace in the lives of the believers was
deep, and was expected to be lasting.[25] Another FFMU missionary,
writing in October 1906, referred to a revival which had broken out
'some months ago'; the instruments used were a national itinerant
preacher and a prayerful young woman. Those attending the meeting
were not conscious of time and could worship for two or three
hours. On one occasion at least, the meeting lasted from 3 o'clock in

the afternoon until 8 o'clock in the evening. There was no doubt in the mind of the missionaries that the revival would continue to spread: 'And we quite expect it will spread to all 24 churches under my charge.'[26]

**Prayer and care**
Unusual manifestations still occurred, and the missionaries had to grapple with influential people in Malagasy society, including the diviner. Such a person was influencing three villages, but Charles Collins, believing in immediate answers to prayer, urged thirty believers to pray for the conversion of the diviner. The group met in prayer from 1 o'clock in the afternoon until 4 o'clock the following morning. They went together to the diviner's home and shared the gospel with him, and he was immediately converted.[27]

Another feature of the revival in one district was a mass movement to Christianity. Elizabeth Rowlands welcomed the turning of a great number to Christ at the same time, but also realised the need for extra care in dealing with converts. There was a greater danger of falling away and a greater possibility for counterfeit experiences.[28] Her husband Thomas Rowlands was the right man to counsel the people. He was not a great preacher, but could effectively apply scriptural principles to the needs of believers and unbelievers. He spent much of his time explaining simply the truths of the gospel and counselling people personally.

Thomas Rowlands' understanding of revival was based on the Scriptures, but he was also interested in the psychology of revival. He requested his son to send him a book on the subject, though he did not specify a title. The Welshman was also aware of the hindrances to revival. In one of his sermons, based on Acts 3:19, he discussed some of them:

- Pride, especially trusting in church membership—but were the names on the book of heaven?
- Traces of the old pagan life in the believer.
- Lack of respect for the Sunday.
- Coldness, having lost the first love.[29]

What was important for Thomas Rowlands was not the form of godliness but the experiencing of its power, which brought forth the fruit of the Spirit.

Thomas and Elizabeth Rowlands' furlough was due, and they began their journey to Wales in April 1906. On their way to the port, they attended the half-yearly services of the churches of Imerina, and realised that they were enjoying the same enthusiastic worship as they had done in Betsileo[30] in the south. Though numbers were not so high as on previous occasions, that was not due to any slackness, but rather to the prevalence of malaria in the district. The missionaries were sorry to leave—not only because of the revival, but also because Robert Griffith was already on furlough and D. D. Green was due to leave before the end of 1906. During a time of explosion in church membership, good teachers, preachers and counsellors were scarce.

There was some consolation, however, in the return to Madagascar of D. M. Rees and his wife, who were in Wales during the Revival and had taken part in it. When they arrived in December 1906 they marvelled at what had been accomplished. The central church in Ambalavao was prospering. Good progress was made in the catechumens' class, the Bible class, the Christian Band and the Christian Endeavour meetings.[31] When D. M. Rees sent his first report home after returning from Wales, he had only visited three of the seven centres under his care, but even so was thrilled with what he saw:[32]

> At one centre where eight churches were gathered together, I had the privilege of welcoming fifty-six new members to the church. Some of these had surrendered to the Saviour since May last, but were only now admitted to the church. I also baptized fourteen. It was a memorable day. The church was much too small to contain the people, so we had four different congregations. It was a touching sight to see some old gray-headed Betsileo, who had listened to the Gospel for years, but had only now been moved to confess Christ, sitting beside and rejoicing with prodigals who had been in the far country, but now surfeited and sick of the husks of sin had returned to their Father's house. It was a time of 'gathering in the sheaves'.

In Ambalavao itself, the church membership had increased steadily; the Sunday school had gone back a little was 'now improving'. In the whole district a hundred and ninety-seven new members had been received into the church during one year.[33]

Other missionaries bear witness to the steady progress of the revival. Arthur Huckett in the South drew attention to the determination of the Christians to 'follow the Lord fully',[34] while one village had lost its sorcerer when he was converted—'the greatest trophy' of the Revival.[35] This meant they had lost their spiritual leader, but Huckett was hoping the void would be filled by the Christian faith.

The same missionary commented on the number of Scriptures that were sold:[36]

> After the revival of 1905, when we found new converts seeking to possess a Bible, and some fairly advanced in years making up their minds to learn to read it, we have been led to hope that they will hold on and remain faithful; and of all the lapses which we have had, the fewest, I believe, have been amongst those who still possessed, and could read, the Word of God.

The Paris Missionary Society sent word to Huckett that they were sending four men to him to collect Scriptures, because their stock had been exhausted.[37]

H. T. Johnson, another LMS missionary, was convinced that

> The result of the revival is seen in a fuller life in the church, a greater desire on the part of the members to be taught, and a keener relish for the Bible classes. There are now a large number of adults able to read, and who volunteer for Sunday school work.[38]

The Norwegian Missionary Society could speak of 'wonderful progress' in Imerina, and claimed that the revival of 'past years' in Betsileo had started in places under the care of the Mission.[39] J. Edwin Orr accepts this claim, as presented by *The Missionary Review of the World*. But he does not make it clear that the mission field was divided by the coming of the French, and it is an exaggeration to say that the revival spread over the whole of Madagascar.[40]

One fruit of revival was evident in the giving of the churches. They gave to support home and overseas work. Mrs Collins commented of a Harvest Thanksgiving service, 'Never in all my life have I seen such giving.'[41] A pastor contributed 16s (80p), which amounted to half a month's salary, children gave from 2d (2p) to 1s.8d (13p), and a tailor gave a new suit of clothes and calico. Others gave in kind: geese, ducks, fowls, potatoes and milk.[42]

The progress in Madagascar was remarkable, especially in view of the past history of Protestantism there. It had known periods of bitter opposition, and clashes with a religion of idol worship with its belief in fate. Then, from 1895 it had faced a new pressure, when the French took over, appointing as Governor Victor Augagneur with his atheistic views and anti-Christian socialist policy.[43]

# Part IV
# ASIA

# 12
# India (1)

According to Ednyfed Thomas, 'extensive preparations' were made for the revival that broke out in Khasia (Meghalaya) in 1905.[1] There was greater emphasis on prayer (especially from about 1902) and renewed efforts to make the Word of God known, through evangelism, the activity of the Bible women and the work of the Scripture Union.[2] During 1902, two of the lady missionaries visited Calcutta and heard R. A. Torrey speaking on prayer. They returned to Khasia to exhort the churches to pray for revival.[3] From 1903, prayer meetings for this purpose were held in many places, including Laitkynsew, Mawphlang, Pangthong and Mawiang. The missionaries were very much aware of the continuing need to revive the life of the church and believed that a manifestation of God's power was needed to accomplish such a renewal. John Roberts and Robert Evans had been influenced by the 1859 Revival in Wales, D. E. Jones by the revival preaching of Richard Owen, and E. H. Williams had sympathy with the Keswick movement.

Ellen Hughes, one of the lady missionaries, summarises the main events leading to 1905. In doing so, she mentions some friends (unnamed) who were burdened with the need for revival during 1902 and 1903.[4] The summary was given in a letter to Evan Roberts, assuring him that the Christians in Khasia were praying for the Christians in Wales.

## Events in Khasia

As in Wales before 1904, church leaders in Khasia were concerned about nominalism: so many were Christians in name only, but were strangers to the experience of conversion. On the first day of 1904, these Welsh words came into Ellen Hughes' mind: '*Bydd hon yn un o flynyddoedd deheulaw Duw*' (This will be a year of the right hand of the Most High). That conviction was confirmed by the reading of an article in *Y Drysorfa* on the 1859 Revival in Wales, and also by reading Psalm 77. She shared her conviction with others in a number of Christian Endeavour meetings, drawing attention to the words in Malachi, chapter 3, verse 10.[5]

What was happening in Ellen Hughes' experience was typical of the experience of many individuals and groups, both missionaries and national believers. In November 1904 the evangelist Lias Syrder had a vision that assured him of coming revival.[6] In December, while visiting a mission station, Ellen Hughes joined with others in reading accounts of revival in Wales in the *Western Mail*, and reports from Wales were read that month in two Presbyteries and received with unusual warmth by the Khasi believers.[7]

A measure of blessing was experienced in a few areas during 1903, especially Mawphlang and Tynrong, where special prayer meetings were held every Monday night to pray not only for Khasia but for the whole world. More people were taking part in prayer, including the women, and it was decided to hold meetings every night of the week. During the period from 1903 to 1905, eighty candidates were received into the churches.[8] For some time before 1904 the Tynrong church had held meetings 'which received the peculiar appellation as *Spirit Meetings*'.[9] When the news of revival in Wales reached them, the prayer meetings reached a 'red-hot stage'.

## Cherra and Pariong

There was, therefore, a spirit of real expectancy as the representatives of the churches gathered together for the Assembly at Cherrapoonjee on 3-5 February 1905. One of the missionaries present captured the feeling of one of the meetings:[10]

> The news of Wales stirred these people intensely. I could feel it when in the assembly at Cherra, in February. We had a striking meeting there. When Dr Roberts gave an account of the *Diwygiad* [Revival] at home, the meeting was thrown open for prayer, and a large number prayed without being called—a strange and new thing, comparatively, for the Khasians.

Two representatives from the Presbyterian Church of Wales were present and were very impressed with what they saw and heard. They knew, as did the others who were there, that the 'explosion' or 'tidal wave' was imminent. Indeed, the two visitors believed that the district 'was ablaze with religious fervour, caught from the reports of the great doings in Wales'.[11]

Many of the Mawphlang people returned from the Assembly at Cherra more determined than ever to seek God in revival. On Sunday 5 March, the Sunday school was studying John chapter 1, giving particular attention to verse 33, which dealt with the baptism of the Spirit.

A prayer, 'Break hearts, O Lord', touched almost all present. U Olik, a national believer, related some of the events in Wales, and this moved many to further prayer in numerous homes and in the village school.[12] On that same Sunday, the believers in Nangspung were surprised by the freedom they enjoyed in worship. A few days later they were joined by Christians on their way to the Presbytery at Pariong. They continued on their journey singing hymns, and marvelling at the singing they heard in the air, though there were no others nearby.[13]

The Christians flocked to the meetings at Pariong.[14] It was here that the red-hot heat was fanned into flames. A prayer meeting was held on the Friday and the chairman had difficulty in bringing it to a close. Another meeting on Saturday was devoted to prayer for Khasia, but the most wonderful service took place at 4 o'clock on the Sunday afternoon. Babu Elik preached a powerful sermon based on I John 4, verse 19, and Babu Joel an equally powerful message from Psalm 144, verse 15:[15]

> We then sang a hymn and the preacher was about to pronounce the benediction when we were startled by hearing someone beginning to pray most earnestly, in the midst of the congregation. He prayed that God would not let us leave without the blessing, we had been expecting Him to reveal the power of His Spirit amongst us all day, and now we had come to the end of the day without the great blessing, 'O God, pour down Thy Spirit upon us all now, whilst Thou art blessing the people of Wales so much, do not send us away empty.' While this brother was praying, others also began to pray at the same time, both men and women, and then it is difficult to say what took place—many were praying; some were crying aloud for mercy; some men were fainting; nearly all were weeping; and some were praising God. Then someone began to sing: '*Dyma gariad fel y moroedd*' [Here is love vast as the ocean] and this was taken up and repeated time after time, until some were nearly dancing with excitement. While the people were singing we could hear others praying, 'O Lord, pour down a still greater blessing.'

At 7 o'clock, Robert Evans endeavoured to stop the meeting so that the worshippers could have something to eat. Some left, but the majority remained to sing and praise. Such was the power of God's presence that many were overwhelmed physically and their friends had to support them, otherwise they would have fallen on the ground.[16]

It was decided at Pariong to set apart Sunday 26 March as a day of prayer for revival. But the impact of the Presbytery was immediate:

'When the first news of the revival at Pariong became known, an intense desire was manifested in all the churches to obtain a similar blessing, and prayer meetings became the best attended meetings of all.'[17] One evening, soon after the Presbytery, a missionary and his wife visited Nongkasen. All the village turned out to welcome them, and one wall of the chapel had to be taken down in order to accommodate the crowd.[18] In another area, Robert Evans left a meeting on 19 March to write a letter to Wales,[19] having no idea when the service would finish; while at Changpoong it was the children who had been the means of revival.[20]

The Cherra Christians were looking forward to Sunday 26 March, the day that had been set apart for prayer. It was also their communion Sunday. A preparatory meeting was held on Saturday, when there was open confession and fervent prayer. Believers met for prayer on Sunday morning, and listened quietly to a good sermon. The Lord's Supper was celebrated at 10 o'clock, when a feature of the meeting was the silent weeping of so many in the congregation. Another meeting followed later in the afternoon:[21]

> The last meeting commenced at five o'clock, and it was in this meeting that the heavenly fire broke out. Several had spoken, men and women, expressing their feelings and deep joy they had when partaking of the Lord's feast. In tears, and with effort, were their words brought out—words of love, words of praise to Him who had loved them and had bought them with His blood—lisping, broken words of praise, but very acceptable we think, to the Father's heart.

A young girl started to pray, followed by five or six others. The women on one side were crying aloud, and suddenly the spirit of wailing, and then rejoicing, swept through the whole congregation. All remained for about four hours, singing and repeating well-known hymns. It was 'the counterpart of what had taken place in Wales'.[22]

The revival spread rapidly, to Jowai[23] and even to the Bhoi country, especially Nongbah. Robert Evans had asked the people of Wales to pray for the Bhoi in the north of Khasia, and by the middle of 1905 the church at Mynnar had experienced a burst of new life and the church at Mawden had been powerfully shaken by the Spirit of God. Cries for mercy were heard in many meetings and, as in other areas, it was difficult to bring them to a close. Even after the closing of a meeting, the people would go outside to hold a service in the open air.[24]

The revival did not continue with the same power week after week, but waves of spiritual blessing were experienced at varying intervals. In Cherra the blessings of February and March 1905 were followed by a period of tension because of strained personal relationships. This quenching of the Spirit deeply hurt John Roberts and his wife Sidney, but they and others continued to pray, and during the month of June a second wave swept over Cherra. When Sidney Roberts was sending her report to Wales, the church at Cherra was experiencing the fifth night of 'red-hot meetings of praise and rejoicing'. She was sure that Evan Roberts would love to have been present.[25] The missionary was travelling home on furlough, and had intended staying overnight in Cherra before continuing her journey. But in the first meeting she knew that she would be staying for a few days.

**Letter from Cherra**
Sidney Roberts sent her account in Welsh, and the following is a translation with an occasional précis:[26]

*Thursday.* Prayer meeting and the place was full in spite of the terrible weather; people weaving past each other, waving their arms and their books; some on the floor, others in the pulpit, others on the pews, singing and praising because of the joy of fellowship with Jesus. They repeated the first verse of a hymn a number of times; the bell was rung to stop them in order to continue praying, but this caused them to sing more loudly. Eventually there was silence and Dr Roberts asked someone to pray, two or three stood up, but a young lady was the first to take part . . . It was morning (about 4 o'clock) when many of them arrived home.

*Friday.* For a considerable time before the meeting was due to start, they sang with fervour the old hymn '*Gwaed y Groes*' [The blood of the cross] &c, and the line '*Tyred Arglwydd mae dy gwmni yn well na'r gwin*' [Come, Lord, your company is better than wine], was repeated scores of times. Considering the meeting as a whole it did not reach the same heights as the one on Thursday, but they were there until the early hours of the morning, some sleeping, others in a trance, not gaining consciousness for a long time. They were still singing when I went to bed at 2 o'clock in the morning.

*Saturday.* Very early in the morning Dr Roberts went to the chapel, which was always open for anyone, and found three of four women sitting, but they did not see him in the front pew; he saw an incomparably beautiful sight—a child resting his elbow on the bench (that is, on the wood at the top), with both hands and face pointing heavenwards, praying silently at the dawn of the day.

[*5 o'clock preparatory meeting for the Lord's Supper on Sunday, the first for three months.*]

It was pouring with rain all day, but it could not prevent the people from coming. A long time before the start of the service the people were arriving with their lanterns, knowing that it would be dark when they would be returning home. They started singing and it was obvious that their hearts were full. Only four or five were dancing, while the others were singing in the pews, their faces shining with joy. Dr Roberts asked for silence in order to start the meeting properly, and asked someone to come to read while the hymn '*Ai am fy meiau i*' [And was it for my sins] was given out. O! singing from the bottom of the heart, the prayers watered by tears, while they were endeavouring to sing; others so full of joy and thanksgiving because of the blood and cleansing that they were swimming in peace. Some verses were repeated a dozen times finding it difficult to stop. When on the last line two young, strong men broke out in loud prayer, heart-breaking indeed, begging again and again for forgiveness. Their fears were stilled, but the stronger of the two fell into a kind of trance while the reading was being taken. In the trance he prayed loud enough to be heard, but this in no way affected the person who was reading. [Many took part in prayer.] After four or five prayers the place became absolutely quiet, hearts being so full that they could not pray nor sing. There were a few terrible moments, all ready to burst forth knowing that the Holy Spirit was present. A young girl got up but was overcome with emotion and could only say Oh! Oh! Oh!—and then the dam broke—the whole place was boiling, and broken hearts groaning, it was enough to overpower the strongest person . . . A hymn was given out which was like refreshing waters to many a soul—the medicine needed in that time of need. Hymn 751 was sung many times; and I cannot say how often the last 2 verses were sung, especially the words, '*Tyred Arglwydd, Mae dy gwmni yn well na'r gwin*' [Come Lord, your company is better than wine]. The meeting lasted 5 hours and it was one to be remembered forever.

*Sunday.* Communion was celebrated in the morning; the meeting was to start at 10.30, but, as usual, the congregation was singing before that time. The opening Hymn was 402 and it had to be sung many times [two ladies started to weep loudly]. Dr Roberts read

Isa. 53, deeply moved, and could not continue because of his feelings. He said a few words, brief because it was felt that this was not the time for talk. With the help of U Sang Bin, the elements were distributed and Hymn 98 was sung '*Yn Eden cofiaf hynny byth*' [In Eden, I always remember]. Dozens in the congregation wept quietly, and very often they were unable to hold the cup because they were trembling and the missionary had to help the poor souls. [A leader restored.] To close the meeting '*O Gariad, O Gariad anfeidrol ei faint*' was sung [O Love, O Love, of infinite measure]. In the third verse the Casi rendering is '*jop ia U. Soitau*', '*jop*' meaning conquer, and '*Soitau*', Satan. It would have been worthwhile for you to be present to see and hear the repeating of '*jop ia U. Soitau*'.

3.30 p.m. Came together again with the purpose of discussing the work of the church, but the meeting was turned into a time of prayer and praise. Hymn 489 was sung, '*Ni redwn yn wrol mae'r Brenin o'n blaen*' [We will run bravely for the King is leading]. [Words of exhortation; many praying]. Hymn 251 was given out to close the service, '*Wrth fy nghuro gan y gwyntoedd*' [While being beaten by the winds], all of which was repeated many times, but especially the words, '*Tyred Arglwydd, Mae dy gwmni yn well na'r gwin*', which was sung scores of times. Every time they came to the words '*Alle Kynrad*'—'*Tyred Iesu/Arglwydd*' [Come, Lord], the fire possessed them anew and they could not be stopped. The meeting lasted for about 4 hours.

*Monday*. My last meeting in Cherra. [Same characteristics as in the other meetings.][27]

### Assembly, Presbytery and local church

Christians could gather together in the local congregation, as in Cherra, and also in a Presbytery or an Assembly. A local presbytery like the one that was held at Marngor, Mawphlang, in April 1905 would have far-reaching results. Thirty churches were represented, and the news from different areas gladdened the ears of the congregation. When a meeting finished at 11 p.m., many believers would remain to pray:

Many were unwilling to leave the Chapel at 11 p.m. and gathered together in the Teachers' House and spent the whole night in prayer and praise. About 3 a.m. while singing the favorite hymn in these parts, [28]

*Rejoice, oh world, the Lord has come,*
*All people praise his name.*

such a powerful wave of feeling came over them that they all
danced with joy and ecstasy.'[29]

Even after the delegates had left, a prayer meeting was held, and
soon the place was in a 'holy confusion'.[30] Since that meeting (the
account was written in May), thirty-eight had professed conversion.

Many of the members at Lawbyrtun were present at Marngor and
returned carrying the fire with them. Revival broke out the very day
they arrived home. On the second day many unbelievers came in of
their own accord and experienced deep conviction of sin, including
those who had come to the meeting in an angry, rebellious spirit. In
one month the church received thirty-nine members, doubling its
membership.[31]

The Presbytery at Shillong, 12-14 August 1905, was another event
that had a significant impact on many churches. Shillong was an area
in which revival had been experienced since 1 April. Two characteristics of this awakening were the reconciliation of divided families
and the sighting of objects in the sky. Some saw a cloud hanging over
a person who was praying, symbolising darkness or fire. One person
was sure that she had seen the suffering Saviour, not in the sky but in
the church.[32]

The Shillong church, therefore, had already had three months'
experience of revival before the Presbytery meetings in August.
Hundreds of people were present, the majority of them under thirty
years of age. Business matters were discussed in the 7.30 a.m.
Saturday meeting, while reports from the districts were received in
the 1 o'clock meeting. At the 4 p.m. service, two were to speak on
'The Holy Spirit and His Work', but the second speaker could not
take part because of the intensity of prayer and praise.[33]

On Sunday, three meetings were held between 10 o'clock in the
morning and midnight, with two one-hour breaks. Three sermons
were delivered, and plenty of time allowed for singing and praying.[34]
Meetings continued throughout Monday and Tuesday. On the
Tuesday evening a most unusual thing happened. After the meeting
had finished at midnight, the missionary and others were asked to listen to the testimony of two girls. One of them spoke of the great
themes of Scripture, God's love and the covenant, and sang hymns
oblivious of all around her. The other girl appeared to be in a trance
and sang unknown hymns to familiar and unfamiliar tunes. She also

composed hymns herself, producing them like water bubbling from a spring. After a while, the evangelist prayed and the company sang, '*Dyma gariad fel y moroedd*' (Here is love vast as the ocean).

On Wednesday, a striking address was delivered by a young labourer, relating how God had answered his prayers; while another young man gave an account of a revival meeting in the village schoolroom, when eleven persons came to a saving knowledge of the Lord Jesus Christ. When the evangelist heard the news he sprang to his feet and gave out a hymn, '*Dyma gariad fel y moroedd*' (Here is love vast as the ocean). The meeting finished at 2 o'clock in the morning.[35]

Revival could also break out spontaneously, unrelated to a denominational event, as was the case in Laityra on 15 August 1905. This was the very day of the Shillong Presbytery.[36] The village overlooked the Plains and was a centre of Hindu worship, which made it very difficult for the church to make progress. A church meeting was held on 15 August, commencing as usual with catechising the children and repeating the texts of the previous Sunday's sermons. Some of the older members had been to Khasia and related what they had witnessed there. A young girl shared what she had seen in a trance during the meeting, and many sprang to their feet to give thanks to God, a number of them dancing with joy. Others were wailing and weeping so loudly that they were heard outside, and people rushed in to see what was happening. When they entered, the place was covered with a bright, shining light, which to some was lightning and, to others, fire. Singing was resumed and the service continued until near dawn the following morning.[37]

The presbyteries continued to make an impact on the churches, and at the Mawphlang Presbytery in October 1905 'the most staid pastors and deacons were simply carried away with the joy that characterised the meetings'.[38] The congregation gave vent to its feelings, but also listened intently to the preaching of the Word of God. A missionary rejoiced at the outcome of the meetings: 'I am glad to say that the revival broke out in several churches in the district, after the delegates returned to their homes.'[39] These churches included a few that had been in a low condition spiritually, like Mawkyllei and Laitkseh. Both churches were transformed and became vibrant with new life.[40]

Prayer was one of the main reasons for the effectiveness of the meetings. Even in places where there was no powerful revival, prayer meetings were held regularly. In Sylhet (now in Bangladesh), where J. Pengwern Jones laboured, many Christians opposed the idea of revival, but the missionary and others met for prayer every morning at 7 o'clock, and 'with the exception of a few days at the beginning of April, the meetings have been carried on daily ever since, and also we have had regular services every evening in the week besides'.[41] It was not until 1906 that some change happened in Sylhet—described as 'copious rain' rather than a 'torrent of rain'.[42]

## Mairang (1906)

Expectations were still high as the revivalists attended the presbyteries and assembly of 1906. Mairang was a small place with a comparatively small church, but the believers and the Rajah of the District (a church deacon) persuaded the authorities that the Assembly in March should come to their village. Travelling there was not easy: [43]

> Men have to find their way to Mairang on horseback or be carried on men's backs, or by walking, as there is only a bridle path from the Shillong main road to the village, a distance of 15 miles. Some few had ponies and a few were carried in a kind of basket-chair on men's backs, but most of the people walked, some of them travelling for four or five days in order to reach there in time.

The hospitality was remarkable. The Rajah himself procured cattle, rice and other supplies from the surrounding villages and personally provided for the needs of two thousand people. It was impossible to provide accommodation for the five or six thousand visitors, and many had to sleep in cowsheds or goat-houses. The missionaries were allocated to the schoolroom, but when they saw many women and children without a place to sleep, they vacated the schoolroom and were glad to find any spot where they could rest.

The chapel was also too small for the meetings (even after removing a side-wall and the pews), but no discomfort was felt as they all joined together to worship and, in the first meeting, sang one hymn for nearly an hour. They also sang hymns composed by girls in a trance. In addition to these girls, 'hundreds went into trances and the way they trembled and shook was extremely painful to witness, but they seem quite unconscious of it'.[44] One missionary suggested that this was happening because their weak bodies could not take the strain of the spiritual experiences.

A long ordination service was held in the open air on Saturday afternoon, in a cold wind, with five thousand present. One of the national pastors was supposed to preach on 'Church Polity', but he preached instead from 1 Kings 18, verse 21. A letter from a minister in New Zealand was read, asking for prayer for the Europeans in his parish, and this request was included in the prayers.[45] A sense of conviction fell on the congregation: 'The scene was awful, it was not excitement but agony, anguish, excruciating pain.'[46] The anguish became more profound when a young man interjected his prayer a number of times with the cry '*Waw, Waw, Waw*' (used by Khasis in a time of distress). His cries shook the whole congregation.[47]

On the Sunday, meetings started before dawn, and during the day thousands continued to arrive. About 8,000 attended the open-air meeting held at 10 o'clock. There were to have been two preachers, but because of the praises of the crowd a few short addresses were delivered. The meeting lasted four hours. The afternoon and evening meetings were held in the chapel and the schoolroom, and 'The earnestness and joy were beyond description.' In one of the meetings, after the sermon the congregation gave vent to its feelings by singing '*Ble'r enynnodd fy nymuniad?*' (What is the source of my desires?), and the worshippers could not stop repeating the last two lines. Another meeting held in the schoolroom finished at 2 a.m., but the women continued to sing all night, had their breakfast and then returned home, still singing.[48]

The influence of the Mairang meetings spread. At Rangthong, the teachers, husbands and wives confessed their sin, and 'These open confessions cast a powerful dread over the Christian community of these parts.'[49] When Robert Evans and others returned to Jowai, attendance at the prayer meeting showed a marked increase. There was also a renewing of the work that had been started amongst the children and young people twelve months previously. At that time, the enthusiasm had been carried to an extreme that many of the Christians found unacceptable, so the work did not develop. But after Mairang it was reinstated on a firmer basis.[50] There were also at Mairang a few representatives from Lushai, whose story will be told later.

Generally speaking, apart from Mairang, the revival meetings of 1906 were quieter than those of 1905. Mrs Robert Jones attended the Shillong Presbytery in August 1906 and described the work of the Spirit as 'the dew from heaven', but the meetings were not 'boiling'.[51] According to Robert Evans the great stirrings had ceased, but there were still unusual meetings in a number of areas. Many of them were characterised by visions, and Mawphlang was particularly noted for such a phenomenon.[52]

## *Shangpoong (1907)*

The wind of revival was still blowing during 1907. The assembly of February of that year was held at Shangpoong, a large village in the

Jaintia Hills, bordering on the North Cachar Hills.[53] The inhabitants had suffered terribly during 1906 because of lack of rice, made worse by a plague of rats. Having had such a bad year, the local Christians had to inform the churches that representatives would be provided only with sleeping accommodation and cooking utensils. Yet, despite all the difficulties, about three thousand gathered together on 7 February, full of zeal, for the first prayer meeting.

The first thing that J. Pengwern Jones heard on entering was a national believer speaking in tongues, but there was no interpreter. 'This gift has not been common in this Revival, I have only heard two or three different persons who have been thus gifted.'[54] Another feature mentioned by the missionary was the 'hissing sound' that many made before speaking or praying. It would last for five to ten minutes, and then the person would cry out before going on to speak or pray.[55]

J. Pengwern Jones had no doubt that the Holy Spirit had taken control of the meeting. He felt that the first part of the meeting on Saturday afternoon was monotonous, but then a missionary who had just returned from Wales witnessed to what he had experienced on furlough. This sparked new life in the worship; the hissing sound returned again, a young man gave out a hymn, and the effect of the singing was like an electric current going through the congregation. Evening prayer continued until midnight, but this did not prevent the missionaries from getting up early for the activities of the following day: prayer, praise and preaching.[56]

*The later period*

J. Pengwern Jones compared and contrasted the experiences of 1905/6 with those of 1907. At the first Revival Assembly in 1905 the Spirit of God came like 'a mighty flood', but since then the water had been channelled in such a way that a deeper work of grace was being wrought in the lives of believers. In the past, the preacher's voice had very often been drowned. By contrast, 'The preaching of the word this year was quietly listened to, but the feeling at times during the preaching was intense and the fervency of the prayers indescribable.'[57] In the sermons there was a strong emphasis on the speedy coming again of the Lord Jesus Christ.

A characteristic of the later period of the revival was the restoration of those who had, in biblical terms, 'lost their first love'.[58] Many who had professed conversion had lost their enthusiasm for spiritual things. The coldness of heart was now turned into glowing love for the Saviour. Not only were individuals restored, but churches as well:

places that had neglected the prayer meeting became resolute in their determination to make it central in the life of the congregation. The hymns composed during the earlier period of the revival were very popular and were sung over and over again, but by 1907 the central themes of the Bible—grace, atonement and blood—were the source of joy in the hymn-singing. Many of these hymns were translated from the Welsh.[59]

J. Pengwern Jones also offered proofs for the genuineness of the Revival:

- The Christians are living on a far higher level than they ever lived before.[60]
- The heathen have been impressed with the truth of Christianity. Between 7,000 and 8,000 have been brought to the Saviour within the two years, and Christians realise their responsibility towards the heathen as they never realised it before.
- The burden of souls for India and other countries has been taught . . . [word lost in report] people and weighs heavily on their hearts.
- The Revival Thank offering Fund of Rs 10,000 has already been subscribed and much more is expected before the Fund is closed.

Revival meetings were still held during 1908, on roughly the same pattern as in 1907. From 1908 the 'rice money' was used to support new schools, which were set up in areas where there was need to teach and evangelise. In the same year Dr John Roberts died, soon after his return from Wales. He was one of the outstanding leaders of the revival. During his furlough he had shared with his fellow countrymen concerning the work of God in Khasia, and his return strengthened the bond between his mother country and the land of his adoption. His inspiration fed the optimism of the missionaries and churches as they looked to the future.

## The work in Lushai (Mizoram)

William Williams, the Welsh Presbyterian missionary, visited Aijal (Aizawl) in Lushai in 1891 and urged the Foreign Mission Committee to adopt the country as a mission field.[61] It decided to do so, but no Welsh missionary arrived there until 1897. Two men who volunteered for work in Lushai were D. E. Jones and Edwin Rowlands.[62]

In the meantime, J. H. Lorraine and F. W. Savidge had started work in Aijal, supported by the Arthington Trust.[63] They remained there for nearly four years—that is, from 1894 until 1897, when the work was transferred to the Welsh Presbyterians. D. E. Jones arrived in Aijal before Savidge and Lorraine left, and so had the benefit of their experience for a brief period.

The Presbyterians were anxious to extend their work to the south of Lushai, but the Baptist Missionary Society (BMS) was also seeking opportunity to work there.[64] In 1901 it was decided that the BMS should concentrate on the south, and when Savidge and Lorraine returned in 1903 they found a Christian community of a hundred and twenty-five, 'the fruit of annual visits by the Welsh Presbyterians from the north'.[65] All the missionaries shared a common background of evangelicalism and concern for revival.

**Visit to Mairang**
The missionaries continued to pray for revival, and the Welshmen working in the north were keen to send some Lushai believers to the Mairang Assembly in February 1906.[66] Four men and three women were chosen. D. E. Jones also sent a telegram to Lorraine in the south to tell him of the proposed visit, and the Baptist missionary sent four people to join the Aijal group. (The four set out as soon as possible, as the hundred-mile journey would take four days, but one of them injured a leg and was unable to proceed.) While the company were away, a prayer meeting was held at Aijal every evening.[67]

On their way to Mairang (a journey of two to three weeks), the travellers were full of expectation. This was strengthened by seeing the outward manifestations of the revival in Khasia, especially the cheerfulness and praising spirit of the believers. As they approached Mairang, the Lushai people were thrilled to see hundreds of believers hastening to the Assembly. The first prayer meeting was devoted to interceding for the church in Lushai. Before the end of the meeting, Khuma, one of the Lushais, knew that the spirit of revival had fallen upon him. That became the experience of Nanchung, another of the company, the following day. He felt that he was burning inside, went stiff all over and started to breathe heavily.[68] The climax for the small group was the open-air service on Sunday, when Robert Evans, who was presiding, called them to the front and asked the congregation to pray for them. All present were filled with joy.[69]

When they left the following morning, the Lushai believers did not feel the joy they had known in the Assembly and tried to recapture it by praying together. They visited a mature Christian in Cherra, who gave them his blessing for the journey but warned them against the wiles of Satan. They also visited Dr John Roberts to ask for money for the journey. This enabled them to take a train for part of the way, but there was no choice but to walk from Silchar. They soon experienced the attack of Satan, as a bitter disagreement broke out amongst them. A few miles from Aijal they agreed to stop and pray. Each prayed in turn, and as they continued in prayer a tongue of fire appeared above them. When the last person finished praying it disappeared, but they believed that the tongue had entered into each one of them. Reconciled, they continued on their way, singing a hymn that they themselves had composed.[70]

The group reached Aijal on 4 April 1906. They were welcomed that day and, on the following day, gave an account of their visit. They found the response disappointing, especially the criticism of the Mairang Revival expressed by some of the Lushais. On Sunday 8 April, D. E. Jones announced a farewell meeting for those who were travelling on to the south. When this brief service was over, the children began to sing 'God be with you till we meet again'.[71] One of the speakers began to speak for the second time, a hymn was given out, *'Cenwch, glychau'r nefoedd, llawenydd yma sydd'* (Sing, bells of heaven, for there is joy here), and the singing became sweeter and sweeter:[72]

Someone began to sing a ringing Hymn of Victory, and the whole congregation joined with great rejoicing, waving their hands, swaying their bodies, and many keeping time with their feet. Then someone would ask for prayer and the whole congregation would plead with God for that soul, then another Hymn would be sung. In this way prayer and praise continued for hours. The meeting which had started at 8 a.m. did not finish until 2 o'clock and all felt that the Spirit of God was present.

Mairang was being repeated in Aijal!

Another service, lasting six hours, was held in the evening. Two of the people present in that meeting went home to their respective villages and were the means of revival there. By July, the missionaries were receiving news of revival from a number of villages. But with the good news came bad news of persecution, and during October 1906 this became even more severe. Many believers were forced out of their villages, but as they moved away they established churches in other villages.[73] Like the scattered saints in the Book of Acts, they went forth gossiping the gospel (Acts 11:19-20).

What happened to the three that returned to the south? The church warmly received them, but their reports did not lead to revival as in the north. Some degree of interest in revival was created, but it was not until 1907 that the south experienced a day of God's right hand. Two or three groups had persevered in prayer, one of them including some lads from Savidge's school who had been attracted to the Christian faith by the reports from Mairang. They, with others, looked forward to the annual meetings of the churches—the 'Great Gathering', as it was called—due to be held in April 1907 and lasting four days.[74]

**The 'Great Gathering'**
During the four days, prayer and business meetings were held, and worship services on Sunday 7 April. In one of the Sunday services, the 216 converts who were present marched to the Mission Station. After a service there, they gathered for a baptismal service on the compound: 22 candidates were baptised, and later in the day another 85 from a demon-worshipping tribe. Yet it was not regarded as revival, and there was disappointment when some had to return home because of the lack of accommodation.

Another meeting was arranged, addressed by three evangelists.[75] The last of the three exhorted the hearers to open their hearts to the Holy Spirit. A hymn was sung, and during the singing a little boy, who had been praying earnestly, went up to the front and sat down:[76]

As he sat down he was seen to bury his head in his hands, and presently there were sounds of low sobbing heard during the pauses in the hymn. The evangelist who had last spoken led the meeting in prayer, and, as he did so, the little boy behind him could be heard sobbing out in broken sentences his sorrow for sin. Suddenly, as at Pentecost, the Holy Spirit took possession of the audience and almost everyone present bowed his or her head and prayed in a low voice. The murmur of prayer pervaded the whole room, rising louder and louder as some with tears cried to God for pardon, and others sprang to their feet to make public confession of their faults. The few who had been praying God for long months to visit South Lushai knew that their importunity had been rewarded, and that the apathy of the many was melting away beneath the influence of the Holy Spirit.

As well as confession, there was restitution and restoration. What some of those present had stolen in the past was paid back, and backsliders were restored.

The church in the south of Lushai was strengthened, and a year later they were praising God for what had been accomplished in the lives of believers. They also gave praise for the eighty-three converts who had been drawn to the church during a period of twelve months.[77]

In the north, on the other hand, the work suffered because D. E. Jones had to return to Wales. Edwin Rowlands was under a cloud at that time.[78] The missionary who had charge of the work, although successful in his own field, found it difficult to make progress in Lushai, which was strange territory to him.[79] There was renewed hope when D. E. Jones returned at the end of 1908. He brought two other missionaries with him, and another worker not associated with the Presbyterian Mission.

# 13
# India (2)

Gary B. McGee suggests three main reasons for the beginning and progress of revival in India at the beginning of the twentieth century.[1] First of all, the missionaries were very much aware of the slow growth of the church; secondly, the Indian believers desired an indigenous form of worship and leadership; and thirdly, news of revival from Wales. McGee also comments on the significant contribution of Robert Wilder during the 1890s, because he 'accentuated the Higher Life view of baptism in the Holy Spirit'.[2] However, he does not mention the prominence given to prayer from 1897, which led to the formation of prayer groups in 1902; nor does he mention the visit of R. A. Torrey to Calcutta that year.[3]

McGee's article makes a few references to Mrs Penn-Lewis, but not to her visit to India in 1903. This visit made a real impression on many Christian workers, especially Dr Rudisill of the Methodist Episcopal Church and superintendent of the bookshop and press in Madras, and F. Kehl of Calcutta, both of whom were revival men. The two men continued to correspond with Mrs Penn-Lewis and distributed her literature in India.[4]

## Mukti

One centre of interest for Mrs Penn-Lewis was Mukti, where revival broke out in 1905. It started as the result of the work of Pandita Ramabai, who had visited Keswick in England and had a deep desire to promote personal holiness and to improve the social condition of her people.[5] She had a background of Hinduism, was an able person intellectually, and was a woman. Proving that a woman from a downtrodden caste could identify with the needs of others, she gathered round her a large group of widows (between 1,500 and 2,000) and also a number of orphans, creating a home for them at Mukti (which means 'salvation').[6]

On approaching Mukti, thirty miles south of Poona, a visitor would see a long row of houses built for the workers, and rooms to receive the visitors who came from all parts of the world. Behind the houses were compounds to accommodate the widows and the (115) boys.

There were other compounds for the workshops and schoolhouse, and one for the baptistry. Added to these was the Rescue Home, a centre for girls rescued from immorality.[7]

It was in January 1905 that Pandita Ramabai, her daughter Manoramabai, Miss Minnie Abrams (a missionary from America) and others in the centre heard of the Welsh Revival:[8]

> The news of the Revival in Wales brought gladness to Ramabai. In January 1905 she told her pupils about it, and called for volunteers to meet with her daily for special prayer for a Revival in India. Seventy came forward, and from time to time others joined.

The news from Wales was soon followed by news of revival in Khasia, and this brought even greater joy, as it was another part of India.[9]

On 29 June 1905 one of the girls at Mukti was baptised in the Holy Spirit. The following day she shared her experience with the other girls, and this led to cries for help from them. Miss Abrams was called and came to counsel them. The following day, as Pandita Ramabai was expounding the eighth chapter of John's Gospel, the Spirit fell on all present, and a number of girls were stricken under conviction of sin. They continued in prayer all night. As many as five hundred and thirty people were formed into prayer bands, and many of them were also sent out to preach. They would wait for the coming of the Spirit before setting out on a journey.[10] Pandita Ramabai was initially reluctant to publicise these events, but eventually agreed with the missionary R. J. Ward (another correspondent with Mrs Penn-Lewis) to include a report in the *Bombay Guardian*.[11]

When Panditai Ramabai's people informed Mrs Penn-Lewis that Pentecost had come to Mukti, she recognised in the accounts some of the characteristics of the Revival in Wales, especially the fact that great numbers were taking part in prayer without any sense of disorder. One of the correspondents referred to the Bible School in Mukti:[12]

> The Bible School is full of Spirit-baptized girls, only a very few are left, and they are seeking. I think at least 400 have received the Holy Spirit. Many are seeking. The inquiry-room is seldom vacant. Often the work goes on half a night, or begins at two or three in the morning, and twice it has gone on all night. I spent all Thursday in the inquiry-room. All night long the matron kept sending in stricken girls. They came into great joy.

During one day only twenty-five to thirty received the baptism of the Holy Spirit.

The revival spread from Mukti to Poona, Dhond, and even to Telegaon, a hundred miles east of Bombay. At Poona a hundred and twenty girls were described as in a 'state of Revival'.[13] They were shaking, laughing, agonising in prayer, and many of them had a vision of Jesus. Miss Abrams took a group of eleven girls to Telegaon, and there in the Famine Orphanage witnessed scenes similar to those in Mukti.[14] Miss Abrams was also invited to Ratnagiri. Missionaries of the American Presbyterian Mission Station had been to a convention in Coonoor, and had returned determined to pray for revival. They invited Miss Abrams and a prayer band to hold a series of meetings. Even on the first night the outbreak of prayer was 'a Niagara on a small scale', and there was a 'storm of prayer' in the meeting on Sunday.[15] On Monday again there was intense prayer, one meeting lasting from 8 until 11 a.m. The evening service lasted four hours. The climax came on the Wednesday:[16]

Wednesday, November 30 was the greatest day, and the scenes of the day were simply indescribable. One woman had an awful fight. It was a real case of demonical possession. Nothing else explains it. She was tossed here and there, over the seats and on the floor. For a long time the demon refused to depart, but at last after much striving in prayer, in the name of Jesus the demon fled, and the woman had some peace; but not for long. The same thing was repeated four different days, until we began to think their name was Legion; but when the fourth demon was cast out, the woman found peace, and she is still rejoicing with exceeding great joy. When they found peace they would jump up and begin to sing and dance, their faces beaming with the light and radiance of Him who had met and conquered them. But soon they would be on their knees again, not for themselves now, but in awful agony for others. One woman who had found peace in her own room, after a long and hard struggle, came rushing into the meeting and told the leader that she was so happy that she had to sing and dance, which she actually did, and was not only encouraged but was assisted by the leader.

The staid Presbyterian ministers believed they had to allow freedom in the meeting so as not to quench the Holy Spirit.

Meetings continued after Miss Abrams left on 18 December, but a change came over the services. There was little agonising for sin as in the earlier days, but more rejoicing and praising. A popular hymn was 'Let us with a gladsome mind', often sung to the 'Hallelujah Chorus'; on one occasion it was sung for an hour, with hand-clapping and dancing. Another feature of the meetings was the giving up of things that were regarded as bad habits, especially smoking. One teacher brought in six hundred cigarettes, which were taken outside and burned.[17] Prayer continued to be central; even in a Sunday school there would be prolonged times of prayer.[18]

### The spreading flame

The arrival of Dr Howard Agnew Johnston in Ratnagiri on 21 December 1905 linked it with Wales as well as with Mukti.[19] The American had been authorised by the Presbyterian church in the USA to travel the world for two years (1905–07). 'On his way to the East he visited Great Britain, and had an interview with Evan Roberts, the after results of which have been far reaching.' Dr Johnston gave nine addresses at Ratnagiri. 'The Lord blessed these addresses very much, and chose for him the addresses that the people needed at the stage of the revival that they had reached.'[20] Acknowledging its debt to the American, one Presbyterian church said: 'Most of the church members attended Dr H. A. Johnston's meetings in Ratnagiri, and some of them sold Gospels to the passengers on the cargo boats out in the harbour.'[21] Within a short period of three days the Doctor was able to influence a great number of people. He had come from revival in Wales to channel the revival in Ratnagiri, before moving on to other parts of India, Korea and China.

To the west of Poona was Bombay, where the *Bombay Guardian* carried news of what was happening in Mukti and other places. In the city itself prayer meetings were held throughout 1905. During 1906 there were awakenings in the English Methodist Missionary Society, the Girls' School belonging to the Church Missionary Society, and in the YWCA.[22] The revival spread throughout most of South India. Within the geographical triangle from Poona to Visakhaptnam to Nagercoil (on India's southern tip) numerous centres were affected. A letter sent to Mrs Penn-Lewis expressed joy at 'the special blessing granted' at the conventions in Coonoor, Ootacamund and Ratnagiri.[23]

The convention at Ratnagiri was held in a hotel because the bishop would not give permission for the use of the English church. Two of the main leaders, Thomas Walker of Tinnevelly and R. J. Ward, were not deterred; they not only made other arrangements but also announced plans to build a convention hall. Both Walker and Ward followed events in Wales, and Thomas Walker believed that 'it was undoubtedly the tidings of the Welsh Revival which excited new desire and stimulated fresh hope in India'.[24]

Thomas Walker was optimistic about revival in India, but cautious too. He pointed out that most of the blessing was being experienced in schools and institutions, but there was need for it to spread to all the churches in India. The CMS missionary took advantage of any sign of revival, visiting Mukti and many places in Kerala where they anticipated an awakening.[25] According to Mr and Mrs Wills in the Girls' School in Travancore, 'The revival in Wales has been full of interest to our boarders.'[26] George Parker informed the Directors in London that the revival had started in Nagercoil and that it had 'borne much fruit'.[27] The young people responded with enthusiasm, but it took some time for the older people to embrace the movement. At Neyoor, the converted village boys were meeting for prayer and holding meetings in the open air.[28] P. J. Joshua organised a meeting at Kunnankulain, 'where a rapt audience heard an account of the Welsh Revival'.[29] Thomas Walker, always ready to help, accepted an invitation from the Mar Thoma to hold a series of meetings with his support.[30]

News of the Welsh Revival reached Bangalore and Bellary early in 1905. At the New Year a real Welsh Revival prayer meeting was held in Bellary, during which an account was given of some of the events in Wales. One of the missionaries described what happened:[31]

In the meeting I told them of the Revival in Wales, especially dwelling on the power of prayer on those absent. I thought some would once pray for those they knew were wandering from the right path, but to my astonishment, those who were the most Christ-like, seemed so suddenly convicted by sin, confession of sin was made, old quarrels were made up and women who for years had misunderstood each other, became friends. From that time on our meetings have been quite different.

Apart from the impact on the lives of individuals, another fruit was the formation of a Women's Christian Endeavour Society.

Answered prayers in Wales encouraged prayer at the Mysore Convention;[32] there was a concentration of prayer in Vellore,[33] and at Atmakur the answer to prayer was realised in a peculiar way.[34] The missionaries here had received a request from Pandita Ramabai for the names of all the children in the station, so that those in Mukti could pray for them. The children in Atmakur responded by getting up themselves during the night to pray for revival, and the missionaries believed that the dreams and visions experienced by them, and others, were a fulfilment of the prophecy of Joel. The impact, generally, was twofold: the nationals were taking more responsibility in conducting services, and they were eager to take the gospel to others, including the Sudras caste. There was already a spirit of enquiry amongst that caste, and 'we cannot but feel that the day for the coming of the Sudras has dawned'.[35]

Wales had a direct influence on the revival movement in Ongole.[36] In the autumn of 1905 a missionary sent some Telugu tracts on the Welsh Revival to J. A. Baker. They had been translated from articles by Mrs Penn-Lewis in *The Life of Faith*, and some articles in the *Western Mail*.[37] To some of the missionaries the content seemed strange, but when J. A. Baker explained to them the nature of revival, slowly there was a change of heart, resulting in much prayer. In the Quarterly Meeting in April 1906 prayer was intense, and even more so in the June meetings, which started on the last day of that month:[38]

> On Sunday morning, July 1, we had a powerful sermon by a native brother. At 3 p.m. our revival prayer meeting was continued two hours instead of one, and some hearts were powerfully affected, so much so that one brother did not leave the church for some time, but kept pleading with God in prayer. In the evening Rev. W. Powell, a native of Wales, who was in the heart of the great Revival there, told without excitement the simple story of God's dealing with His people. After his talk we were to have a few minutes of silent prayer, and then those who wished were to offer prayer. During the minutes of silent prayer there was a dead silence, and then the spirit of confession broke on the great Indian congregation of about 1,000 souls.

The noise was tremendous, making it impossible to speak to individuals, and when, after an hour, a group attempted to sing, their voices were soon drowned. After about two hours the spirit of song did prevail, and the singing continued until 1 o'clock in the morning.

The Sunday night meeting was described as a 'cyclone', but when the meetings continued the following week they were quieter. They were still crowded, many were converted, and unbelievers attended in large numbers, anxious to see what was happening. Unlike the Revival of 1878, which brought the heathen into the church, the 1906 Revival renewed believers and gave them a spiritual dimension which they did not have before the awakening.[39]

William Powell was a Strict Baptist missionary working with the Telugus in Bapatra.[40] Another member of a group of three was John Dare Thomas, who was, as his name suggests, a native of Aberdare, South Wales.[41] He and his wife left Wales when the revival was a few weeks old. They had oversight of St. Thomas' station and Poonamallee, where they lived in a bungalow. The husband also visited Tinnevelly occasionally. Like J. A. Baker, John Dare Thomas refers to the translation of the Welsh Revival accounts 'unto several Indian languages' at the Mission Press in Madras, adding, 'Even here in India, the movement is a general topic of conversation.'[42] The Welshman welcomed the revival in India because whole churches were being renewed, and, therefore, there was real hope for more aggressive evangelism.[43]

The Spirit of God invaded many schools. At Ongole, forty-eight were baptised in a brief period,[44] while in Nellore the awakening spread from the church and the boarding school to the village churches.[45] It created more seriousness and diligence amongst the girls, and some of them received an unusual ability to understand the Scriptures.[46] It was, however, impossible to avoid problems. The high number of converts made it difficult to deal with them personally. In addition, the missionaries were in the process of decentralising the 10,000-strong Ongole Church.[47]

*The Canadian field*
The Canadian Baptists rejoiced to hear of what was happening in Wales and Khasia. A missionary working among the Telugus referred to the awakening in both countries. He was also encouraged by the fact that the American Baptist Telugu Mission was enjoying revival during October 1905.[48] Another Canadian said that the news of revival in Wales and Khasia was creating 'unutterable longings' for revival in India.[49] The Canadians experienced a measure of blessing during 1905, but it was 1906 that proved to be a special year for them.

Revival broke out spontaneously and separately in many places on the Canadian Telugu field. When a missionary visited Chettipelt on 1 August 1906, revival had already broken out, on the very day that the Baptists in Toronto were praying for the Telugus.[50] On 11 August the Spirit of God fell suddenly on the worshippers in Yellaman and Akidu. It followed the confession of a Bible woman that had humbled the congregation, and it led to spiritual renewal.[51] Three days later it was the turn of the Girls' School at Cocanada to experience the extraordinary work of the Spirit, and 'food and rest were forgotten

while God dealt with souls'.[52] Daily meetings in some areas lasted
from five to seven weeks.

Looking back over this time of spiritual refreshment, the Canadian
report summarised the characteristics of the work:[53]

> A new and awful sense of the holiness, majesty and sovereignty of
> God, coupled with such a view of the exceeding sinfulness of sin
> as awakened terror and anguish in every heart, was undoubtedly
> the chief characteristic of the Revival. While confined chiefly to
> the workers and more intelligent of the native Christians, and as
> yet not exercising any appreciable influence, except indirectly,
> upon the great masses of heathen, it has nevertheless proved a
> wonderful blessing for which our missionaries have never ceased
> to thank God.

Although there was much excitement and expression of strong
emotion, according to the missionaries there were no excesses.[54]
Men, women and children came under the influence of the Spirit of
God, and, generally, the work was lasting. It was acknowledged that
there were lapses, especially in the southern part of the Canadian
field where cholera raged early in 1907. Many lapsed because they
wanted to please the cholera goddess, but when the cholera ceased
some of them renewed their Christian profession.[55]

Like the Welsh Presbyterians, the Canadian Baptists worked in
parts of Assam. In Upper Assam it was Nowgong that was first
stirred by revival, followed by North Lakjimpur and Golgoht. One of
the Mikir villages was won to the Christian faith, and the singing of
hymns could be heard in the homes and in the fields. The physical
needs of the villagers were not neglected, and the missionaries,
although not medically trained, did everything possible to relieve the
suffering of the people.[56]

### Dr Rudisill

Missionaries of the American Methodist Episcopal Church were keen
to promote revival. It had one of its centres in Madras, where Dr and
Mrs Rudisill superintended the Mission Press.[57] This was the couple
who had visited Wales and corresponded with Mrs Penn-Lewis. They
had returned from Wales in the company of another missionary, H. E.
Dunhill, who, having spent 'four wonderful weeks' visiting places in
North and South Wales,[58] wrote to the Rudisills, who were staying
with Mrs Penn-Lewis in Leicester, informing them of her intention to
visit Leicester and to return to India with them.[59]

The three of them arrived in India, the husband and wife going to Madras and the lady missionary to Bangalore. By that time there had been much prayer in many areas.[60] Early in July 1905, J. Pengwern Jones had received a telegram with news that revival had reached South Arcot.[61] R. J. Ward was zealously exhorting believers to prepare for the week of prayer at the beginning of 1906. During January, a Christian worker attended a meeting where about a hundred nationals were present, Hindus and Mohammedans: 'I told them of the power of the precious blood of Christ to release from sin, and related what was being done in Wales. They listened with breathless attention and a crowd was outside unable to get in.'[62]

The Rudisills took an active part in revival meetings and in the distribution of literature. The husband also visited many areas around Madras, but he was anxious to see for himself what was happening in Mukti. When he visited Mukti he was favourably impressed and had to acknowledge that this was a genuine work of God. He was sceptical about speaking in tongues, but was assured by Pandita Ramabai that she did not insist on tongues as the initial proof of the baptism of the Spirit.[63]

*The Kurkus*

Inland, between Bombay and Calcutta, half a million thinly clad Kurkus lived in forests and hills.[64] A few people who took a prayerful interest in their spiritual welfare had met with Albert Norton near Ellichpur to discuss possible action.[65] Albert Norton left for London, and arranged for two ladies from Mrs Baxter's Training Centre to go out to minister to the Kurkus—Miss Sharpe and Miss Roberts, a Welsh girl.[66] Thus, in 1889, the Kurkus and Central Hill Mission came into being. The early missionaries and their successors were evangelical, with a deep concern for revival, and fifteen months of regular prayer meetings preceded the revival that broke out amongst the Kurkus in October 1905.

**Calcutta and beyond**

Calcutta with its teeming thousands was regarded as a hard place for missionary work. The missionaries believed, however, that their God could accomplish great things even in that city. They knew that he had answered prayer in Khasia and Wales, and they must depend upon him. So they persevered in prayer, and by November 1905 there were reports of crowded revival meetings in some places. W. B. Byers of the Methodist Episcopal Church was convinced that revival had broken out in Asansol, just like the movement of the Spirit in Wales,

Khasia and Mukti.[67] Writing in January 1906, he described what was happening in South Arcot as a fulfilment of Malachi chapter 3, verse 10. At the time of writing, the meetings had already lasted seven weeks.[68] The prominent leaders were Bishops Robinson and Warne, and among the visiting preachers was the Welsh missionary J. Pengwern Jones, Sylhet.

When a missionary (probably J. Pengwern Jones) arrived on the Saturday, he was taken to an upper room where about thirty pastors and missionaries were present with Bishops Robinson and Warne.[69] Much time was spent in self-examination, and confessing lack of faith and prayer. When they met on the Sunday morning the response to the call to prayer was rather slow, so W. B. Byers gathered a small group around him and exhorted them to pray fervently. J. Pengwern Jones joined Byers to meet with the teachers and national pastors. This meeting concentrated on prayer for the evening meeting.

Another meeting was held at 4 o'clock in the afternoon, when groups for prayer were again arranged. 'The volume of prayer that went up from the three groups was deafening at times.'[70] Bishop Robinson made an appeal for all those who wanted to consecrate their lives to Christ to come forward, and large numbers responded, singing a hymn of praise in Bengali:

> *Rejoice and be glad! It is sunshine at last!*
> *The clouds have departed, the shadows are past.*

This was taken up by the whole congregation with 'indescribable enthusiasm'.[71] Other hymns were sung, including the 'Glory Song' in Bengali, and many were repeated a hundred times. It was after 7 o'clock when the meeting closed, but the singing continued among the young people to the accompaniment of drums and cymbals.[72]

During the hot season, the missionaries in Calcutta and district would move to a cooler place, usually to Darjeeling. One of those who went there in 1906 was Emlyn H. Davies, an LMS missionary from Machynlleth, North Wales.[73] During his stay at Darjeeling he gave three addresses, the third of which was an account of the Welsh Revival—'a movement which in its democratic, enthusiastic, & powerful sides was perhaps difficult to be understood by a high caste Hindoo audience'.[74] The Welshman had a memorable Sunday also, when Brockway of Calcutta and W. B. Byers of Asansol led the meetings: 'Many believe that we have had a breath of the real Revival.'[75]

Emlyn H. Davies had left Wales 'full of the fire of revival'.[76] That is how Miss E. M. Lloyd (CM), Sylhet, referred to him when she heard he was coming to India. She had the news from F. Kehl, the publisher in Calcutta (already mentioned as one of Mrs Penn-Lewis's correspondents and a close friend of J. Pengwern Jones).

When Emlyn Davies returned to Berhampur, Calcutta, he shared his optimism for revival with Brockway, minister of Union chapel, Calcutta.[77] Both men believed there was a readiness for revival, and their hopes were quickened by the recent formation of the Bengali Convention League. Their dreams were realised in August 1906, when for nine days the people found it difficult to leave the services. Emlyn Davies and many others could spend as long as six hours each day in the chapel, not only leading the services but counselling enquirers as well.[78] In the homes, the Women's Home, and amongst visitors, the revival was the topic of the day. The Welshman was not surprised: prayer had been offered ever since they had heard of what had happened in Wales during 1904–05. Meetings were also held for different groups: the Christians, those who had broken with Hinduism, those born in Christian homes, and the 'pagans'. Emlyn Davies pinpointed two characteristics of the meetings—their intensity and the spirit of unity.[79]

**Conventions**

As in South India, to the north and west of Calcutta there was a cluster of revival centres. In many of these an annual convention was held, in which revival could be discussed and prayed for in the hope that this would lead to actual revival. To the west was Jabalpur, where the first convention was held in 1906. About a thousand people attended, some of the nationals having walked almost a hundred miles to be present. Two of the Indian speakers held the congregation spellbound, and they were followed by others, including J. Pengwern Jones, Sylhet. After one meeting the convention members marched through the streets, waving banners and singing a Punjabi revival hymn.[80] Arrangements were in the hands of Mrs Hensley (CMS), whose roots were in Wales.[81]

A contributory factor to the revival in Allahabad was the Christian Endeavour Convention held in December 1905. In India, as in Britain and China, Christian Endeavour meetings were congenial to revival. The central theme at Allahabad was 'the Revival that is upon us'.[82] Speakers included Dr J. P. Jones (an experienced missionary who was born in Wrexham, Wales, but moved to America), J. Pengwern Jones and Dr H. A. Johnston, who had already spoken at Ratnagiri. It must have been during his visit to Allahabad that J. Pengwern Jones visited one of the schools where the head teacher was from Wales.

*Welsh Students at Spurgeon's College, 1905*

*Revd Caradoc Jones at eighty*

*Pastor Reuben Saillens*

*Her Highness Princess Lieven and family*
*Prince Paul and Prince Anatol*
*Princess Alicia*
*Her Highness Princess Lieven*
*Princess Mary and Princess Sophie*
(by permission of Mayflower Christian Books)

*Mrs Jessie Penn-Leiws, October 1925*
(by permission of *The Overcomer*)

*Miss Arianwen Jones and Mr and Mrs Griffiths*

*Pastor William Fetler,*
*St Petersburg, Russia*

*T. B. Barrett, Norway*

# THE MICHIGAN
# CHRISTIAN HERALD.

Price $1.50 a year.
Price per copy 5 cents.

DETROIT, MICH., FEBUARY 9, 1905.

VOLUME XXXVI
NUMBER 6

## Story of Evan Roberts, the Welsh Evangelist

### An Example of God's Methods.

#### The Story of Evan Roberts.

The child is father of the man. Wordsworth. It is good that a man should both hope and quietly wait for the salvation of the Lord. It is good for a man that he bear the yoke in his youth.—Lamentations iii. 26, 27.

A servant of Jesus Christ called . . separated unto the Gospel of God.—Rom. i. 1.

One of the concomitant features of the revival is the attention it receives from the daily and weekly press. Evan Roberts has been represented as a young man of 26—a miner—who had devoted to become a preacher, and was a student in a school preliminary to his entering college, when suddenly he was pressed with a desire to go forth, and thrust forth, into remarkable prominence, for which there seemed to have been no adequate antecedent preparation.

#### God's Methods.

But that is not the way of God with regard to his servants. If ever a witness of Christ seemed to be suddenly thrust out unprepared into a place of testimony and notoriety, it was the Apostle Paul. But he tells us that he was separated even prior to his birth unto the Gospel of God, until he called him by his grace, and revealed his Son in him, that he might preach him among the Gentiles.

But not only Paul, but David and Solomon, Isaiah and Cyrus, Amos and Jeremiah Ezekiel and

EVAN ROBERTS.

## Prayer For an Awakening.

youthful tyrants who would take advantage of them.

As he grew he found many little ways of being useful to his mother, when he was 12 years old, his father's foot was hurt by an accident in the mine, but as soon as the injury permitted of his return to work Evan begged to be allowed to go also. Thus it was found that he could be helpful to his father who held a responsible position, and could not be spared longer than was absolutely necessary. Describing the position at this time of the future evangelist, a contemporary says.

So Evan Roberts, the little Welsh boy of 12 laid aside his childhood. Almost literally he became his father's right hand, until Mr Roberts recovered from his accident. Even began to know the hard, perilous life of the miner for after some months under his father, he commenced regular work as a mine boy.

. . . it was at this time, apparently that his thoughts began to turn to religion. He did his work underground at a pit on the colliery cheerfully and well, and always a put on the ordinary shifts.

Now, his father told a man at work in the same stall with him "the lad belongs to no choir or club. He just goes home and works at his books. It's hard to get him to bed before three or four in the morning."

One day came his first opportunity for doing active religious work. The Wesleyan chapel at Gorseinon did not include in the Sunday school a min-

*Converts of the 1904-5 Revival in Gaiman, Patagonia*
(by permission of the National Library of Wales)

*Eluned Morgan, Patagonia*

*Elizabeth Rowlands*

*Revd J. Pengwern Jones, India*     *Mrs Sidney Roberts, India*

*Welsh Presbyterian Missionaries, Nongsawlia, 1905*

*The first seven Presbyterian ministers in Korea 1907*
(by permission of The Banner of Truth Trust)

*Revd Howard Agnew Johnson*
(by permission of the Presbyterian Historical Society, USA)

# AMONG THE RUSSIAN REFUGEES.

The Story of the remarkable work
now being carried on in Poland.

## Come and hear the thrilling account
to be given by
## Pastor Fetler's Missionaries.

Also
**Mr. F.
Spencer
Johnson,
Special
Missioner**
to the
**Y.P.A.**
Russian
Missionary
Society.

**Mr.
Spencer
Johnson**
(formerly Society
Entertainer)
**will
speak
and sing.**

Mr. and Mrs. DAVID T. GRIFFITHS,

who have just arrived in this country; they have had twelve months
strenuous labour among thousands of destitute Russians, including
noblemen, officers, professional men and outcasts.

Free-Will Offerings will be taken in aid of this needy work.

Mr. and Mrs. Griffiths represent the
Young People's Auxiliary of the Russian Missionary Society,

Gifts of clothing can be sent to the Offices, The Evangel House,
350, Christchurch Road, Boscombe.

The visit led to a revival that was reported later by the missionary Ellen Hughes.[83]

Darjeeling not only provided shelter during the hot season but it was also the home of a convention. J. Pengwern Jones was one of the speakers in 1905, and he returned the following year as one of the main speakers, joined by R. McCheyne Paterson (Sialkot) and W. G. Proctor (Asansol). Even the older, more experienced missionaries were surprised by the high spiritual tone of the meetings.[84] A significant happening at the convention was the formation of the Bengal Prayer Union, and it was a tribute to J. Pengwern Jones that he was made secretary of that Union.[85]

Although the Christian Endeavour meetings were contributing substantially in creating a spirit of revival, there was a feeling in Pilibhit that they were becoming superficial. It was believed that too many nominal Christians were joining the Society. In July 1906 the Society was dissolved and reorganised. A prayer band was formed to concentrate on prayer for revival:[86]

> When we read of the revival in Wales and Assam we longed to see with our own eyes and hear with our own ears such glorious things and now God has let us see them in our own work. We have seen his power. For a week but little progress was made. We realized the difficulty was with the workers themselves, and told them so. There were things they needed to confess. This was hard for them but there was no going forward otherwise. The Holy Spirit prevailed, and they were broken down and confessed many sins.

Confession at Pilibhit was sustained for an unusually long period. There was also a case of demon possession; but some of the leaders had heard of the work of Pastor Hsi in China and were prepared to meet with such a crisis.[87]

Enthusiasts could be critical of those who were lukewarm about revival. One LMS missionary thought the directors in London were sleeping:[88]

> I am quite sure if there came a day when the board of directors were all down on their knees with streaming eyes, and forgot they had to catch a train, and just broke down under the burden of the world's sin and sorrow, that day would see all our difficulties melt away in the field in a Baptism of the Spirit.

While this was, perhaps, a necessary stricture on the directors, the missionary was rather optimistic, because all difficulties do not melt away during a time of awakening.

Another enthusiast, Thomas Walker of Tinnevelly, included north India in his preaching tours. He visited Agra, where the Welshman Daniel Jones (BMS) was labouring, a man in full sympathy with Thomas Walker's work.[89] According to one report, 'The ten days ministry left an indelible mark.'[90] The proof of new life in Meerut was the fact that so many believers were meeting in each other's homes to sing and pray.[91]

Letters and newspapers were continually used to spread news of revival. In Ludhiana a young lad received letters from Assam, and when revival broke out he wanted Praying Hyde to send the news to Assam.[92] Eleanor Soltau in north-west India received a copy of *The Christian* containing reports of the Welsh Revival, and these were read to the railwaymen. This led to a meeting taken by James Lyall, who sent the report to Mrs Penn-Lewis.[93]

*Sialkot* (now in Pakistan)
The Punjab had its convention centre, and Sialkot brought believers together from many parts of India. The foundation was laid in 1904 and confirmed in 1905. What was expected of the supporters was made known in a list of questions:[94]

- Are you praying for quickening in your own life, in the life of your fellow workers and in the Church?
- Are you looking for greater power of the Holy Spirit in your life and work, and are you convinced that you cannot go on without this power?
- Will you pray that you may not be ashamed of Jesus?
- Do you believe that prayer is the great means for securing this spiritual awakening?
- Will you set apart one half-hour each day as soon after noon as possible to pray for this awakening, and are you willing to pray *till the awakening comes*?

Prior to the convention, Praying Hyde (American Presbyterian), George Turner (YMCA), McCheyne Paterson (Church of Scotland) and Ihsan Ullah (Anglican Church) had spent much time in prayer seeking God's blessing on the proceedings.[95]

As in other conventions, J. Pengwern Jones played a leading part at Sialkot. He was a close friend of Praying Hyde and McCheyne Paterson. The Welshman, who would share a room with Praying

Hyde during the convention, bears witness to his prayerfulness: 'He was always on his knees when I went to bed, and on his knees long before I was up in the morning though I was up with the dawn.'[96] This is some testimony, coming as it did from a man who knew what it was to persevere in prayer in difficult situations. J. Pengwern Jones believed that McCheyne Paterson was 'one of the most wonderful and powerful men in India'.[97] This was the man who had Mrs Penn-Lewis's Motto and a photograph of Evan Roberts on his desk: 'God fills my heart with praise for them and Wales.'[98]

The booklet *India Awake* had heralded the coming of its editor (J. Pengwern Jones) to Sialkot. James Lyall had received advanced copies of the book while attending the Darjeeling Convention and, on his way back to the station, he had left a copy with A. P. S. Tulloch at a missionary centre. He in turn had sent a copy to a college friend, George Turner of the YMCA in Punjab, who was one of the Sialkot organisers. George Turner offered to be the agent for the booklet in the Punjab and sent off three orders for a hundred copies each, arranging also for the work to be translated into Persian Urdu. Reports of revival from different parts of India were therefore being read in the Punjab before J. Pengwern Jones arrived at Sialkot in 1905.[99]

Both the Welshman and Praying Hyde spoke at Sialkot. When the former finished speaking, the whole congregation was humbled and there was a general confession of sin. Many of the confessions 'shocked the hearers but later were found hard to remember'.[100] Praying Hyde was supposed to speak a number of times on 'The Holy Spirit', but he only succeeded in doing so once because the Spirit of God took over completely and there was much singing in the informal meetings. 'During the last days of the convention the place became veritably a garden of singing birds, for everywhere the voice of song was heard.'[101]

The meetings created a spirit of expectancy to see increased numbers at the 1906 convention. Attendance in 1905 had been in the region of 300, but in 1906 about 3,000 gathered together, plus 60 to 70 missionaries. J. Pengwern Jones doubted if he could afford to go, lacking both the time and the money, but his friends felt strongly that he should attend. A missionary and 'my friend Kehl' offered to help, and George Turner (YMCA) mentioned the need to one of his friends, who sent J. Pengwern Jones a gift of £10. In the absence of other means of help, the Sialkot organisers would have paid his expenses.[102] The eagerness to assist reveals how highly Sialkot valued the Welshman's presence and contribution.

Feelings were intense during the first Sunday in Sialkot, but it was at the prayer meeting that followed the evening service that revival was really experienced. Both in the Prayer Room and on the Mission compound generally, large parties, or groups of two or three, were praying earnestly, the more experienced believers leading others into a fuller experience of God. Such was the compelling power of prayer that the women set up an extra tent, and the Scottish Presbyterians opened their chapel as another prayer centre. Many believed that their calling was to pray rather than to attend the meetings, and a number of them continued to intercede for a period of ten days. Friends would take them food, and they would sleep in turn, ensuring that a few people were always awake.

The missionary from Sylhet notes three particular characteristics of the revival meetings at Sialkot: intense praying, confession of sin, and praise. Confession very often issued from being convicted of a critical spirit and an awareness of past sins, causing those present to hide their faces in shame. A committee member spoke, reminding the convention of some biblical principles. Confession was usually made to God privately, but if a believer wronged another believer they should meet each other. Another consideration was the leading of the Spirit of God. If the Spirit prompted confession it was acceptable, but no human pressure was to be exerted in any way. This talk had a healthy influence on the convention, and the people became rather reluctant to confess sin publicly.[103]

A feature of the meetings was not only general intercessory prayer but a 'burdened prayer'. A 'burden for souls' was laid on the hearts of many, causing them to pray specifically for people. The burden was referred to as an experience of Gethsemane, but they would then be led on to Calvary and Pentecost. J. Pengwern Jones describes such an experience at the close of the convention, when many felt it for the first time:[104]

At the last service or rather after the last Service, almost all the Missionaries and some of the Indian Christians moved towards the Prayer Room and there we had a memorable time together. God was evidently in our midst, what earnest prayers were offered, what anguish some passed through on account of the hardness of hearts, but when an Indian sister asked for prayer on behalf of a near and dear relative, that the Spirit of intercession seemed to be poured on all present, and many had an insight into the agony of Gethsemane which can never be forgotten. How one after another prayed for that misguided sinner. Some of us realized for the first time how sins of an entire stranger could become a real burden to us. On the heart-rending cries of many present for that person, many wept like children, others groaned under the burden and most of us had the assurance that God had heard our prayers.

Greatly inspired, and endued with fresh power, the believers returned to their homes, churches and stations expecting much spiritual fruit in the immediate future.

The main influence of the Sialkot Convention was on the Christians, though Hindus and Muslims were influenced to some degree.[105] Those returning from the convention were the means of spreading the revival message, and were able to share their Sialkot experiences with others. The impact was felt in Jamma in the north-east and Ludhiana in the north-west.[106] Missionaries, including J. Pengwern Jones, returned to their stations to discover that news from Khasia was still encouraging believers. This was especially true in Delhi.[107]

There was a further development in 1907. Until that year the CMS missionaries had stayed away from Sialkot, but that year many of them attended the convention. Not only were they present, but they were also an integral part of the proceedings: 'the barriers were down & bigoted Churchmen became one with us, oh it was glorious, glorious'.[108]

They were rejoicing in Sialkot because Christians of different backgrounds were dwelling together in unity, but already divisive forces were at work in India. These had begun to appear at the beginning of 1907.

## Division

As in Germany, 1907 was a crucial year for evangelicals in India. J. Pengwern Jones was in Calcutta in early February, and was taken by George Wilson to one of A. G. Garr's meetings. Alfred Goodrich Garr was one of the first to be baptised at Azusa street (1906).[109] He and his wife arrived in India early in 1907 and arranged meetings according to the Azusa Street pattern.

In the first meeting, J. Pengwern Jones was impressed by Garr's earnestness. The second meeting was led by Max Moorhead, and when he commented on the Spirit of God in revival, J. Pengwern Jones thought it was a 'mistatement' and attempted to correct the speaker; but he was prevented from doing so. A. G. Garr arrived and objected to an 'outsider' taking part in the meeting. Whenever the Welsh missionary tried to explain his stand he was not allowed to

continue. 'The third time Mr Garr interposed shouting him down
and working himself up into such a rage that he lost all balance and
self control.'[110] This scene took place in spite of the fact that J.
Pengwern Jones had been invited there by R. J. Ward, who at that
time accepted A. G. Garr's teaching on the baptism of the Spirit with
tongues following.

An anonymous writer described one of A. G. Garr's meetings. It
started in prayer and prostration.

> Then came a constant rubbing of the throat, and arms and shoul-
> ders; which they called the laying on of hands, or anointing in the
> name of the Lord. As soon as this was done there was a trance-like
> state produced, then would come on a violent shaking and groan-
> ing, and sometimes shrieks and cries as of one in hysteria.[111]

Another source revealed that some were barking like dogs and lowing like cattle.

Commenting on the Calcutta meetings, J. Pengwern Jones
believed that Satan 'was playing his best cards'.[112] The missionary did
not doubt A. G. Garr's sincerity and believed that the American
demonstrated a supernatural gift in his meetings. He was unhappy,
however, with the insistence on tongues as being the proof of the
baptism with the Holy Spirit. He also believed that there was an
apparent show of the gift in some of the meetings and reminded the
believers that quaking and shaking had been experienced in other
parts of India. It was wrong to value the gift of tongues so highly,
because of all the gifts of the Spirit it was the lowest. On the other
hand, J. Pengwern Jones warned against a critical spirit that would
mar relationships between fellow Christians.[113] He was being cautious,
critical and gracious.

The Garr group moved to Fernwood, Mukti and Coonoor. The
party included Mr and Mrs Garr, R. J. Ward, Mr and Mrs Groves,
Miss Gardiner, Miss Orlebar (the Superintendent of the Alliance
Missionary Home) and a few others. The Christian Missionary
Alliance in India was deeply influenced by the Garr movement.[114] Its
founder, A. B. Simpson, acknowledged the gifts of the Spirit but did
not insist on speaking with tongues as proof of the baptism of the
Spirit. The meetings at Coonoor were quieter than those in Calcutta,
and the Mukti people welcomed the group to that area.[115]

Some church leaders thought that Pandita Ramabai and her people
were too sympathetic to the Garr movement. One of them, George
Wilson, visited Mukti in order to see for himself, and he was assured

that the work there was of God.[116] He spent much time with Ramabai and her daughter Manorabai. In a meeting, both would sit on the floor, Ramabai taking notes and the daughter passing messages to her mother because she was deaf. In one of the meetings George Wilson spoke from 1 Corinthians 2, verse 15, on 'spiritual discernment'. Speaking to the mother, the missionary could see clearly that her concerns were the spread of the gospel, the circulation of literature and the printing of the Murathi Bible with references. He did discuss tongues with the daughter, and she insisted that speaking in tongues was only one sign of the baptism of the Spirit. She also acknowledged that errors were creeping into some movements in India. George Wilson was glad of this response, both for the sake of India and because so many visitors from other countries were coming to Mukti. It was his personal hope that believers would assess the tongues movement critically.[117]

The critics of the tongues movement were helped in many ways. The extreme claims of Garr and the excesses of the meetings turned many away from him. Garr had believed that tongues had a missionary function, and that when he visited a particular country he would be able to speak in the language of the people. That did not materialise, and he had to acknowledge his failure. The critics were provided with ammunition from outside, especially from A. T. Pierson and Mrs Penn-Lewis.[118] Their articles were sent to India and distributed by F. Kehl, Dr Rudisill and R. J. Ward, who had turned against Garr.[119]

It seemed that the work of the Garr group would be discredited, but the Pentecostal cause had a new champion in T. B. Barratt.[120] He was invited to India by A. N. Groves, Maud Orlebar and Max Moorhead. In the letter of invitation A. N. Groves referred to the intensive interest shown in the Garr movement but admitted that there had been bitter criticism as well. Some of the criticism, he claimed, was not only biased but malicious, and the critics included a 'Mrs–.' This was most probably a reference to Mrs Penn-Lewis,[121] who made an uncompromising attack on the tongues movement.[122]

Minnie Abrams in Mukti welcomed the visit of T. B. Barratt, while F. Kehl made use of Mrs Penn-Lewis's articles to oppose him. F. Kehl thanked the Welsh lady for a letter in which she explained her 'victory when you met the tongues people. It will be a sort of standard letter for reference in the months to come for all leaders who will have to face the Barratt teaching in their station.'[123] When Barratt was asked to speak at the Belgaum Convention with J. Pengwern Jones and George Wilson, F. Kehl became more concerned. He said that Max Moorhead was behind this unwise move, as he had been the 'leading and misleading spirit in Colombo'.[124] Two ladies, Miss Gardiner and Miss Knight, spoke glowingly of T. B. Barratt, even after his first meeting. 'He has arrived and begun meetings. He is most pleasing and loving, saying nothing that could offend anyone. A great contrast to what I have heard of Mr Garr.'[125] Evangelicals in India were divided, and T. B. Barratt's visit did not unite them.

# 14
## China, Korea
## and Manchuria

At the beginning of the twentieth century China was in turmoil because of the Boxer Rising of 1900. Foreigners had been put to death, including missionaries, and the CIM suffered terribly during that year.[1] In many areas in the north of the country, churches were rased to the ground.

Much good, however, came from the unpleasant events, because local officials, realising that their country was being weakened, changed their attitude towards missionaries. So the rebellion that could have seriously harmed the Protestant mission in fact turned out for good. 'The suppression of the Boxers was followed by greater opportunities than ever and many new recruits came to fill the gaps left by the martyrs.'[2] Yet, though there was room for optimism, the missionaries knew that they were in a precarious position. They would have to continue to depend on spiritual weapons, the most effective of which was prayer. From 1900 to 1905 a prayer movement spread through large parts of China, and the formation of Fukien Prayer Union in 1903 stimulated further intercession on behalf of the country. Local revivals were experienced in Foochow in 1900, in Amoy in 1904,[3] and also in the west under the ministry of Samuel Pollard.[4]

Individuals and groups were of one mind in seeking God for a widespread revival. This desire was strengthened by news of revival from Wales. Benjamin Williams,[5] a CIM missionary from Swansea, South Wales, received clippings from the South Wales Daily News from his minister in Cwmbwrla, Swansea.[6] When E. Marshbank, another CIM missionary, heard of events in Wales, her cry was 'Oh that some of the Blessing might come to China',[7] while T. Howard Smith, an LMS missionary, believed that there was a harvest to be reaped but bemoaned the lack of workers.[8] A CMS missionary corresponded with Evan Roberts, seeking prayer for China,[9] while a missionary from China was present at revival meetings at Nant-y-moel, South Wales, pleading before God for revival in China, as in Wales.[10] Even greater interest was created when some of the reports from Wales were translated into Chinese.[11]

**Beginning of blessing**

There were awakenings during 1905, but it was in the following year that they became more general and powerful. T. N. Thompson arrived in Tsintau, Shantung, in the autumn of 1905 and witnessed a work 'truly born of the Spirit of God'.[12] One pastor was in charge of forty villages, and had created a centre for twenty-six of them where a church was built with a membership of two hundred. Within three months three more churches were built. This surprised Thompson, as the area was a new mission field. He left in February 1906 to visit other districts and was continually conscious of the manifest presence of God. What happened at Ta-hsin-t'an is typical of many areas:[13]

> At Ta-hsin-t'an, where there has been a woeful lack of harmony among the Christians and even open quarrelling, the people were greatly moved by the Spirit of God. Falling to the floor and crying out to God for mercy because of their sins. Many of the night meetings were held till nearly midnight. The people quickly raised the money to call a pastor. He is now with them. Besides this they raised a sum to help the poor in other parts of the field. Since then eleven have been added to the church.

Thompson left that village to take part in a series of meetings in Liu-kia-ch'ioa, where six hundred people gathered together. A feature of the series was the 'Sunrise Prayer-meetings', starting at 6.30 a.m. and on one occasion continuing until 1 p.m.

Those outside the church came to the meetings. Under the ministry of the Word of God many of them became catechumens and candidates for membership. Apart from the preaching services there were opportunities to discuss problems that worried people, such as foot-binding, domestic difficulties, and lawsuits that had been carried out in the name of the church. Many of the women had their feet unbound, and lawsuits were abandoned. In one church the members would not even take care of the building, and there was also a case of immorality that created a division in the church. As a result of revival, the members came together, supported the pastor financially, some of the women prepared to be Bible-workers, and the roof of the building was repaired.[14]

Missionaries were willing helpers in revival, but were careful not to take the central place:[15]

> These meetings were entirely free from false excitement. The Spirit of God was recognized as the leader throughout. As far as

human leaders were concerned, we foreigners, only two in number in most places, let the Chinese pastors manage it all and the Spirit of God used them as His own. The people have been taught here for three or four years that they must not depend upon the foreign church as heretofore for aid especially in financial matters.

The missionaries were convinced that the revival was bearing fruit.

### Howard Agnew Johnston

Another person to visit Shantung was Howard Agnew Johnston (who had been to Wales and had just arrived in China from India). This 'Special Commissioner to the Missionaries in Asia'[16] began his tour in Shanghai, and from 4 to 8 May 1906 was in Weihsien, where, besides the mission station members, representatives from four missionary societies were present. During those five days, eighteen services were held in all.[17]

When Howard Agnew Johnston began his ministry in Weihsien the missionaries were rather downcast, but the very first address given by the American changed the whole atmosphere. He spoke in a quiet, simple manner, his message abounding in scriptural references. In that service there was 'a sense of the reality of God, which made us feel that the Holy Spirit was in our midst'.[18] There were about three hundred students in the compound, and 'Dr Johnston was able in a remarkable manner to reach the heart of his student audiences.'[19] The preacher had such an impact that nearly two hundred of those present expressed a desire to spend the summer holidays preaching the gospel.

Much time was spent in prayer. On the Monday, the college boys spent all day in prayer—from 8 a.m. until midday, from 2 p.m. until 6, and the whole evening.[20] Many of the boys had come to Weihsien to obtain Western education, but they made it known that they had now found wisdom in Christ. It was not only Dr Johnston's preaching that was welcomed in China but his books also. Mrs C. W. Mateer translated his *Studies for Personal Work* (New York, 1905) into Chinese, and a volume based on his works was in preparation by a national believer in the north.[21]

The port of Tsingtau was considered a hard place to work in because of its cosmopolitan character. During Easter (and more so during Whitsun), numbers at meetings grew, and in one of them a person was released 'from terrible sins'. It was just for one night that Howard Agnew Johnston visited the Union Theological and Lay Preachers' School, but during his brief stay numerous backsliders were restored and the faith of many strengthened. As at Weihsien, a number of the students committed themselves to evangelistic work during the summer.[22]

The visiting preacher was able to spend more time at Chefoo, arriving on 15 May and leaving six days later. During this time he spoke at a number of schools and colleges. One of the preaching centres was the American Presbyterian Mission, and the congregation on one occasion included students from a nearby school established by Chinese gentry who had returned from Japan. Other schools were visited, including CIM schools and a centre for deaf children, where the preacher was able to communicate with them by means of sign language he had learned in New York. In one of the meetings, Spencer Lewis gave an account of revival at Foochow College, and Howard Agnew Johnston of revival in Weihsien and India.[23] As in other countries, Christians in China believed that telling the story of revival in one place could lead to revival in other places.

On the Sunday afternoon of his visit, Howard Agnew Johnston preached at a large meeting for nationals at the Union Chapel. The church was full:[24]

He spoke at our regular Chinese service, and our church, which seats 500, was filled to overflowing. Many were much impressed and no doubt this helped greatly towards the results of revival meetings held here in connection with a normal class during the summer.

The women's meetings also benefited, and after the American preacher left, they arranged four days of prayer.

As a strong believer in prayer Dr Johnston welcomed the week of prayer for China. During that time prolonged meetings were held at Yan-chow. On the Friday there was a real sense of God's presence; a cloud of darkness came over them on the Saturday, but renewed blessing came on Sunday as a result of a meeting for humiliation.[25] The visiting preacher moved to Chihli, where he addressed a number of schools. At Paoting-fu, all those 'old enough to understand the step, but still undecided, stood up to confess Christ', while at the Girls' School he encouraged believers and helped others to come to faith in the Lord Jesus Christ.[26]

### The spirit of revival

While the American was touring Chihli, the spirit of revival was spreading rapidly from place to place. At the Roberts Memorial

Hospital in the LMS station, Tientsin (Tianjin), missionaries and other believers were seeking revival. The Chinese preachers had met in Pehtaiko in the summer, and this was followed in October by the annual meeting of the LMS. In both meetings there was concentration on prayer for revival.[27] On 15 November, Mr Yang spoke at Tsangchow Training Institute. He read 2 Thessalonians 1, verses 11 and 12, and commented on them. When he finished, he requested personal testimonies from the congregation, and this was followed by a time of prayer.[28] As at Tsingtau and Weihsien, many were inspired to go out as evangelists. Further inspiration was received when news of revival in Wales reached them, and they arranged a meeting to relate the story of what was happening in that country.[29]

Another memorable day was Sunday 1 January 1906, when the believers had a 'blessing beyond expectation'.[30] At the Roberts Memorial Hospital, where Dr Peill and Mary Roberts worked, the experience of revival began on that day. Mary Roberts was the sister of Frederick Charles Roberts (after whom the hospital was named), the missionary who had worked with James Gilmour. Brother and sister had been born of Welsh parents in Manchester, and she was glad to continue the work started by her brother.[31] Dr Peill refers to a particular meeting when many strangers attended the hospital for eye treatment. The Christians shared the gospel with them, and many believed on the Lord Jesus Christ. Mr Yang spoke in a very direct way, warning his hearers that God wanted resolute determination to be faithful rather than words and tears.

Dr Peill describes the result of Mr Yang's meeting:[32]

From that meeting onwards began a striking progression in the minds and prayers of the people, which filled one with awe, and gave a distinct impression of the wisdom of God. The first night people were mostly concerned about personal guilt and cleansing. On Monday they had started, with keen solicitude, to pray for the saving of others, and were full of trouble for the need and sin of their friends and families. On Wednesday the prayer was more striking still in this land till of late unpatriotic. Mighty gusts of prayer literally shook the room; for the Emperor, for the High Commissioners of Europe too, that they might be led to give due placc to the influence of Christ in their report to those who sent them; and for all Christians in the eighteen provinces who, that day, were praying for 'Nations and their Rulers', that this subject, especially in regard to their native land, might be deeply laid upon their hearts.

During the service a man would go round the congregation to see if all were praying earnestly, and he was assured that they were praying in the Spirit.

The meeting on the Thursday was devoted to foreign missions, a subject very meaningful to many of the missionaries in Tientsin and district. Mrs Murray had a brother serving as a missionary in New Guinea; Mrs Peill had a brother in Africa, and Dr Peill's parents had spent some time in Madagascar. Others present spoke of revival in India, Madagascar and Khama's land.[33] Mary Roberts was not the only representative of Wales, for the Welsh Revival was represented in the person of S. J. W. Clark from Upton, Chester. (He was a deacon at the Congregational Church whose minister, D. Wynne Evans, was one of the group that prepared the way for establishing Keswick in Wales.) [34] Clark had visited Wales during the Revival, and had come to China to visit Griffith John, the missionary from Swansea— a man who was thrilled to hear of what was happening in his mother country during 1904–05. Clark spoke in the Thursday meeting through an interpreter, but even so his message went forth with power. But for the language, he could have been in Wales.[35]

Like India, China had her conventions, though not so numerous. One important centre was Kuling, a valley opened up by the missionary Griffith John.[36] The Keswick representatives at the 1907 convention were W. B. Sloane and F. S. Webster. Webster had taken part in revival meetings in Wales and he and Sloan had represented Keswick in overseas conventions.[37] Another 'Keswickian' was Charlotte Featherstone, who had visited Keswick in 1905 when a strong revival contingent from Wales was present. She returned from England to Kiang-si, China, and exhorted her fellow workers and friends to pray for revival. In a few weeks time they experienced the melting ministry of the Holy Spirit and had much joy in singing, especially the refrain from Wales, 'Blessed Jesus! send a breeze from Calvary'.[38] As in other places, evangelism was given an impetus and the 'All For Jesus Army' was formed. This was made up of young boys, but they would take Blandford, one of the missionaries, with them on their journeys. Apart from evangelism, much good work was done to help those in the opium dens.[39]

Charlotte Featherstone had returned to southeast China, and there, as in other parts of that land, schools and colleges were centres of revival.[40] During the winter of 1905 stations of the Methodist Episcopal Church enjoyed seasons of refreshing, and Bishop Blaskford was the instrument of revival in school and college. In some of the CIM stations the Holy Spirit 'brooded' over the meetings,[41] and at Hinghwa they were fasting—a feature not often found during the revivals of the period.[42] At Hinghwa also they were aware of what was happening in Korea. Events that took place in that country during 1907 were to determine the spread of revival in China and Manchuria in 1908.

# Korea

Writing in 1890, the American missionary Henry Appenzeller expressed his desire for Korea: 'I want to see Korean sinners alarmed because of their sins . . . I want to put a premium on praying for a mighty baptism of fire for Korea. Nothing else can save the Hermit Nation.'[43] Appenzeller,[44] his fellow Methodists and the Presbyterian missionaries shared this hope for Korea.[45] After initial progress a paralysis had taken hold of the work, and R. A. Hardie, another American missionary, was overcome with a sense of personal failure.[46]

**Signs of change**

A partial answer came in 1903 when a group of Methodist missionaries met at Wonsan. During the meetings a marked change came over many of the missionaries, including R. A. Hardie. He echoed the words of Appenzeller in 1890, that he would like 'to see Koreans convicted of sin and to see them have actual and living experience'.[47] Hardie himself experienced a spiritual transformation and shared his experience with the congregation on a Sunday morning. He told them that he had claimed the gift of the Holy Spirit.[48] Another meeting was held in Wonsan in 1904, and also in Pyangyang and Jemulpo.[49] By early 1905 there were reports of revivals in many areas, especially Pyangyang. In Korea as a whole the churches harvested more souls during 1905 than during the whole twenty-year period of Protestant mission.[50]

While the revival movement was gaining momentum, there were fears that developments in Korea would hinder the advance of Christian work and, possibly, ruin it in some parts of the country. Korea had been humiliated by the Russo-Japanese War, but with the humiliation came a new spirit of patriotism. The missionaries believed that this spirit, if governed by Christian principles, would help the country; but if controlled merely by political considerations it could be a danger. Now was the time for God to intervene, and William Blair had faith that this would happen. 'For years now she has been sitting in the dust. Mourning not only her personal present misfortune, but her past sins. Over such a stricken people has God so often stretched his hands in blessing.'[51]

The churches persevered in prayer, and there were signs of changes. This was so even in a neglected area like King-won, while in Makpo[52] the Presbyterians had to double the size of their church building, and there was a substantial increase in the sale of Scriptures.[53] When John R. Mott visited Seoul he addressed a congregation of six thousand, and G. H. Jones, who until that time had not known of a single convert, estimated that the Christians in his area (Ch(J)emulpo) numbered ten thousand.[54]

## 1906

A meeting was arranged at Pyangyang in August 1906, and as the missionaries gathered together they had mixed feelings. On the one hand they had hope, because God was already working in their midst: on the other hand, they were conscious of the insecure future of the country. The conference study was based on 1 John chapter 1, with the emphasis on fellowship with God that should bear fruit in love and righteousness. It was a time for personal heart-searching. As they went from those meetings the missionaries were more convinced than ever of their need of the baptism of the Spirit. Koreans should not only repent of hating the Japanese but should see it as a sin against God. Before righteousness and justice could be established in Korea, a holy people had to be formed.[55] J. R. Moose, a Southern Methodist missionary, was convinced that 'It is so urgent a time that we must pray for all workers in Korea to experience revival in this coming New Year so that the Korean Pentecost may truly come.'[56]

Following Pyangyang, the Presbyterian Mission held a week of meetings from 2 to 9 September. One of the speakers was Howard Agnew Johnston. His account of what he had seen in Wales and India came as a fresh challenge to the missionaries: 'His telling of it gave some of the people a great desire to have the same blessing.'[57] He moved on to Taegu, where the Christians were thrilled with the same story. When they came together for prayer they asked their God to grant them the blessing he had already given to the people of Wales. The Presbyterian Board of Foreign Missions in the USA reported enthusiastically on Johnston's visit: it had stirred the missionaries, and 'His addresses to the Koreans have also been most helpful and his visit will not soon be forgotten.'[58]

The Koreans in their local congregations and in conferences would set apart time for concentrated Bible study and prayer. 'Just as the Jews kept the Passover, the Korean Christians keep these days sacred to prayer and the study of God's word.'[59] One of those most zealous for prayer and study was Sun-fu Kil, an elder in the Chang Dae Hyun church who was regarded as 'our most gifted Korean preacher'.[60] Under the ministry of Howard Agnew Johnston he had received the baptism of the Spirit and became even more zealous for the things of God. Not only did he discipline himself, but he would call his fellow believers together for prayer, and that early in the morning. The experience of Kil is another instance of Howard Agnew Johnston's crucial role in the development of revival in many countries.

## Bible Conference, 1907

Elder Kil believed that the discipline of prayer and study was the best possible preparation for the Bible Conference in January 1907.[61] William Blair, Graham Lee and elder Kil led the January meetings, which were attended by fifteen hundred Christians. William Blair preached in the Saturday meeting on 1 Corinthians 12, verse 27; Sunday's meetings were lifeless, and on Monday the missionaries came together to humble themselves before God.[62] When they arrived at the Monday evening service they knew that things would be different. A spirit of sorrow and mourning came over everybody and the whole congregation was weeping.[63]

Tremendous spiritual power was released in confession, especially when an elder confessed that he had fostered hatred against William Blair. The elder prayed for forgiveness, but could only say 'Father', and then:[64]

It seemed as if the roof was lifted from the building and the Spirit of God came down from heaven in a mighty avalanche of power upon us. I fell at Kim's side and wept and prayed as I had never prayed before. My last glimpse of the audience is photographed indelibly on my brain. Some threw themselves full length on the floor, hundreds stood with arms outstretched toward heaven. Every man forgot every other. Each was face to face with God. I can hear yet the fearful sound of hundreds of men pleading with God for life, for mercy. The cry went over the city till the heathen were in consternation.

Quiet was restored when Graham Lee gave out a hymn, but immediately afterwards there was a stream of confession.

Confession very often shamed the congregation, as they heard of hatred, lewdness and two cases of killing—one of an infant and the other of an infirm mother. Some, who could not find relief, would bang their heads against the floor, while others were writhing in anguish. Preaching was not neglected, however, and Kil 'was so set on fire with purity and holiness when he preached he looked like Jesus himself not Kil' and was described as 'The Messenger of Fire'.[65] The preacher could adopt an unusual way of presenting the gospel. In one meeting, 'He had himself tied with ropes and in his preaching frantically broke loose to illustrate how the sinner should break away from his sin.'[66] Typical titles of his sermons were: 'Choose either heaven or hell', 'Open the door of your heart and accept the Holy Spirit', and 'Strange visitors and unusual master'.

The influence of the Bible Conference of January 1907 was widespread. The women, who were rather isolated in Korea, were blessed in their meetings,[67] and so were the colleges and schools. In most meetings confession continued to be prominent: what was acknowledged in one meeting was described as 'hell uncovered'.[68] Theological students, who were better trained than most believers, could preach, visit other places, counsel and lay the foundation for future development. William Blair was also busy visiting, and he expressed amazement at what he saw in Nam San Maru, where the church had 'wept its sins out before God'.[69] In that place the spirit of conviction was exceptionally strong.[70]

By this time the Japanese were occupying the country by force, but they made improvements as well. When John R. Mott visited Seoul in 1907 he travelled on the new railway line opened by the Japanese. He found the Koreans the most receptive of all the Oriental people.[71] During 1907 there was a marked increase in church membership. It was said of one area that before the Revival one-sixtieth of the population was Christian, but immediately after the Revival the proportion was one-sixth.[72] In many areas church buildings had to be enlarged. During the same year the revival fever in Korea had crossed the boundary to Manchuria and China.

## Manchuria and China, 1908

The Presbyterians from Scotland, America and Canada had entered Manchuria before 1900 and some progress had been made, but in 1908 there was a change. 'In 1908, moreover, largely through contact with a revival in Korea, a remarkable religious movement broke out in Manchuria.'[73]

In the spring of 1907, the Canadian Presbyterians authorised Jonathan Goforth and Dr Mackay to visit Korea. On his return from Korea, Goforth visited George Douglas, of the United Free Church of Scotland, at Liaoyang, south of Mukden. Douglas invited Goforth to return as soon as possible. In the meantime, Douglas sent two men to Korea, who were warmly welcomed by Dr Moffett. On their return the two related what they had experienced in Korea. As a result of the meeting, prayer groups were formed and men sent out to invite as many as possible to attend Goforth's meetings, as he had promised to return in February 1908.[74]

The visit was a turning point in Jonathan Goforth's ministry. He had been concerned about revival for a number of years, though confined in his ministry to Changteh and the mission to the north.[75] He read the works of Charles Finney,[76] and news of the Welsh Revival had a lasting effect on him. Rosalind Goforth explains how this happened. 'We were living as a family at one of the out centres, when some unknown friends in England began sending us pamphlets on the Welsh revival.'[77] Jonathan Goforth was thrilled with these, and they gave him 'a new conception' of the work of the Holy Spirit.[78] As he himself said, 'The reports of revival in Wales caused us great searching of heart, and we were led to pray more intensely for China.'[79]

**Liaoyang and Mukden**
In Korea, Jonathan Goforth witnessed what happens when God comes in revival power. He experienced the same manifestation of God's Spirit in Manchuria, first in Liaoyang, and then in Mukden. In a sermon, to the surprise of the congregation, he concentrated on the scandalous sins that haunted that area.[80] The missionaries were dismayed, and some of them angry, but they soon realised what the preacher was doing. He was following the methods adopted in the revival in Korea. The Spirit of God was the spirit of conviction, and because this was so evident he was asked to preach in the evening. The 'tenor of his address was once more that of Romans chapter 1.'[81] D. T. Robertson, one of the missionaries, regarded Jonathan Goforth as a John the Baptist sent to break up the fallow ground ready for sowing, watering and harvesting.

Jonathan Goforth had postponed his return to Manchuria until he was convinced that 'the thing was of God'.[82] The scenes in Manchuria confirmed his conviction. Even the Christians did not know what to expect. In Mukden the sceptics believed it was the 'alleged instability' of the Korean people that had led to revival. Others thought that 'political instability' was the explanation for the emotional upheaval.[83] The ministry of Jonathan Goforth and the vivid descriptions by Chang of what he had seen in Korea soon silenced the critics. In one meeting, after Jonathan Goforth had spoken for almost an hour on 'Prayer', one after another in the congregation took part in prayer.[84] All were convinced that they were in the midst of a great work of grace.[85]

A central theme in Jonathan Goforth's preaching was 'Not by might, nor by power, but by my Spirit, saith the Lord'. While he spoke there would be complete silence, leading to outbursts of prayer, praise and confession. James Webster expresses wonderment at what was happening: 'To see seven or eight hundred people gathered together after sunset, a thing almost unheard of in China, to listen to a foreign missionary setting forth the doctrines of sin and righteousness, seemed to me to be something miraculous.'[86] Another missionary refers to Goforth's preaching topics: he majored on sin, prayer and the power of the Holy Spirit. The same missionary had seen men and women falling down on their faces confessing their sins, their cries being lost in the 'swelling tide of general weeping that gradually rose and culminated in a shout'.[87] The noise brought those in the streets to the church door.

Mukden was on the 'high tide of revival' when Jonathan Goforth left.[88] During the farewell meeting a long list of freewill offerings were read out: these included money, rent on land, gold ornaments and, from one elder, a two-roomed house as a place of worship.[89] Meetings continued at Mukden: they took the form of prayer for named people, confession, an address and singing ('I need Thee every hour' was a particular favourite).[90] Volunteers were sent out to seven districts to evangelise, starting on 10 March 1908. 'So, on the morning of Tuesday, March 10, a cavalcade of carts left the church premises at dawn, bearing messengers of good tidings north, south, east and west.'[91]

## Other visits

Jonathan Goforth travelled from Manchuria to Tientsin (Tianjin), Peking (Beijing), Chihli (Hebei), a number of places in Shansi (Shanxi) and Honan (Henan). He did not enjoy the same degree of blessing in Peking and Tientsin as in other places,[92] and an LMS missionary had mixed feelings about the evangelist's visit. Revival had taken place in the church of Pastor King, with scenes like those in the Welsh Revival, but the missionary felt that generally 'there was the feeling that the expected visitation of God's Spirit did not materialize'.[93] In Shansi it was different: in many CIM stations the manifest presence of God was experienced, especially in Taning[94] and T'aiyuen-fu. In the last meeting Jonathan Goforth asked for prayer for himself, as he was returning to Honan. In response, 'They all began to pray aloud, earnestly but quietly, each one uttering his or her own petitions, and it harmonized into a perfect blending of sound, through which one felt the breathing of the Holy Ghost.'[95]

The Canadian Presbyterian missionary was glad to be back in Honan, and in his ministry there he made use of his experience in Korea and Manchuria.[96] Often the Spirit of God would come with 'the suddenness and violence of a thunder storm'.[97] On one particular Sunday, meetings were held all day, each of them lasting three hours, with intermissions for food.[98]

In the midst of revival, the missionary left for Britain. He reported on revival in China when he spoke in London on 20 April 1909, and in August he was one of the main speakers at the Keswick in Wales, Llandrindod.[99] He had now arrived in the country that had meant so much to him during 1905 and 1906.

Meanwhile, in China the revival was continuing. The key men in the spiritual movement were the evangelists. An outstanding example was Dr Yao, who had responded to the call to be an evangelist by reading of how Evan Roberts of Wales had been filled with the Spirit of God. Dr Yao was no great preacher, but when he spoke the Holy Spirit gave him extraordinary power. Meetings led by him reached their climax at Kweikei in February 1909.[100]

# 15
# Japan

Many influences contributed to revival in Japan during the first decade of the twentieth century. Churches and missionaries felt the need for more co-operation, and a conference for prayer was held in October 1900. This was followed by a united evangelistic campaign, the 'Takyo Dendo' (Aggressive Evangelism).[1] A number of denominations joined, and by mid-1901 the movement was described as 'Pentecost in Japan'. Takyo Dendo continued to make progress even during the Russian-Japanese War.[2]

John R. Mott visited the country in 1901 and had a tremendous influence on the young men, especially in the YMCA and the colleges. In one meeting he spoke on 'Be Sure Your Sins Will Find You Out' and he was 'at his persuasive and logical best'.[3] Large numbers responded to his addresses. As many as seventy-five would give their names for counselling in one meeting.

There were also prominent evangelists who preached powerfully. Seimatsu Kimuri, a full-time evangelist, held mass meetings with visible results in conversions. He visited Wales in 1906 and related to the believers at Llandrindod 'how he got the blessing of the filling of the Spirit'.[4] Nakada, like Kimuri a graduate of the Moody Bible Institute, was a dynamic preacher, and taught the Wesleyan view of holiness. Kanamori was diverted from revival for some time because he accepted liberal theology. But later on, restored to his old faith, he became a champion of evangelicalism in Japan.[5]

The British and Foreign Bible Society helped to meet the spiritual needs of the Japanese. The society sent 25,000 copies of Gospels and New Testaments—'some proof that the Spirit of God has been working among the Japanese'.[6] A gentleman from England was sending to missionaries in Japan copies of *The Life of Faith* and periodicals, and these included reports of the Torrey and Alexander meetings and the Welsh Revival. 'The reports of these have been an encouragement to us, and are one of the first things looked for when the papers and magazines arrive from England.'[7] But Korea was much nearer to Japan: 'To the influence of the Welsh Revival upon the missionaries was added the direct influence of the Korean Revival on the Japanese.'[8]

Awakenings continued into 1907:[9]

One missionary writes that during thirty-two years in Japan he has never before seen such a very marked wide hunger for soul food that shall give life more abundantly. At one Church in Yokohama there are more than 70 inquirers; at another there have been 70 baptisms. At one church in Tokyo, there were 78 additions; and at one at Tsuyama, 76; and 120 inquirers at Maebashi. Sixty-one pupils at the boys' school at Nagasaki have decided to become Christians, and 100 at Wakayama. These are but indications of the condition of things in other places.

Church leaders were continually looking for large accessions to the churches.

In April 1907 the Conference of the World Student Christian Federation was held in Tokyo.[10] One of the speakers was Paul Nicolay of Finland and St. Petersburg, and a message of goodwill was received from Prince Bernadotte. They supported evangelical causes and the more ecumenical Student Christian Movement. John R. Mott regarded the Conference at Tokyo as 'one of the most notable events in the history of Christianity in the extreme Orient'.[11]

# Part V
# AUSTRALIA
and
# NEW ZEALAND

# 16
# Australia
# and New Zealand

The background to revival in Australia and New Zealand is the preaching of evangelists and the praying of the churches.[1] Torrey and Alexander, James Lyall, Harry Guinness and others created a stir in both countries. It was prayer in the Moody Church and the Moody Bible Institute that prompted Torrey to visit Australia for the first time. Prayer continued in Australia and New Zealand, and a spiritual quickening was experienced in many churches. The Torrey and Alexander campaign in Australia in 1902 was described as 'evangelism accompanied by revival'.[2]

Welshmen in both countries looked forward to the visit of Maurice Griffiths and W. S. Jones, the two Welsh Presbyterian ministers who had visited India early in 1905. News of the Welsh Revival had already reached them, but they wanted more information. The two ministers failed to reach many areas in Australia, however. The people of Blackstone were disappointed not to have a visit, but accounts in *Y Goleuad* of events in Wales were received and read out to the congregations.[3] The evangelist Cummings from Scotland also prepared the people for revival. His preaching, like that of R. B. Jones in Wales, exposed particular sins, creating a sense of guilt in the hearers, who would then be turned to the grace of God in Christ for forgiveness.[4]

Welsh and English meetings were held during July 1905. On Sunday 23 July there was an exceptional manifestation of God's power. One after another prayed earnestly, many cried, and the congregation joined in singing the Welsh hymn '*Pen Calfaria*' (Hill of Calvary). The result was a series of meetings lasting five weeks, when the church was full every night.[5]

One Australian minister described what was happening in his parish as 'a small Welsh revival'.[6] It happened as a result of the minister and his friends coming together. They sang hymns, prayed, and some of them gave addresses on the Welsh Revival. The Holy Spirit came in power, the spirit of prayer spread amongst them, and many were crying for salvation.

Interdenominational meetings in Redfern, New South Wales, led
to a 'gracious revival'. And a correspondent from Melbourne could
say, 'the pulsations that have stirred Wales are reaching here'.[7]

The denominational spirit was not always overcome. A Baptist
from Newcastle, New South Wales, rejoiced at the success of the
revival in Wales and that so many Baptists had joined the churches.
He also believed that God would be good to them in Newcastle.
There were signs of blessing, but no revival.[8]

## New Zealand

The two Presbyterian ministers from Wales arrived in New
Zealand in the middle of 1905. One of the first places they visited
was the volcanic district of Wanganui.[9] A Welshman met them, a
child of the 1859 Revival in Wales, and he immediately asked them
about the present revival in Wales. The next morning the two visitors
bought a local paper, to find that it included a report of a sermon by
Evan Roberts the revivalist. The daughter of an 1859 convert
provided another report from Wanganui, informing *The Christian*
that 'Christians in New Zealand are still rejoicing over the glorious
news of the Revival in Wales'.[10]

In Wanganui itself, prayer meetings had been held and it had been
necessary to arrange overflow services in many churches. During a
period of two weeks, unceasing prayer had been offered to God, and
every night many would be seeking the way of salvation.

In reporting the revival in Auckland, the *Auckland Weekly News*
drew attention to 'the strong similarity to many of the revival meetings in Wales', especially the lack of human leadership in the after-
meetings.[11] Worship was spontaneous, prayer intense, and sectarian
prejudice was overcome. Businessmen were making arrangements
for their employees to meet together for prayer.[12]

Prayer brought the believers together at Kaitara, eighty miles from
Auckland. They met together in a cottage, and there they experienced
the manifest presence of God.[13]

One correspondent drew attention to the impact of revival upon
nominal church members. Before revival they were 'dumb in regard
to religious experience', but conversion had transformed their lives.[14]
Another feature of revival was the work amongst the children. A
'notable' work was accomplished in one church among the 13-16
age group:[15]

A week ago a Presbyterian minister met with 60 boys and girls in
connection with his own church. In response to his questioning,

one after another of the young people rose and spoke in simple child-like fashion of their love for Christ and desire to serve him.

Generally, the influence of revival was felt within the churches, but some outsiders were coming to the revival meetings. Believers also felt the need to reach the mining community.

The three truths that were emphasised during revival are reminiscent of the four points presented by Evan Roberts during the first week of revival in Wales. They were the confession of sin and forgiveness, surrender to the power of the Holy Spirit, and acceptance by simple faith of the Holy Spirit, that he might fill and control a person's life.[16]

**Part VI**
**INFLUENCE**
and
**EFFECTS**

# 17
# Continuing Impact

The Welsh Revival of 1904–05 directly influenced most of the countries that have been mentioned. It was only in a minority of cases that the influence was indirect. In some countries it was the main cause of revival: in others it was the means of strengthening the desire for revival, or sustaining revival where it had already broken out.

News from Wales reached other countries through newspapers, letters, visitors, or accounts read in services and prayer groups. And Evan Roberts wielded a powerful influence, through his work in Wales, his messages to different countries, and his personality. He never went abroad, and yet it seemed as if he were personally present in some countries, and his name was revered. Respect could turn to hero worship. For example, a photograph of the Welshman was on the desk of McCheyne Paterson at Sialkot. Some examples of how the Welsh Revival influenced overseas countries will be explored in this chapter.

## Church matters

Revival was a phenomenon within Protestantism. Roman Catholics were affected as individuals by attending revival meetings, but officially the Church stood aloof, and it could also oppose what was regarded as foreign to its tradition. In France, Protestants were encouraged and strengthened, and this led to more unity amongst them. Reuben Saillens acknowledged that the influence of the Welsh Revival had not reached the whole of France, but he and others were greatly indebted to it:[1]

And through the men who brought some of the fire from Wales, evangelistic campaigns have been conducted, in places where no such thing had ever been witnessed; conversions have taken place in many towns and villages; Conventions of Christian people have been organized, both in France and Switzerland, at which hundreds, and even thousands are attending year after year, each time receiving new light and new grace.

Chexbres continued to be one of the main centres, and Morges in Switzerland could attract as many as fifteen hundred to its Convention.

Pastor Saillens was the 'head and heart' of the conventions, and he also organised a three-week Bible school in Paris. France lacked the preaching and Sunday school tradition of Wales, and Saillens believed that the best way to confirm the Revival was to seek to make the Bible central.[2] One of Saillens' co-workers was H. Johnson of Leicester, one of the group of people close to Evan Roberts. Johnson was also distributing copies of Evan Roberts' articles printed in *The Overcomer*. Writing to that magazine in 1909, he informed readers that ever since the Revival in Wales a weekly prayer meeting had been held in Paris.[3]

Mrs Penn-Lewis continued to correspond with her friends in many countries. Her works were being circulated in France, Germany, the Scandinavian countries, Russia and Poland.[4] Her contact in Poland was Pastor Lubeck.[5] A Russian contact (in addition to William Fetler) was I. V. Neprash, one who became acquainted with Evan Roberts after the Revival period. Fetler and Neprash worked together for a while, but Neprash then established another society, the Russian Missionary Service. After further division the European Missionary Fellowship was formed. Two Welshmen, Ionawr Williams and Omri Jenkins, were prominent in the development of that work.[6]

In Germany, where there was a State Church, the leaders were wary of any change that could disturb the status quo. Those in sympathy with the revival could meet across denominational boundaries and find a spiritual home in the fellowships. The open spirit of these fellowships spread to the churches and helped believers to be more flexible in their churchmanship. It helped them to think of the congregation 'as united by personal conversion and faith in the atoning death of Christ', and not territorially in terms of a parish.[7]

The Presbyterians had an advantage over other denominations. Their people were used to coming together in presbytery and assembly. Such gatherings proved crucial in the development of the revival in Khasia and Lushai in India. The believers would go home from denominational revival meetings to their congregations and kindle a fire in their midst. Their organisational structure also enabled leaders to keep a close watch on what was happening during the revival; and as the Presbyterians had a large area of Assam to themselves, this could be done without any denominational tensions. The churches flourished and saw spiritual and numerical growth.[8]

The Presbyterian churches in Korea were quite young, but the Revival of 1907 led to the formation of the Presbyterian Church of

Korea and the first Assembly of 1912. The growth in the Church has been described as a 'volcanic upheaval'.[9] Membership doubled between 1905 and 1910; it increased sixfold between 1910 and 1935, and doubled again between 1935 and 1960.[10]

In both Khasia and Korea, the revival led to further occasional awakenings in the history of the two countries. The revival in Shillong (India) in 1910 was considered to be as powerful as that of 1905. Between six and eight thousand gathered together at the Assembly in March of that year. One evening meeting was so crowded that many brought ladders to scale the walls and reach the windows. F. Kehl of Calcutta was overwhelmed by what he saw and heard—'Such preaching, such praying, I had never heard before.' And he was a person who had known revival in Calcutta and other parts of India.[11]

The Welsh Revival made a marked contribution to Pentecostalism. The Apostolic Church was born in Pen-y-groes, Carmarthenshire, and it has become a worldwide movement. Its Bible School and Convention Centre are still located in the village of Pen-y-groes.

During revival, an increasing number of people were able to take part in the meetings in various ways. One result of this was the emergence of new leaders in the churches. Many noble examples were found in Khasia, Korea and Madagascar. Women were among the participants; they had opportunity to contribute extensively in revival circles—in prayer, as soloists, giving testimony, leading services and addressing convention meetings. The revivals of the period made a positive contribution in this respect, and the prominence given to women helped to create a conducive atmosphere for the Suffragettes. A number of women ventured to preach—Mrs Penn–Lewis, for example, Elizabeth Rowlands in Madagascar and Pandita Ramabai in India. In strong Presbyterian countries like Korea and Khasia there were a number of lady workers, but no woman was set apart to the office of minister in the church. During its early stages, even the Pentecostals in California were reluctant for women to enter the professional ministry.[12]

Those who took part in services did so in their native language. They also saw the importance of having the Scriptures in their own language. Individual believers needed the Word of God, and it was essential in the church for teaching, for worship and for Sunday school work. Revival created a hunger for the Word of God, and a body like the British and Foreign Bible Society was glad to meet that demand. In Patagonia, and in the Welsh churches in the USA, revival quickened interest in the Welsh language. At the same time, the

Welsh of Patagonia acknowledged the need to use some Spanish in some services. The Welsh in the USA faced a similar problem with the English language. On the one hand the revival was furthering the Welsh language, while on the other hand it was bringing the Welsh into closer contact with other languages. This contact, eventually, made it more difficult for the Welsh language to thrive. There is a parallel in what happened to the Welsh-speaking community in the Rhondda, Wales.

**Revival hymns**

Welsh hymns and tunes were introduced to a number of countries during the revival period. Reuben Saillens was anxious to translate Welsh hymns into French. When he crossed to Wales in 1905 he immediately translated '*Dyma gariad*' (Here is love)—his French version begins, '*Torrents d'amour et de grâce*'. While visiting Aberdare he gave the proof copy to a friend, who in turn gave it to Dan, Evan Roberts' brother.[13] Although Saillens speaks of 'translating', he explained in his published collection that the French versions had rather been 'suggested' by the Welsh hymns. Echoes from the Welsh originals can be discerned in many of Saillens' Collection, especially those set to Welsh tunes. '*Torrents d'amour et de grâce*' is set to 'Ebenezer' (Tôn y botel) by T. J. Williams (No. 352), and the Frenchman's words '*Jehovah, vers toi je crie*' to 'Bryn Calfaria' by William Owen, Prysgol (No. 185). Saillens also wrote words to the tune 'Deemster' by William Owen, and to Joseph Parry's tune 'Aberystwyth' (Nos 46 and 92). Another author, A. Palez, contributed (to the tune 'Caersalem') words that are described as the 'official translation of "Diolch Iddo"' (No. 92).[14]

Rogues de Fursac was also interested in the musical Welsh, devoting a chapter in his work to music in Wales.[15] He commented on the hymns of the Revival, especially '*Dyma gariad*' (Here is love), and pointed out the custom in Welsh homes of gathering round the piano to sing. He was also aware of the musical and bardic traditions of Wales.[16]

The Frenchmen came to Wales to hear the hymns, but Welsh-speaking missionaries could take the hymns with them to various countries. In Khasia, Sylhet and Lushai, the ground for revival singing was well prepared. J. Pengwern Jones was an accomplished musician. He composed and translated hymns, setting them to Welsh tunes and airs. He also carried a little organ with him, to help with the singing.[17] Edwin Rowlands, too, was an able hymn-writer and translator. In 1903, he and D. E. Jones published a hymn book of 81 hymns, many of them translated by the nationals themselves.[18] Realising that the simple words and rhythmic tunes of Sankey and Moody appealed to the Mizos, D. E. Jones, like revival leaders in Wales, made use of that collection.[19] John Roberts was a prolific author of hymns, and translated many into Khasi from both Welsh and English. Out of the 411 hymns in the 1922 Khasi hymn book, he was the author/translator of 73.[20]

There was a time when music meant very little to the Mizos.[21] The children sang some lively songs, but not the adults. Edwin Rowlands succeeded in writing some of the children's tunes on paper. In arranging tunes for words he faced a problem: the Mizos had a five-note, not a seven-note, scale, so he had to change many of the Welsh tunes. The revival was a golden opportunity to further the cause of hymns and congregational singing. 'On one particular day in 1906 he produced seven first class hymns, all of which are still now among the most popular in our hymnbook.'[22] Apart from his original works, Edwin Rowlands translated some of the well-known Welsh hymns, including '*Efe yw'r iawn fu rhwng y lladron*' (He is the propitiation between the robbers), '*Pam y caiff bwystfilod rheibus*' (Why ravenous beasts), '*Cul yw'r llwybr*' (The way is narrow) and '*Dyma gariad*' (Here is love).[23]

Hymns catered for children as well as adults. One of the children's hymns written by J. Pengwern Jones was a favourite during the revival. It is a hymn of praise. The first verse praises the Saviour for coming from heaven to die on the cross; the second praises him as the one on the throne, while the third praises Father, Son and Holy Spirit. During visits to his homeland, J. Pengwern Jones would teach Bengali hymns to Welsh children.[24] Children and adults would have their favourite hymns; also, different areas would have their own popular hymns. It was 'Great Redeemer, Friend of sinners' in Nongspung; 'Rejoice, oh world, the Lord has come' in Mawphlang, while the Hills of Khasia and Jaintia echoed with 'The love that Jesus had for me'.[25]

In Wales, the revivalists sang hymns both in the church and in processions along the streets. They did the same in parts of India, but they did something else too. In some areas, the women would travel from village to village chanting the story of Jesus. This was a method that appealed to the villagers, and it also presented them with basic information.[26]

Some hymns and tunes were produced in unusual circumstances. Many were composed while their authors were in a trance: an individual would fall into a trance, and as that person gave out the hymn it would be taken up by the congregation. In Mairang, one such hymn became known as the 'Angel Hymn':[27] three verses describe Christ interceding for the sinner, and in the other three the sinner is beseeching Christ for mercy.

Peter Frazer of Lushai tells of a significant dream he had. He could see himself in a meeting in Wales, and the congregation was singing 'When I survey the wondrous cross'. As he listened, a tune to suit the words came to him. When he woke, he sang it to his wife, and she wrote it down.[28]

Hymns sung in Khasia spread to other parts of India. A hymn composed by a Khasi girl in 1905 was being sung in other areas in India many years later. Edwin Rowlands had translated '*Dyma gariad*' (Here is love), but 'The love song of the Welsh Revival finds its counterpart in Telugu and Tamil, Maharthi and Hundustani.'[29] The English version mentioned by the writer was the one by William Edwards:

> *Here is love vast as the ocean*
> *Loving kindness as the flood;*
> *When the Prince of Life, our ransom,*
> *Shed for us His precious blood.*

In Wales, the 'Glory Song' (When all my labours and trials are o'er) was popular in both English and Welsh, and believers in Germany, Russia, Denmark and Bengal sang it in their own languages.[30] In India it would be accompanied by hand-drum and cymbals. Another popular Welsh hymn, '*Yn y dyfroedd mawr a'r tonnau*' (In the mighty surging waters), was translated into German and Arabic.[31]

Many themes are common to many countries. Evan Roberts would continually point to the blood of Christ.[32] Revival hymns in India, China and Korea give thanks for the blood. In Korea, for example, one of the most popular hymns was 'There is a fountain filled with blood'.[33] Revivalists would agree with a missionary from India that it was not 'the example' of Christ that should be proclaimed, but 'the blood of Christ'. Atonement should be at the centre of the Christian message. Other hymns emphasised the gospel call and obedience to Christ (an example would be 'I will follow Thee'),[34] while assurance of heaven was expressed in the 'Glory Song' and 'There's a land that is fairer than day'.[35]

*Welsh churches*
In the Welsh churches in Patagonia and the USA it was possible to sing revival hymns in Welsh. Heading the list in Patagonia was

# "WONDROUS CROSS."

P. FRASER.

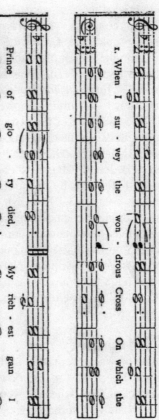

1. When I sur - vey the won - drous Cross On which the

Prince of glo - ry died, My rich - est gain I

count but loss, And pour con - tempt on all my pride.

(by permission of The Overcomer)

## NOTE.

Dr. Fraser writes concerning this piece of music: "The other night I had a vivid dream. I was in a large meeting in Wales, and the congrega-tion was singing "When I survey the wondrous Cross" to a tune which was new to me. I could hear them so plainly, and was much moved by the singing. When I awoke the tune was ringing in my ears, and I sang it to my wife, who has written it down, and I send it on to you. . ."

Lushai Hills,
Assam, India.

'*Dyma gariad*' (Here is love), sung not to the usual tune 'Lament of Britain' but to 'Casllwchwr'.[36] The hymn '*Am Iesu Grist a'i farwol glwy*' (Jesus Christ and his mortal wound) was sung to the tune 'Diadem'. Added to these were '*Hapus awr*' (Happy day), '*Y cysur i gyd*' (All the comfort), '*Am wirionedd boed ein gweddi*' (May our prayer be for truth), and '*Gelwaist Mathew gynt o'r dollfa*' (You called Matthew from the receipt of custom). '*Taflwch raff bywyd*' (Throw out the lifeline) was not only sung but also recited in a meeting.[37]

Surprisingly little is said of popular hymns in the Welsh churches in the USA. It is no surprise, however, to learn that '*Dyma gariad*' (Here is love) was one of the favourites.[38] As in Wales, there were a number of soloists in the churches. One of them was the Baptist pastor Teifion Richards, and he was a hymn-writer as well.[39]

When R. B. Jones of Porth, Rhondda, went to the USA in 1907, he made use of his own hymn book, *Prayer and Praise/Gweddi a Mawl*.[40] This contained 109 Welsh and 50 English hymns, and was made up of original compositions and translations from the English. The translations were mainly from *Hymns of Consecration and Faith* and *Sacred Songs and Solos*. A good number of the Welsh hymns are based on passages of Scripture. Not many of R. B. Jones's hymns are sung today, but a few translations have remained popular through the Ammanford Whitsun Convention and were included in *Clychau Seion* (1952).[41]

## Revival and Pentecost

The people of Wales were used to thinking of revival as God coming down upon his people in the power of the Holy Spirit. It was a sovereign act of God, when he would come not to a few individuals but to many. It was something corporate. During such a time of spiritual refreshing, God would accomplish in a very short time what would usually take a number of years. Revival was extraordinary, accomplishing extraordinary results. The best way to describe such a movement of the Spirit was to refer to Pentecost. Many in other countries, including the Welsh missionaries in Madagascar and India, would agree with that concept.

The Welsh Revival of 1904–05 could be interpreted as Pentecost in the traditional sense, but it was interpreted in other ways as well. What happened in Wales strengthened many of these interpretations.

### Continual Revival

The Welsh Revival renewed the hopes of those who believed in continual revival. R. A. Torrey had been praying for revival for a very long time before 1904. He had prayed that God would raise up men mightily anointed by the Spirit of God. It was a great joy to the evangelist to hear from many sources of what was happening in Wales through Evan Roberts.[42] Hopes for continual revival were quickened. Torrey expressed his view in an interview with George T. B. Davies:[43]

> I know that when a company of God's people—not necessarily everybody in the whole community who profess to be Christian—but when even a small company of God's people get really right with God, and begin to cry to God for an outpouring of His Spirit in mighty power, I know God hears.

God desires to bless his people, and it is their duty to humble themselves and cry for the coming of the Spirit.

When there is repentance, crying unto God, and (Torrey would add) witnessing to the gospel, God will answer. There is no reason at all why revival should not be perpetual. 'A Revival ought to be the normal condition of the Church of Christ, and not merely a spasmodic outburst.'[44] Willam Fetler agreed with him. From his college days in London he had practised the presence of God, and he knew in his own experience the fullness of the Spirit. He presents three central considerations:

- Absolute *necessity* of a Revival as being the normal condition of the Church.
- Truth of a *perennial* revival as the only state compatible with the character of God.
- Strict observance of the condition that Achan cannot remain in the camp.

The way to take these considerations seriously is by coming to repentance and faith in Christ. Repentance includes breaking with all known sin, separation from the world, and a complete change of tastes, views and aims in life. Faith in Christ means listening to him and obeying him as Lord.[45]

In the writings of both Torrey and Fetler there is an emphasis on conditions, reminding us of the four points laid down by Evan Roberts during the first week of revival in Loughor. William Fetler could say, 'A genuine revival is the natural result of the meeting and carrying out of definite conditions laid down in the Word of God.'[46] The words echo those of Charles Finney, who said that revival takes

place when we make the best use of the best means. Fetler's theology, however, is far removed from that of Finney. Fetler took sin and
the Fall seriously.[47] He would point out that one of the main weak-
nesses of modernism was its superficial view of sin. There is a tension in his thinking. Conditions are laid down, but it is God alone that
can bring revival. The same tension is found in the thinking of
Jonathan Goforth.

*Pentecost*

Stephen Neill claims that 'The emergence of the Pentecostal
Churches and their mission was among the most striking phenomena
of the Church history of the twentieth century.'[48] Not only did
Pentecostalism spread quickly, but it also introduced a radical change
into the thinking on Pentecost. All the children of the revival were
agreed on a number of points. They regarded revival as an extraordinary work of God, accepted the physical and mental phenomena
witnessed during revival, and gave a central place to the Second
Coming of the Lord Jesus Christ. The Pentecostals insisted on inter-
preting Pentecost (Acts chapter 2), literally. They claimed that
speaking in tongues is an integral aspect of any revival, after the pattern of the first Pentecost. Healing was also given a prominent place
in their thinking.

There was some difference of opinion. It was possible to
acknowledge the gift of tongues without insisting upon it as the initial
proof of the baptism of the Spirit. This was the opinion held by
Pandita Ramabai in India. A correspondent from China expressed
his view thus:[49]

  I gladly welcome what is of God; I stand for all that fullness of
  God; believe intensely that since the beginning of the Welsh
  Revival God is seeking to do a new thing in all the earth; that the
  whole body of Christ needs apostolic gifts; that God wants to add
  new chapters to the Book of Acts.

During the Welsh Revival, God had opened up a new period. He was
doing a new thing, and restoring not just one of the gifts of the Spirit,
but all of them.

What happened in Germany is representative of what happened
in India and the Scandinavian countries. By the end of 1908, both
parties were considering their position seriously.[50] There was a
temporary ceasefire, but in 1909 hostilities were resumed. The
evangelicals who were against the tongues movement drew up a

statement on 15 September 1909 in Berlin. The signatories included well-known names from the revival period: Dallmeyer of Leipzig, Dolman of Wandsbeck, Korff of Hannover, Mascher of Steglitz, Viebahn of Stettin and Tiele-Winckler of Rothenmoor. The company in Berlin came to the conclusion that 'The so-called Pentecostal Movement is not from above but from below.'[51] They claimed that the manifestations had much in common with Irvingism, Christian Science and Spiritualism. As for the twitchings, tremblings and screamings, it was difficult to decide whether they were demonic, hysterical or soulish. There was no doubt that they were not of God.

Much of the criticism was levelled at Jonathan Paul and his teaching concerning the 'clean heart'. According to this teaching, inbred sin is removed when a believer is sanctified, and that happens in a crisis experience following conversion. Paul did acknowledge the possibility of sin; but there was no need for any believer to sin; he could be kept from sin. To the Berlin signatories this was contrary to Scripture. 'It cannot be sufficiently insisted upon that we must preserve an eye for sin which is not dimmed through a man-made holiness, or through a fantastic teaching of the taking away of the sinful nature.'[52] The Berlin brethren declared publicly that they could not acknowledge Jonathan Paul as a leader in the Church.

The distinctive teaching of the Berlin group appears at the end of the manifesto:[53]

> We believe there has been only one Pentecost given. Acts ii. We believe in the Holy Ghost, who will remain in the Church of Jesus forever; cf. John 14:16. We are clear that the Church of God has received, and needs, ever fresh, gracious visitations of the Holy Spirit. The apostles' command, 'Be ye filled with the Spirit', Eph. 5:18, is to every individual believer. The way thereto is, and remains, *full* fellowship with the crucified, risen and exalted Lord. In Him dwells the fullness of the Godhead bodily, from Him we receive grace for grace. *We do not look for a new Pentecost, we wait for the returning Lord.*

The emphasis is on the 'filling' of the Spirit. Pentecost was a unique event. Tongues are not a continuing gift to the Church, and its real hope is the coming of the Lord Jesus Christ.

Mrs Penn-Lewis was very sensitive to these developments in Germany. She had been to revival meetings in that country and had described them as 'Pentecost'. She had also been welcomed in the conventions as a lady speaker. A few years later the leaders were wary of speaking of 'Pentecost' and were reluctant to see women and young girls taking a prominent part in meetings. The Welsh lady continued to speak of Pentecost (which for her did not include tongues) and, like the Berlin group, deplored the growth of Pentecostalism.

Mrs Penn-Lewis related the work of the Holy Spirit first of all to regeneration, when he indwells the believer. This experience, she argued, should lead on to a crisis experience, which she described as death with Christ, a crucifixion. Crucified with Christ, the believer can receive a fresh experience of the Holy Spirit. She agreed with the way in which Dr Beck had presented the matter. As Christ's death was potentially for all, so was the Spirit of God poured out potentially for all. As Christ's death has to be applied to the individual by faith, so must the Holy Spirit be received by faith. There is an 'objective universality', but 'subjectively' very few have been endued with power for service.[54] It is wrong to 'tarry' for this experience, because the command to tarry was given before Pentecost. The dispensation of the Spirit was ushered in on that day, thus making the command irrelevant.[55]

Passive tarrying had been used as a channel by Satan to attack the Welsh Revival of 1904–05. Mrs Penn-Lewis claimed that there was an outbreak of demons 'which followed the outpouring of the Spirit of God in Wales', and many in Germany believed that the devil had silenced Evan Roberts.[56] This is why she collaborated with Evan Roberts in writing *War on the Saints*. From the Welsh Revival 'developed the joint-witness and co-service of the collaborators of the Book *War on the Saints*'.[57] The authors were right in calling attention to the spiritual battle raging in heavenly places, but they dwelt so much on this theme that it became an unhealthy preoccupation. They also lost sight of other considerations in dealing with revival, including the sense of the presence of God, conversion and social impact.

Furthermore, there was a tendency to make a particular doctrine of holiness the only path to blessing, that doctrine being crucifixion with Christ. Bound up with the doctrine was the tripartite view of man, that is, that he is body, soul and spirit. True revival takes place when the Spirit of God reaches the spirit of man. He moves from the physical and the soulish to the spiritual. Mrs Penn-Lewis's assessment of revival and the path to blessing was accepted by a group of her friends in India, including R. J. Ward, Dr Rudisill and F. Kehl.

It is possible to understand this clash between the Christian faith and culture in a country like India. It is difficult to understand it in a country like Wales. Here many children of the revival turned away from a culture that was basically Christian. This escape into piety is a pity. The revivalists had the basis of a Christian world-view. They had the Word of God, the doctrine of conversion, and an awareness of the cosmic significance of what was taking place in revival. The same negative attitude was adopted in Germany and Scandinavia.

In overseas countries the work of evil spirits was made manifest. They were visible. The missionaries in Madagascar regarded the 'Bilom-Bara' as 'demoniacal possession'.[58] So often it was evident during, or after, a time of revival. Individuals would come under the spell of a spirit and would be completely controlled by him. The nationals were terrified of this power, and many of them attempted suicide in order to escape the spell.

In the Khasi Hills it was the 'Shakers' who were the problem. Their leader was a man who had professed conversion and was regarded as a Christian. He and his followers would tremble, use terrible language, grind their teeth and scream in 'a hellish way'. The leader had complete control of his followers. If anyone disobeyed him he would say that God was angry with him. There was no need to read the Scriptures and preach the gospel, because the Spirit would come and reveal everything necessary to them. J. Pengwern Jones was convinced that 'Satan is wild, mad with rage at the influence the Khassee Revival has had in India in drawing men to pray.'[59] The Welshman looked upon the development as something blasphemous, and was convinced that 'These things goeth not out but by fasting & praying.'[60]

The Swadeshi and the Seng Khasi were different. They aimed at safeguarding the traditions of the Khasi, creating a better society and reviving the faith of the fathers. These were commendable aims, but the Swadeshi fostered hatred against all foreigners,[61] and both the Swadeshi and Seng Khasi were anti-Christian.[62] The society they wanted to create was essentially religious, but missionaries regarded the religion, whatever it might be, as anti-Christian. The clash between the Christian faith and other religions was an aspect of the cosmic struggle between God and Satan.

Another development was the taking over of revival by the Holiness Movement. What happened in Wales happened in other countries also, especially in India. Not only did this movement prepare the way for revival, but it controlled its development as well. A change of emphasis took place. There was a moving away from the corporate emphasis to concentrate on the individual. The Holy Spirit was asked for in the context of sanctification, and not conceived of as a sovereign act of God coming upon a number of people.

Later writers endeavoured to redress this emphasis, particularly J. Edwin Orr and Martyn Lloyd-Jones. Both men had deep sympathy with the Welsh Revival, but acknowledged the problems bound up with it. Orr joined regeneration with the baptism of the Spirit, regarding the filling of the Spirit as revival. Lloyd-Jones related the filling to sanctification and regarded the baptism of the Spirit as revival.

# 18
# Revival
# Doctrine and Society

While the anti-Christ was at work in the world, the Holy Spirit was advancing the kingdom of God. The kingdom of God was manifested in power in the revival of 1904–05, but that was related to what God was to accomplish in the future. Greater blessing was to come before the Second Coming of the Lord Jesus Christ.

## Eschatology

Eschatology was the background to revival. The Advent teaching that became popular was that of premillennialism, with two main traditions, the futurist and the historicist. The former looked to the future, because the prophecies of Daniel and Revelation had not been fulfilled, while the latter looked to the events of history to read the signs of the times.

Evangelicals and Pentecostals believed in the personal, visible return of the Lord Jesus Christ. The Pentecostals regarded the outpouring of the Spirit as a sign of the end. They interpreted the restoration of tongues 'as the key indication that God was about to initiate the much anticipated revival ("the Latter Rain")'.[1] The doctrine of the 'Latter Rain' was based on Joel, chapter 2, and Zechariah, chapter 10. What was experienced on the Day of Pentecost was the 'Former Rain'. The 'Latter Rain' would be given immediately before the Second Coming and before the Rapture.

The Welsh Revival was significant for the Pentecostals because they could see God at work in an exceptional way. It also gave them a desire for a greater blessing. What had taken place was only a shower compared with the downpour that was to come. A. A. Boddy, the pioneer of Pentecostalism in Sunderland, had visited Wales during the Revival and met Evan Roberts. After his return, Boddy was helped in revival meetings by the Welsh soloist A. M. Rees and a Welsh evangelist. The English clergyman was convinced that 'The Welsh Revival was surely intended by the Lord as a preparation for this further Outpouring.'[2]

Those who did not accept the restoration of tongues laid great stress on the Second Coming of Christ. A. T. Pierson had been a convinced premillennialist before 1904, and R. B. Jones accepted the doctrine during the Revival of 1904–05.[3] Many ministers and church members in Wales rediscovered the doctrine during that period.

Premillennialists were criticised for their lack of social involvement. There is some truth in the accusation, but care must be taken not to generalise. A. T. Pierson exhorted believers to be responsible citizens and to be involved in society: 'Missions begin in evangelization, but have *everything* to do with Christian education, and the printing press, and the organization of churches, and the training of a native pastorate.'[4] The belief in Christ's return does not make social progress superfluous. F. B. Meyer would be of a similar mind.

### Kil and 'Messianic Nationalism'

There is an intriguing example in Korea. The eschatology of Kil, a prominent figure in the 1907 Revival, has been described as 'unique and creative'.[5]

Kil, a Presbyterian, accepted premillennialism, but he assured his people that this was not a means to escape from the world. Rather it was a way of facing the problems of the world. The kingdom of God was continually coming into being, but would be consummated at the end time when Christ would return to reign for a thousand years. More precisely, it would be the first step, because Christ would judge the world at the end of the thousand years. The coming of Christ was imminent; there was not much time to evangelise and work for the Saviour.

Believers should look for the coming and prepare for it (Matthew 25). They should be active in all spheres of life:[6]

> The spiritual and the material are not separate. The material world will be spiritualised and the earth will remain forever. Christianity affirms the resurrection of the body and the recovery of the material world, so the material world must not be devalued.

At the end time Eden will be restored and there will be perfect happiness. Until that time there is a fierce struggle between good and evil. Korea was involved in that struggle. Not only were there anti-Christian forces at work in the country, but the power and tyranny of Japan were marshalled against Korea. The country had to be won for Christ. That task would involve evangelism and influencing every aspect of the life of the people. The Koreans were like the people in the Old Testament. They should come out of Egypt and pass through the Red Sea. Revival is a time when this coming out happens on a large scale. Men and women are removed from the kingdom of Satan into the kingdom of God. It is the citizens of this kingdom that will work for the good of Korea. When Koreans were praying for revival, they were also praying for the good of their country. Kil's teaching was a kind of 'Messianic Nationalism'.[7]

*Eberhard Arnold and the kingdom of God*
Another man that demands attention is Eberhard Arnold, a product of one of the revival groups in Germany. Like Kil, his thinking is strongly theological. Arnold was not a premillennialist but related his eschatology to society. He refers to John, chapter 3, where Jesus refers to the new birth and the kingdom. The new birth is central in the Christian faith, but what the Saviour told Nicodemus goes beyond the individual.[8] A new-found faith had led many in Germany to an experience of revival, but this experience had not been applied to the concept of the kingdom.[9]

The life of the risen Christ is lived out in the individual Christian. It is the life that was made manifest on the Day of Pentecost. On that day, the Spirit of God transformed individuals and also made them one. 'And so this unity in the Spirit was there the moment the Holy Spirit was poured out at Pentecost.'[10] The relationship of individuals with their God must be reflected in the oneness between believers. Love is the hallmark of this relationship, a love for God and man's neighbour. This is the life of the kingdom.

God will bring in the kingdom finally at the end of time, but it is also coming continually. Pentecost, according to Arnold, 'was God's way of bringing about His future kingdom'.[11] God is working against evil, and so must believers work against evil—everything that is contrary to God's will. A clash between the kingdom of God and the kingdom of evil is inevitable. 'We oppose outright the present world order of society. We represent a different order, that of the communal Church as it was at Jerusalem after the Holy Spirit was poured out.'[12] The present order is characterised by selfishness and love of money, and it also has a demonic dimension. It is the power of Jesus and the Holy Spirit that can overcome all opposition.[13]

Two closely related themes appear in Eberhard Arnold's works: they are the kingdom (based on Matthew, chapters 5 to 7), and that of community. His wife describes the feelings of those who had been studying the chapters in Matthew with her husband:[14]

'The Beatitudes', the words of Jesus about loving our enemies, the 'Our Father', giving charity, seeking the kingdom of right- eousness—all these struck us like a bolt of lightning. After the injustice of the war and the years leading up to it, Jesus' words burst on us with a force of a thunderclap. We felt we could not go on living as we had. Faith must lead to action, and we must set out on new ways.

Because of this emphasis, Eberhard Arnold clashed with Karl Barth. Both of them were speaking on 'The Christian in Society' at a meeting in Tanbach in the late summer of 1919.[15] Barth was not well known at that time, but his message was clear. It was the *'totaliter aliter'* of God. Man is insignificant: God is everything. It was useless trying to do something to bring in the kingdom of God; God must do everything. It was a brilliant lecture, 'And it is impossible to avoid the impression that Barth had his fun in taking the wind right out of the sails of his learned assembly.'[16]

Eberhard Arnold followed him, and he refused to give in to Barth on two central points. They were the literal interpretation of the Sermon on the Mount and the reality of a personal relationship with God.[17] Arnold was grappling with Barth's theology. If Barth was right, was it possible to have a saving knowledge of God? And this was in 1919.

The Sermon on the Mount was central in Eberhard Arnold's thinking. It was the basis of life for the individual believer, for social justice, for pacifism and his concept of a Christian community.[18] The idea of community developed into that of the 'Bruderhof' (The Brotherhood). The first one, in the tradition of the Hutterites, was established at Sannerz in 1920. Organised on the basis of common goods, as found in the Book of Acts, the community was self-supporting in every respect.[19]

Many influences contributed to Arnold's thinking. He acknowl- edges his debt to Johann Christoph Blumhardt and his son Christoph Friedrich Blumhardt. Both father and son taught a kingdom theology and were not afraid to deal with the demonic aspect of the kingdom of evil. The son became a member of the Württemberg Parliament.[20] The early influence of R. A. Torrey lingered with Arnold through- out his life, reminding him that it is the Holy Spirit that provides power for service.[21] The Anabaptist tradition moulded his thinking on community.[22]

The German also responded to events, especially the 1914–18 War. He was horrified by the atrocities, but his reaction was different from that of Barth.[23] Arnold wanted action. Barth overemphasised the transcendence of God; the modernist overemphasised the immanence of God; but Arnold made a real effort to balance both aspects.

## Revivalists and Modernists

The leaders of revival were convinced that God only blesses what is in accordance with his Word. They defended orthodoxy not for its own sake but because it was bound up with vital spiritual life. Truth and life were inseparable. They were alarmed at the headway that theological modernism was making at the beginning of the twentieth century. Modernism was endangering the lives of individual believers and spoiling the fruit of revival. Most revivalists were glad to identify themselves with the Bible League, which had been formed in 1892 to wage war against the Higher Critics. A close companion was the Baptist Bible Union, whose official organ was *The Bible Call*. Its co-editors were John Thomas, the Welshman, and James Fountain.

The Bible League and the Baptist Bible Union were concerned with modernism at home and abroad. Three former missionaries— J. Macdonald, D. T. Morgan and Watkin R. Roberts—supplied information on developments in India and other countries. The Baptist Missionary Society was the main target of criticism, and a Bible Missionary Trust was set up 'to divert funds away from the BMS'.[24] Watkin R. Roberts, who was resident in Sutton, Surrey, at the time, was made its temporary secretary. The committee included R. B. Jones of Porth (Rhondda), and Dinsdale Young of Westminster Hall, London.

John Thomas, a Baptist minister, expressed his concern in a series of articles written during 1922, whose titles included 'The Axe at the Root', 'The Gospel Travested', and 'Hunted by Heresy'. The August issue of *The Bible Call* drew attention to Watkin Roberts' address at the Bible Union meeting of 11 July 1922. In this address (and also in various articles) he voiced the opinion that 'fifty per cent, at least, of the Missionaries in India, Ceylon and Burma are Higher Critics'.[25]

During that same year (1922), R. Wright Hay criticised George Howells (BMS) for his modernism. *The Bible League Quarterly* appealed to all missionary societies to declare their allegiance to the inspiration and authority of Scripture. It published the names of the missionary societies that had responded to the appeal and those that had not done so. The BMS was one society that did not respond. It explained its refusal by pointing out that it was happy with the state-ment drawn up by C. H. Spurgeon during the Downgrade controversy. It affirmed the divine inspiration, authority and sufficiency of the

Scriptures. W. Y. Fullerton, the BMS secretary, was sure that all its missionaries were faithful to Scripture.[26]

R. Wright Hay was unhappy with the BMS defence, and he and Watkin Roberts made use of pamphlets to publicise and defend their views. The former produced *Untrue to the Bible*, and the latter *The Ravages of Higher Criticism in the Indian Mission Field*. Articles by Watkin R. Roberts and John Thomas could also be read in *Yr Efengylydd*.[27]

Another means of furthering the cause was by arranging meetings. J. Cynddylan Jones (Cardiff), Alan Stibbs and B. F. Atkins addressed the Meetings of the Bible League on 6 June 1924, and at the Great National Bible Day in 1925 the main speakers were E. A. Carter (Pioneer Mission), T. G. Pinches (University College, London) and Reuben Saillens of France. Reuben Saillens was not the only speaker from overseas at such meetings. The main speakers at the Bible League meetings in June 1925 were Paul Kanamori (President of the Japan Bible League) and Robert Dick Wilson, author of *Is The Higher Criticism Scholarly?*[28] Journeys were made into other parts of Britain, including South Wales, where the main centres were Porth (Rhondda), Bridgend, Llanelli and Ammanford (the Whitsun Convention).[29]

The Bible League and the Baptist Bible Union supported the Thado-Kookie Mission working in north-east India. It was a Mission formed by Watkin R. Roberts and mainly led by him, and R. B. Jones, Porth (Rhondda) was on its committee. The Bible Missionary Trust sent out D. T. Morgan, who had resigned from the BMS, to work with this Mission. D. W. Bebbington rightly says that Morgan was the Bible Missionary Trust's only missionary and comments critically, 'Once more a Fundamentalist campaign produced scant results except ill feeling.'[30] Although Morgan was the Trust's only missionary, the work of the Thado-Kookie Mission with which he served was thriving. In 1926 (renamed The North East India General Mission) it had forty churches, eight thousand members and a hundred and twenty workers.[31]

In both the pamphlets and the addresses India received much attention . One reason was the influential position of the missionary George Howells, 'the most prominent representative of advance theological views within the Society'[32] (BMS). His modernistic views coloured his approach to other religions. The Hindu could speak of the incarnation of Vishnu, and this finds its fulfilment in the historic incarnation of Christ. Propitiation by sacrifice has 'much that the Christian conscience would condemn', but God's love is made known in the death of Christ as a sacrifice. Christ showed God's love by giving himself as a sacrifice, but in no way did he turn away the wrath of God. Salvation according to the Hindu had three aspects, work, knowledge and faith, and, according to George Howells, 'this is not something to reject as false and worthless'.[33] His critics felt that George Howells was denying the uniqueness of Christ and the doctrine of justification by faith alone.

*Effects of Modernism*
The critics were agitated by the visit of Leslie Weatherhead to India. In dealing with the Old Testament his main authorities were A. S. Peake and S. R. Driver. *The Bible Call* believed that their teaching was 'blasphemous'.[34] It was even more harmful because the visit was arranged by the Christian Literature Society, and such a body could spread the teaching through the sale of its books. Watkin R. Roberts received a report from India that some Indian Christian leaders had denounced faith in the deity of Christ. A number of Christians were returning to Hinduism.[35]

The same warning cry came from Japan, Russia, Korea and China. Paul Kanamori was a Professor of Theology in Japan. He became a convert to the 'new doctrine' (Higher Criticism) and translated Dr Pfeiderer's *Philosophy of Religion*. In his own words, 'I was introduced into the Christian religion by the front gate of orthodoxy, and led out of it by the back gate of New Theology into my old heathen doubt and unbelief.'[36] Restored to a living faith in Christ, Kanamori wrote on a decision card, 'I believe in the one true living God; I repent of my sin; I accept salvation through the Cross of Christ; I follow Christ even unto death.'[37]

William Fetler detected liberal tones in the preaching of visiting preachers to Russia. In his opinion, Sherwood Eddy was recommending an 'improve yourself prescription'.[38] It was more of a surprise to find modernism among the Baptists in the USA, even amongst the committee of the Russian Baptist Seminary in New York of which he was Dean. One member thought highly of W. N. Clark's *Sixty Years With the Bible*, but Fetler believed that the title should have been 'Sixty Years Away From the Bible'. Staff and students stood with him, but because the committee would not accept a doctrinal declaration, Fetler resigned from the committee. He remained a Baptist, but formed the Russian Missionary Society.[39]

Missionaries in China tried to retard the growth of modernism. Sixty missionaries in China sent an appeal to missionary societies in Britain and America imploring them to send no more Modernists to

China.[40] Henry Woods prepared a *Chinese Encyclopaedia* to expound the Scriptures and 'repel the attacks of Modernism'.[41] Both he and his wife supported the Bible Union of China—a Union formed in 1920 when Griffith Thomas and Charles Turnbull visited China. The Fundamentalist and Modernist controversy reached its climax during that time. 'Meetings were held almost every day, with the result that the cleavage, deep and wide, was made between the two factions.'[42]

Mr and Mrs Woods were convinced that revival would change the whole situation, and in 1924 the wife formed the Worldwide Revival Prayer Movement. George T. B. Davies, who had visited Wales twice during the 1904–05 Revival, was one of the original group.[43] Mrs Woods wrote an account of the Revival that broke out in Shanghai in 1925 under the title *The Half Has Never Been Told*. This account was distributed by F. Kehl of Calcutta, as were stories of other revivals. (He had been prominent in revival in India and distributed Christian literature, including Mrs Penn-Lewis's works.) A hundred thousand copies of Mrs Woods' book were circulated.[44] A few years later, she was glad to receive a copy of *Rent Heavens* from R. B. Jones giving an account of the Welsh Revival of 1904–05. She believed herself to have been partly responsible for getting the author to publish it.[45]

Kil, the Korean revival leader, made a thorough criticism of the *Abingdon Bible Commentary*.[46] In his opinion the majority of editors and translators were theologically liberal. He laid three platforms for his criticism: the work was contrary to the teaching of the Presbyterian Church of Korea; the authors made rationalistic assumptions; and many of them denied the supernatural. Jonathan Goforth of China was likewise a staunch opponent of modernism.[47]

*The student world*

The wide gap between the modernists and the conservatives was reflected in the student world. Tatlow could say, 'The senior friends of the Movement in England [SVMU] in its early days were almost all from the conservative school of thought', but added, 'the desire for comprehensiveness was there from the beginning'.[48] The same desire was made known in Conishead in 1907, and even more so in the Missionary Conference in Edinburgh in 1910. 'Edinburgh 1910 was in a remarkable way a training-ground for those who were later to be leaders of the ecumenical movement.'[49] Even those who were one in the early days of student work divided theologically. This was true of John R. Mott and Robert Speer. Speer was happy to contribute to *The Fundamentals*, championing the orthodox faith.[50] Mott never lost sight of his evangelical background, but argued that the social emphasis was an essential aspect of salvation.

The division was not always clear-cut. There were convinced evangelicals present in Edinburgh, and some remained within the Student Christian Movement. Paul Nicolay, a member of the Lieven group in St. Petersburg, remained within the Student Christian Movement but insisted on a Bible-centred faith.[51]

Other evangelicals were perturbed at what was happening in the student world, including members of the Royal family in Sweden, Robert Wilder and Karl Heim.[52] A statement made by John K. Fairbank needs to be qualified: 'The tendency of Speer, John R. Mott, Sherwood Eddy and Robert Wilder, and the other great missionary recruiters of the era was to walk the tight rope of the theological centre.'[53] Speer was not walking a tightrope when he agreed to write to *The Fundamentals*, and Wilder regarded the Inter-Varsity Fellowship as the organisation that was faithful to the early vision of the SVM and SVMU.

### The central truths

Continual attention was given to the inspiration of Scripture and the work of Christ. The revivalists regarded these as central truths of the Christian faith. Although they differed as to the mode of inspiration, they were all agreed that the Bible was God's Word written. Atonement was regarded as Christ giving himself in the place of sinners and turning away the wrath of God. No revival could be expected if these truths were neglected or rejected. *Yr Efengylydd* echoed the declaration made by the Minneapolis Convention for Fundamentalists:[54]

> Real revival must be based upon the supernaturally inspired word—the final, complete revelation of God's will; upon the Holy Spirit's convicting power, upon Jesus Christ and his atonement for sins.

The revivalists held fast to these truths.

The revivalists, especially those labelled as 'fundamentalists', were bitterly criticised. There was some truth in the criticisms. Fundamentalists wasted much energy discussing details of the rapture, made sweeping accusations regarding the critics, painting all of them with the same brush, and were too ready to depend on unscholarly articles to defend their position. On the other hand, their critics tended to concentrate on the weaker articles that were written: for example, the lecture given by Emil Reich, a well-known traveller.

This was a popular lecture, but Reich lacked the intellectual ability to be convincing. *The Expository Times* responded in a sarcastic review.[55]

Others, like E. König of Bonn University, Dick Wilson in the USA and William Edwards in Wales, could not be dismissed so lightly. The tendency of the critics was to isolate the 'fundamentalists' from the 'moderates'. There were differences between them, especially in matters of strategy, but basically they were one. This oneness is expressed in the unanimity regarding the central truths of the inspiration of Scripture and the atoning death of Christ.

# 19
# To the Ends
# of the Earth

The work of God in true revival is both deep and wide. It gives a new dimension to the experience of believers, and it also sends them out into the world as witnesses. The Revival of 1904–05 is no exception. As a result of it, ministers like Cynolwyn Pugh[1] and Peter Joshua went to America,[2] and G. J. Morgan to Brisbane, Australia.[3] Evangelists were thrust out to travel in Britain and many overseas countries. They included David Matthews[4] and the brothers Arthur and Emlyn Davies.[5] The two brothers helped R. B. Jones of Porth (Rhondda), in revival meetings. Arthur had an outstanding ministry in Gilgal, Porthcawl, and travelled with the evangelist John McNeill, spending three months with him in Malta.[6] A number of individuals went to other countries, going 'by faith'—a significant feature of the missionary explosion of the post-revival period.

## 'By faith'

A number of persons claimed that God had called them personally to a particular country and ventured out without any means of support, independent of any denomination or missionary society. The call was subjective, and external only to the extent that friends encouraged them. They were promised prayer support and would receive an occasional gift of money. It also meant going out as soon as possible after the call, irrespective of all possible difficulties.

There are two outstanding examples of this from Cross Hands, Carmarthenshire. Both men belonged to the Mission Hall that was formed by children of the revival who had come out from the Welsh Congregational Chapel.[7]

One was Edward Wilkins. He attended revival meetings in Gorseinon, Ammanford, and the Rhondda, very often in the company of D. P. Williams (later Pastor Dan of the Apostolic Church). They also visited Evan Roberts at his home in Loughor. D. P. Williams was converted at Loughor on Christmas Day 1904, and Edward Wilkins while working underground on 16 February 1905—in a meeting of five persons, one of whom was D. P. Williams.[8]

In obedience to a vision he received, Edward Wilkins left for South Africa in 1908.[9] On arrival in Cape Town he stayed at the YMCA, where he saw an appeal in a local paper for missionaries to be prepared by Dr Karl Kuhm for work with the Sudan Mission. On making enquiries, the Welshman discovered that the college was in Wellington, but Dr Fallows, who was in the office, chatted with him and asked questions about the Welsh Revival. After helping the Salvation Army and preaching for a while, Edward Wilkins left for Johannesburg. Here he would walk the streets in order to meet people and present the gospel to them. Knowing that the Dutch Reformed Church was reluctant to work with dark-skinned people, the missionary became determined to work amongst them. He found employment in the gold mines in Randfontein, and soon he had thirty-six workers under his care, to whom he would witness and teach hymns. Whilst working, they would sing

> *Gla tanda zibenzo*
> S    fmf    rrd    (sol-fa)

The missionary was also welcomed in a village two miles from the mines, where there was no other white person.[10]

Because he was working with people of a different culture, Wilkins faced a number of difficulties. It was customary for men to buy their wives, giving from one to five cows to obtain one. The Zulu war dance not only glorified war but also encouraged loose moral standards. Coming from a revival background in Wales, the Welshman found it hard to live with heavy smokers. His approach was to establish a good personal relationship with the men, without which it would have been impossible to present the gospel to them. Edward Wilkins arrived back in Cross Hands in 1913.[11]

Eliazer Jenkins was also a child of the revival, and prominent in the meetings of the Mission Hall where he worshipped. He too went to South Africa, going 'straight from the pit to the pulpit'.[12] He worked in a gold mine in Rand, Johannesburg, and regularly visited two compounds—one of three thousand men, and the other of a few hundred. In his ministry he experienced the Holy Spirit coming down upon the congregation: 'We have felt just the same here as we used to do in the revival meetings in Wales.'[13] Another aspect of his work was healing, and by 1910 there had already been two examples of divine healing. Unlike Edward Wilkins, Eliazer Jenkins remained in South Africa all his life, and after his death his son followed him in the pastorate.[14]

## Pentecostal Missionary Union

Pentecostals were emerging in the North of England, London and Wales. They formed churches but were also found within the historic denominations. Pentecostal missionaries could work in the context of a wider fellowship of believers. Meetings at Sunderland with A. A. Boddy (Anglican) and the formation of the Pentecostal Missionary Union in 1909 (PMU) brought the Pentecostals together. Being more united, they were able to consider the challenge of overseas witness. Sunderland had direct links with the Welsh Revival: A. A. Boddy had visited Wales, and Welsh revivalists had been to Sunderland.[15] The Pentecostals, including those in Wales, faced the missionary challenge in two ways. They sent representatives to various countries to spy out the land and bring back reports. They also prayed for volunteers to go out to various parts of the world and stay there as long as possible.

One of the representatives sent out was T. M. Jeffreys (Congregationalist) of Waun-lwyd, Ebbw Vale.[16] It was arranged for him to go to Armenia. He was set apart by the laying on of hands at Peniel, Herne Hill, London, on 28 June 1910.[17] His contact was Sister Gerber, an English-speaking Swiss lady who lived in Cesarea and was working amongst Armenian Massacre Orphans. Pentecostal friends from Müllheim-Ruhr sent him a gift of twenty pounds to help with expenses.

T. M. Jeffreys visited Athens and was inspired 'incidentally' when he saw the Acropolis. After visiting the tomb of Polycarp in Smyrna, the Pentecostal moved to Eregh and then to Cesarea (Kaisariaych). He spent a busy month with Sister Gerber in Zingidere: 'I have given a fortnight's Bible readings on Pentecostal truths. Many have been quickened and some have received the Spirit and are waiting for the full manifestation.'[18] His ministry was threefold: to bring men and women to salvation, to a full Pentecostal experience, and to establish relationships with other Pentecostals. On his return, after a delay because of ill health, a missionary was found for Armenia.

There were others in Wales besides T. M. Jeffreys who supported the PMU. The Baptists A. Hill and D. S. Jones of Bridgend, and T. Mercy of Wattsville,[19] together with others, held meetings in Cardiff and encouraged those who wanted to work overseas. The degree of missionary interest at the time is evidenced by the fact that at a meeting in Cardiff in 1910 a dozen young men volunteered for overseas service.[20]

Over forty applicants were interviewed by the PMU during a period of about ten years, from 1914 to 1924. The precise figure was probably forty-four. Seventeen were accepted and twenty-seven turned down (the usual reason given was that they were 'not suitable'). Those accepted were almost evenly divided between India, Africa (especially Belgian Congo) and China. A few stayed only for a short period. One couple had to return because the husband had shot two elephants and was selling the tusks to the nationals. Another had to come home because she had accepted the teaching concerning 'The Bride' (a teaching claiming that a spiritual élite would have a special place in heaven). A few names of people with a Pentecostal background can be added to the PMU list, but no details are given of their preparation.[21] George Jeffreys, converted in the Revival of 1904–05, also trained with the PMU, but he concentrated on the home ministry. He formed the Elim Evangelistic Band in 1915, but the Elim Missionary Council was not formed until 1928.

Missionaries were drawn from areas strongly influenced by the Revival of 1904–05. For example, five people from the Rhondda were accepted and seven turned down, while five from Gorseinon were accepted and three turned down. In the mid-twenties, the Mission Hall in Aberaman had five workers on the foreign field. One feature of this missionary movement is the number of marriages that took place between missionaries. Seven couples are mentioned: in five cases one partner was Welsh, and in the other two, both were from Wales. In 1924 the PMU merged with the Assemblies of God, and about twelve of those who were already Pentecostal missionaries identified themselves with the Assemblies. W. F. P. Burton was also PMU-trained, but he left the Union in 1914 to form the Congo Evangelistic Mission. In 1926, at least four Welsh people were working with this Mission in Africa. They were Garfield Elias Vale and his wife Mary (née Taylor), and Leonard Gittings and his wife. Their spheres of labour were Katenta, Kasongo, Dilomba and Dianda.[22]

### Elim Church, Dowlais

Another name that must be added to these four is that of Cyril E. Taylor. He is mentioned separately because he was a member in the Elim Church at Dowlais, Merthyr. A group of Pentecostals was meeting there in 1907. In 1913 they were described as very different in character, but all one because they were children of the Revival. They were formed into an Elim Church in 1920. When Cyril Taylor left in 1921 he was their first missionary. Elim supported him, but he worked with the Congo Evangelistic Mission. After taking a medical course in Edinburgh he left for Katanga, Belgian Congo. Soon after his arrival, the home was threatened by fire and he suffered from dysentery; yet in 1922 the missionary reported thirty-six baptisms. During the early years Cyril Taylor did much itinerant work on his bicycle.

George Thomas and his wife were also members in the Elim Church, Dowlais. They were prepared for overseas work in an unusual way. A small Spanish community had settled at Dowlais, and the Elim Church was anxious to reach them with the gospel. Dr Murcutt and Miss Luce visited the Spaniards during 1922, and after their mission Elim appointed Mr and Mrs Thomas to continue the work. They started with the help of an interpreter, but soon mastered the language. It was this work in Dowlais that led them to work in Mexico. Initially they worked at San Diego on the Mexican border, because only Mexicans were permitted to preach in the country itself. Concentrating on the Mexicans in their own area, they opened a Bible School that enabled them to send national workers into Mexico. In 1928 they were allowed into the country themselves and settled in Guadalupe Hgo.[23]

*Pen-y-groes*

The Apostolic Church had its origins in Pen-y-groes, Carmarthen-shire, and emerged from the midst of controversy. The children of the revival began to meet outside the denominational churches during 1907, drew up a trust deed in 1909, and a mission hall was erected in 1910. A significant Pentecostal group in the Hall was influenced by W. O. Hutchinson of Bournemouth, founder of the Apostolic Faith Church, and D. P. Williams joined them. Their distinctives were the appointment of apostles and prophets, and acceptance of the gifts of the Spirit, including speaking with tongues.[24] Division took place in 1913 between those who accepted the gift of tongues and those who were critical of it. The trustees locked the gates of the Hall and on the second Sunday of January 1913 the Pentecostals had to hold their meetings elsewhere. The local people looked upon the event as a clash between two revival groups—those that advocated free worship and the 'pentecostal dancers'.[25]

Other groups in South Wales were attracted to the Apostolic Faith Church and responded to the overseas missionary call. Their numbers were not high, but a pioneering work was done in South Africa that prepared the way for the PMU missionaries who went out between 1914 and 1924. It was 'in fulfillment of the prophetic word' that William Roderick and his wife, from Ammanford, went out to South Africa.[26] They were prepared for the mission by W. O. Hutchinson.

He received word from a Welsh missionary that there was need for a white person to take care of a group of thirty-six Ethiopian national churches. Hutchinson gave William Roderick full authority to make all decisions regarding these churches.

William Roderick returned after two years and was replaced by James Brooke. He was from Bournemouth, but was pastor of the Apostolic Faith Church at Bellevue, Swansea. Worsfold assesses Brooke's ministry: 'Brooke proved to be an able minister who gave ten years of faithful ministry and oversight to the developing of Apostolic Faith Church in South Africa and neighbouring states.'[27] In 1913, S. B. Swift and his wife left Wales to work at Boksbury North.[28]

There was further division at Pen-y-groes in 1916, when a group led by D. P. Williams separated from Bournemouth and formed the Apostolic Church of Wales. They also were keen to witness overseas and turned their attention to Argentina, where Joseph Hollis had done some work in the name of the PMU. He joined the Apostolic Church of Wales. His wife Catherine, from Skewen, Neath, was converted during the Revival of 1904–05. Husband and wife, together with D. T. Morris from Trebanos, Swansea Valley, left for Argentina in 1922.[29] Though D. T. Morris was only a child in 1904, he had been brought up in a home influenced by revival.[30] The three were joined by Jim Turnbull, a Scotsman, and George Evans, a Welshman. They were followed by Myfanwy Williams (a niece of Pastor Dan), who was to marry George Evans.[31]

Much work was done at Aquilares, where they were encouraged by conversions but discouraged by the bad roads and the heat. D. T. Morris, however, had purchased a horse and a trilby, which were proving very useful.[32] One conversion is of particular interest. When D. T. Morris was preaching in the open air, a certain Mr Palau was converted. This led to the formation of the Christian home in which Luis Palau, the well-known evangelist, was brought up.[33] D. T. Morris became superintendent of the work, but resigned in 1930 and joined the Plymouth Brethren.[34]

Just as T. M. Jeffreys opened the way for more permanent work amongst the Pentecostals, so did D. P. Williams and his brother W. J. Williams for the Apostolic Church. According to Turnbull, 'They played a major part in the progress of missionary work.'[35] Like his brother Dan, W. J. Williams was indebted to Evan Roberts. In a meeting at Llanlluan, near Pen-y-groes, Evan Roberts asked W. J. Williams if he wanted to be a minister. When he answered positively Evan Roberts told D. M. Phillips—'And both laid their hands on him and asked God to make him a preacher of the Gospel.'[36] The two brothers visited Ireland in 1919, USA in 1922, and the Scandinavian countries and France in 1924.[37]

A close relationship was forged between the Apostolics in Britain and those in the Scandinavian countries through the visits to Britain of Sigurd Bjorner and Dr Karl Naeser. Bjorner, Secretary of the YMCA in Denmark, married Anna Larssen, an outstanding actress and singer. Naeser was a member of the Danish aristocracy and leader of an evangelical group in Paris from which the first Apostolic congregation in France was formed.[38] In 1925 Dr Naeser welcomed two missionaries from Britain to France, one of whom was Thomas Roberts, a Welshman from Skewen, Neath.[39]

**Faith missionary societies**

Two of the original members that met in Pen-y-groes in 1907 were Eben Griffiths and his wife. The husband was one of the leaders from the beginning and continued to lead the non-pentecostals that met in the Evangelistic Hall. His son David Thomas Griffiths responded to the call to be an overseas missionary, doing so in a meeting in Llanelli, Carmarthenshire, on 15 October 1921.

This was a convention meeting, and is another example of the influence of 'convention' on overseas mission. The preachers were Rees Howells (back from Africa) and William Fetler, Russia. Fetler arrived from Porth, Rhondda, where he had spoken at the College with R. B. Jones. This was probably his first visit to Wales since the revival period 1904–05. After preaching at Llanelli on the Saturday afternoon, William Fetler tested the meeting and nine persons committed themselves to overseas mission. David Thomas Griffiths was one, and another was Sally Evans from Cross Hands, one of R. B. Jones's first students at Porth in 1919.

*Eastern Europe*

D. T. Griffiths and Sally Evans were soon married and volunteered to work with William Fetler's Russian Missionary Society.[40] In 1921 the Griffithses left for Baranovitchi, Poland, where starving Russians were continually pouring in. The missionaries would meet with as many as a thousand refugees every Saturday, helping them both materially and spiritually.[41]

During the same year, J. C. Williams of *The Overcomer* (edited by Mrs Penn-Lewis) and the Rev. Arthur Harris, who spent some time in Cardiff, also joined the Russian Missionary Society. These men were very close to Evan Roberts:[42]

The four colleagues or regular prayer partners were Charles Raven and Arthur Harris—when they were free of their commitments; Henry Johnson—who eventually moved to Paris to pioneer a French *Le Vainqueur* and other publications; Mr. Scottorn—who devoted all his free hours to God's service and later became an Anglican vicar; and J. C. Williams (Skewen, Neath).

Evan Roberts personally trained these men in the principles of prayer, especially perseverance, and praying until all prayers were gathered into one. J. C. Williams's centre of operation was Warsaw, and the nature and direction of the work there were determined in discussions with William Fetler. The Welshman, however, was only there for a few years, and then he returned to England (probably in 1923).[43]

By this time the Griffithses had settled down and, significantly, were referred to as 'Stundists'. That is, they were linked with the group of evangelicals that had emerged in Russia during the second half of the nineteenth century. The couple from Wales were working with S. K. Hine, translator of the hymn 'How Great Thou Art'.[44] They moved to Berlin and were joined by another Welshwoman, Arianwen Jones from Cwm-parc, Rhondda.[45] Hine refers to the long meetings led by William Fetler:[46]

In between these long meetings Mr and Mrs Griffiths, Miss Arianwen Jones (a strong Welsh soprano) and I sang as a vigorous quartette at Mr Fetler's meetings in the Wilhelmstrasse YMCA. We had lessons in Russian grammar and diction, invaluable in later years.

In 1923 Hine and his wife left the Russian Missionary Society, soon to be followed by the Griffithses, and the four worked together in Volkynia.[47] The two couples came across an empty brewery and turned it into a Gospel Hall, seating about three hundred. During the opening ceremony a former Roman Catholic priest gave a word that greatly encouraged the four missionaries.[48]

They had to respond to the growth of Pentecostalism, which for a brief period had been raging like wildfire. D. T. Griffiths was of the opinion that it was diminishing 'with the same vigour as it raged', and they were 'reclaiming some fine assemblies from the clutches of Pentecostalism'.[49] Further joy was experienced when L. M. Rees, from the Griffithses' home district, arrived in 1928. She married J. Shneidrook, and consequently there was a strong group involved in the work.[50] Apart from Arianwen Jones, all the others were now under the umbrella of the Open Brethren.

## Africa

The Russian Missionary Society was one of many faith missionary societies formed at the end of the nineteenth and beginning of the twentieth century. Another was the South Africa General Mission (SAGM), which advocated the teaching of the Holiness Movement and prayed for revival. Two of its missionaries were Rees Howells and his wife Elizabeth Hannah Jones.[51] The husband, who was from Brynamman, Ammanford, was converted in the USA. He was blessed in the Welsh Revival of 1904–05 and, in 1906, went through a 'protracted holiness experience' at Keswick.[52] His wife came into assurance of salvation during the Revival.

The crucial influence on their going to South Africa was Albert Head and his wife: the former was chairman of SAGM and of Keswick in Wales.[53] Rees and Elizabeth Howells left on 10 July 1915 and, weeks after arriving, they were experiencing revival. The nationals knew that they had come from the land of revival and Rees Howells was happy to relate some of the events of 1904 and 1905. That was not easy, because there was no word for 'revival' in the language of the people. In spite of this problem, as Rees Howells listened to the singing and praying, he 'recognized a sound he had heard in the Welsh Revival'.[54]

On Sunday 10 October (which was his birthday), Rees Howells had no doubt that the Holy Spirit had come upon them. A young lady had been fasting because she felt unready for Christ's Second Coming. She got up in a meeting to pray:[55]

As she prayed she broke down crying and within five minutes the whole congregation were on their faces crying to God. Like lightening and thunder the power came down. I had never seen this even in the Welsh Revival. I had only heard about it with Finney and others. Heaven had opened and there was no room to contain the blessing. I lost myself in the Spirit and prayed as much as they did. All I could say was, 'He has come.'

That evening there was praying in every house in the district. The revivalists went to Mount Silinda to tell the story, and it led to a series of meetings lasting all day for six days.[56]

A day of celebration was arranged to mark the first birthday of the revival. Communion was celebrated in the morning service, the

afternoon was devoted to personal witness, and at a preaching service in the evening the message was based on Luke 1:74-75. At the
close, the whole congregation stood up spontaneously to claim the
Holy Spirit in revival. They sang a hymn that would roughly correspond to '*Ni bydd diwedd byth ar swn y delyn aur*' (There will be
no end to the sound of the golden harp). The revival spread in two
ways. Believers would visit villages and witness to the gospel, and
evangelists prepared in a class would go out to preach. Half the
class would be out for six weeks, while the other half was trained.[57]

In about two years after the outbreak of revival Rees Howells
toured the stations in five countries. This meant travelling 11,000
miles. The missionary preached and counselled enquirers. On one
occasion the work kept him in the chapel for thirteen hours.[58] A
typical series of meetings were those held in Johannesburg:

> In Johannesburg for instance, Mr Howells conducted revival meet-
> ings for twenty-one days in one of the largest churches and it was
> packed every night. He had to speak through three interpreters
> because there were so many tribes, but that did not hinder the
> Spirit breaking through and hundreds coming out every night for
> salvation.[59]

Rees Howells and his wife were not the only ones that went out
with the SAGM. Evan L. Evans and his wife from Carmarthenshire
reached Portuguese East Africa on 30 September 1923. Both husband
and wife were influenced by the Ammanford Whitsun Convention.[60]
Evan and Florence Howells went with the Angola Evangelical
Mission to Portuguese West Africa. They were followed by Watkin
Edwards of Capel Hendre, Ammanford. The Howellses worked with
the Society until 1952, when they joined the BMS. When Watkin
Edwards returned, he ministered at Caersalem, Gorseinon.[61]

Other Welsh people joined the Heart of Africa, a mission formed
by C. T. Studd in 1912. He travelled in Wales during 1915, visiting
Colwyn Bay, Caernarvon, Bangor, Aberystwyth and the Llandrindod
Convention. When he returned to Africa in 1916, Albert W. Davies
from Llanelli went with him. Albert Davies married Miss Flanhagan,
one of the first missionaries to go out with the Heart of Africa.[62] The
party also included O. T. Jenkins, another Welshman, and Edith
Studd. They received a tremendous welcome at Nala: [63]

> It was like a Lord Mayor's Show in the road to Nala. Four men
> carried a big wooden drum with a little darkie on top beating it for

all his worth. Then there were bugles and throats blending wonderfully and hand-shaking with the 'Nala touch' to it [shaking of the hand and grasping the thumb].

Albert W. Davies was superintendent of the work and remained in Africa for over twenty years. On his return he settled in Barry. Emily Davies, also from Llanelli, joined Albert Davies in 1924 when he returned to Africa after a furlough.[64]

The Sudan United Mission attracted at least one worker from Wales. He was Edward Evans from Merionethshire, who went to Nigeria. He had been educated at Aberystwyth and Bala, and as a student had signed the declaration of the SVMU. One thing that encouraged him as a Welshman was to find an '*ch*' in the people's alphabet! Edward Evans taught in a school, evangelised, took care of a dispensary (partly paid for by friends in Swanage, England) and cared for the Freed Slaves Home.[65]

*South America*

At least three faith missions were formed to enter South America, all of them having links with Wales. The Bolivian Indian Mission had Richard Cory of Cardiff on its Council, and O. M. Owen was a Council member for the Evangelical Union of South America. The third society was the Inland South America Missionary Union, and it was with this mission that Daniel Thomas of Pen-y-banc, Llandeilo, Carmarthenshire, went out with his wife in 1911. They worked in an isolated area in Paraguay, where there was a mistrust of white foreigners. Only one person turned up for the first meeting; a few more came to the second, but when an English hymn was given out they all left. During the third service, a number stayed to the very end. Daniel Thomas's experience was very unlike that of Rees Howells. He did have the company of Jabez Merriman, a fellow Welshman, for a brief period, but he could not settle and left the country.[66]

**Training**

The faith missions and independent churches were aware of the need for some formal training for missionaries. They could not support the denominational colleges because of the inroads of Modernism. The answer was to set up Bible schools of their own. The first was the East London Training Institute. With the growth of Pentecostalism other centres were established, at Preston and Sion College, London.

Ben Griffiths started a fascinating work. He was a London-Welshman and an elder in the Welsh Presbyterian Church in Charing

Cross. Like many other Welshmen, he had gone to London to find work and had a milk round in Notting Hill. Spiritually he was a product of the Revival and experienced the fullness of the Spirit in 1909. In 1911 he established an independent Pentecostal work in his own home. By 1917, the family and those who had joined with them were meeting daily. During the same year two members left for Africa.

The company bought Peniel, Kensington, in 1924 and adopted an aggressive missionary programme. Their aim was to support one foreign missionary for every ten members in the Church. The number of missionaries increased steadily, and at one time nearly ninety workers were supported in different parts of the world. The main centres were Brazil, South Africa, China and Belgium. The training was church-based and practical, including leading and taking meetings in the church and in the open air at Hyde Park. The teaching would be done through the preaching and the Bible studies.[67]

No collections were taken in the services, but boxes were laid out at every pillar in the church, with a scriptural text on each. The money came in consistently throughout Ben Griffiths' ministry, which lasted until 1956. Many Welsh people like Mrs Jose of Kenfig Hill found a spiritual home there. She went from Wales to London in 1927 as a domestic help, and her husband Richard became one of Ben Griffiths's right-hand men. Welsh preachers would be regularly invited, including Pastor Dan and Clement Morgan of Dowlais, Merthyr Tydfil. Another missionary aspect of the life of the church was tract production. Thousands of tracts would be distributed every year.[68]

*Porth Bible Institute*
In Wales itself, the conventions, which were a fruit of the 1904–05 Revival, gave a prominent place to the missionary meeting. At such meetings, news was given of what was happening in other countries, and the challenge of overseas mission presented. Occasionally there was an unusual response, as at the Ammanford Convention in 1921 when twelve people volunteered to go abroad.[69] The convention leaders saw the need for more specific training for pastors at home and for missionaries going abroad. R. B. Jones and W. S. Jones, both of the Rhondda, started a Bible study group in 1916 that developed into a Bible Training School for Christian Workers in 1919 and was later renamed the Bible Institute. During the early period, from 1919 to 1923, at least eleven students left for other countries—India, Poland, Madagascar, Canada and Japan. The majority worked with

faith missions, but three went out with denominational societies (two with the BMS and one with the LMS).[70]

Students from the Bible Institute continued to go overseas after 1923. Tudor Jones and Lilian Jones broke new ground by going to Japan. Bronwen Hale was a lady pastor in Treorchy. She married A. L. Hughes and, later, both of them went to India with the CM (Presbyterian Foreign Mission).[71] Foreign students also came to the Institute. At least seventeen entered between 1924 and 1933, the year of R. B. Jones's death. They included Joseph Schwartz, a factory director turned evangelist at Riga; Ferrazzine, a Swiss from Reuben Saillens' Institute in France, and Jacob Vagar. Vagar was an ex-army officer who became an evangelist. During a period when he was disillusioned with life he found a New Testament at the bottom of a trunk, and the reading of it led to his conversion. He returned from Porth to work in Odessa.[72]

Some of these students were in contact with William Fetler, with whom by this time R. B. Jones had established a friendship. Both men were like-minded, independent, anti-liberal in theology and Baptist by persuasion. The two visited each other on a few occasions, and the Principal of the Bible Institute did not know of anyone, apart from C. T. Studd, who had so impressed him.[73]

*Swansea and Switzerland*

The Bible College at Swansea was another product of the Revival of 1904–05. It was founded by Rees Howells in 1924, the missionary who had spent a number of years in Africa with the South Africa General Mission. He himself was responsible for all arrangements. John Thomas, Liverpool, was appointed Principal, helped by B. S. Fidler, Trelogan, Clwyd. Some of the students from Wales who were there during the early years became missionaries, including Ieuan Jones and Sarah Thomas, who went to China and were later married.[74]

A Bible School in Geneva was influenced to some extent by the Welsh Revival of 1904–05. John Anderson, Principal of the Glasgow Bible Institute, visited Wales during the Revival, and one student who was impressed by the report was Hugh Alexander, who was moved to pray for revival. He had been converted during a visit to an aunt in Coligny, Switzerland, but after hearing of revival had a desire to work overseas. He came across the teaching of Mrs Penn-Lewis and had real difficulties with it. He was so perplexed that he visited her in Leicester, probably just before 1914, and was greatly helped by her. He opened a Bible House in Switzerland in 1917 and a Bible

School in Geneva in 1928. A continuing link was forged through
B. S. Fidler, then a lecturer with R. B. Jones at Porth and, from 1936,
Principal of Barry Bible College. Both men wanted to develop Bible
schools and, like R. B. Jones and William Fetler, were anti-liberal
and pro-revival.[75]

## Denominational societies

Madagascar was one of the early fields of the London Missionary
Society (LMS). After twenty-five years of persecution (from 1835 to
1860), missionaries from England entered once again. It was in 1879
that the Welsh missionaries renewed their interest in the island. The
missionaries who were there during 1905–06 welcomed the revival
and were also glad to be joined by others of like mind. Phoebe Hall
of Penarth was one of those deeply influenced by the Welsh
Revival.[76] It was during one of the revival meetings that she quietly
promised her God that if called she would definitely go overseas.
That call did come, and she went to Madagascar, becoming the second wife of William Evans, who had already laboured there for a
number of years.[77]

Many of the Bible School students went out to the mission field
immediately after finishing their course, while a few went on from
Bible School to receive further education. Brinley Evans, brother of
Sally (D. T. Griffiths' wife), is one example of this. He owed his conversion to his Sunday school teacher, who was a convert of the Welsh
Revival. It took place at Bryn Seion, Cross Hands, the Mission Hall
that had nurtured his sister, Edward Wilkins and Eliazer Jenkins.[78] On
returning from Porth in 1921, the young convert became a member of
a Welsh Congregational Church. After further preparation he left for
Madagascar in 1926 under the auspices of the LMS.[79]

Lewis John Thomas was also an LMS man. Born in Llangefni but
brought up in Blaenau Ffestiniog, North Wales, he was converted in
the Revival while working in Birkenhead. He himself was glad to
say, 'I am a child of that Revival.'[80] As a result of this experience
Christ meant so much to him that he felt compelled to go out to proclaim the good news of salvation. After being ordained in 1911 he
went out to Cudapah, situated between Madras and Gooty. Two
things struck him on arrival: the fluency of the nationals in preaching and their variations in singing—'variations(!) with a
vengeance!!!!!!!'.[81] He spent forty years in India and made a valuable
contribution to LMS work as a preacher and organiser.

The BMS benefited from the Welsh Revival. A few missionaries
went to Africa, and a few to India. Of the African missionaries,

David Jones left the BMS and joined the Apostolic Church.[82] David Christopher (Christie) Davies, from the Swansea Valley, was one of the quartette at Spurgeon's College that took part in revival meetings. While home from college he had attended a meeting underground, joining with the miners in song and prayer.[83] After working for a time in Yalemba, he moved to Kinshasa. While he was there, Belgium colonised the Congo and introduced heavy taxes and forced labour. D. Christie Davies and others put pressure on Brussels to introduce a programme of reform. The Welshman spent twenty-five years in the Congo and, after his return, represented the BMS at home.[84]

Three women, Beatrice James, Mary Ann Davies (Mair) and Lilian Mary Edwards, volunteered for BMS work in India. Beatrice James was a faithful member of a Baptist Church in Barry, but it was the Welsh Revival that transformed her life, giving her a new sense of commitment to overseas mission.[85] Mair Davies was a student with R. B. Jones in Porth before going out to India.[86] Lilian Mary Edwards was the daughter of William Edwards, Principal of the Baptist College in Cardiff. (Her brother Austin Edwards was another member of the Spurgeon quartette.) Among the influences on her life the daughter mentions the following: Daniel Jones the missionary, Amy Carmichael, a book on India given to her by Albert Williams, and meeting Evan Roberts.[87] William Edwards and his wife were prominent leaders during the 1904–05 Revival, and the father regarded his daughter's going to India as one fruit of that work.[88]

Like Christie Davies, Caradoc Jones (another member of the Spurgeon quartette) was a committed Baptist. He joined the Pioneer Mission, an undenominational missionary society.[89] He had pioneered Baptist work in Gabalfa, Cardiff, before leaving for Brittany in 1920, making Paimpol his main base. He kept in touch with Reuben Saillens, the prominent revival leader in France, and one of the girls from Paimpol entered the Nogent Bible Institute, returning to work with Caradoc Jones.[90]

The opening of the first chapel in 1930 attracted many people from great distances, Wales included. Among those present were Pastor Oriol (Paris), who had been one of Caradoc Jones's fellow students at Spurgeon's College; Gerlan Williams, the Welsh Calvinistic Methodist missionary at Quimper, and Charles Phillips of the Pioneer Mission. One of the guests was the wife of Cornelius Griffiths from Cardiff, and she had the honour of opening the doors of the chapel.[91] On the following day, a conference for the Protestant Church of France was held in the new building. This greatly helped the unity of the Protestants.

When war broke out in 1939, Caradoc Jones was imprisoned and spent four years in a concentration camp; he regarded this as 'the most fruitful period of his ministry'.[92] Included amongst the converts were seven women who were later baptised in Gabalfa, Cardiff. The Welshman returned to Brittany in 1946, by which time he was seventy-one years of age.[93]

## Welsh Calvinistic Methodist (CM) Foreign Mission

Of the denominational societies there is no doubt that it was the Calvinistic Methodist (Presbyterian Church of Wales) that benefited most profoundly from the Revival of 1904–05. Only a few went overseas during the period from 1890 to 1907, but from 1908 there was a marked increase. Between that year and 1924 over forty men and women left as missionaries, more than twenty of them leaving during the seven-year period from 1908 to 1914. One lady missionary succeeded in going out in the middle of the war in 1916![94]

Peter Frazer belonged to the first group. He was one of the men that had welcomed Evan Roberts to Caernarvon in 1905. Frazer and his wife and Watkin R. Roberts, an independent missionary, went out to north-east India together. The three of them had an evangelical, revival background. The Frazers were influenced by Gypsy Smith, Watkin R. Roberts by R. A. Torrey and Keswick, and all three of them by the Revival of 1904–05.[95]

Huxley Thomas of Ammanford was a church member, 'But not until the revival of 1904–05 I saw my own personal need of a Saviour.'[96] His reading reveals how his mind was prepared for mission work. The authors included Griffith John, David Brainerd, Pastor Hsi and F. B. Meyer. Like Huxley Thomas, Hetty Evans and Nurse Hopkins were members in Bethany, Ammanford, where Nantlais Williams ministered. Hetty Evans experienced 'unbelievable things' during the Revival.[97] Nurse Hopkins was converted in the wake of the Revival, but other members of her family had been converted during the Revival itself.[98] It was in the same awakening that Elizabeth Radcliffe came to a saving knowledge of the Lord Jesus Christ[99] and Dilys Grace Edwards dedicated herself to missionary work.[100] The medical missionary Gordon Roberts was 'much blessed during the Welsh Revival'.[101]

Florrie Evans was endeared to the Welsh people as the one who had declared her love for Jesus Christ in that meeting in February 1904.[102] She spent a year at Doric Lodge, the Regions Beyond Missionary Centre, and made 'satisfactory progress in various branches of English study'. She returned from India after three years, and some denominational leaders felt she should not have gone, believing her to be unsuitable for work in that land.[103]

Other influences could fuse with that of revival. The evangelistic thrust of the Student Missionary Union was in harmony with the revival. Many missionaries, including Dilys Grace Edwards and Helen Rowlands, received much help from student conferences. Helen Rowlands was also 'grateful' for the revival.[104] Hetty Evans was in touch with the South Africa General Mission and, during her stay with the Faith Mission in Edinburgh, considered going to South Africa with them. Nurse Hopkins attended the meetings of F. B. Meyer while working in a London hospital.[105]

There is no doubt that the Revival had a profound influence on Sidney Evans and his wife Mary.[106] The husband was with Evan Roberts in Newcastle Emlyn during September and October 1904. He became one of the leaders of the revival and married Evan Roberts' sister; and he was one of the group that joined with R. B. Jones to establish the Training School in 1919. Mary Roberts spent five years in the Jamestown Girls' Institute in Nigeria.[107] This was closed in 1918, and she was commended for staying on longer than was expected of her. In 1920, the husband and wife went out to India. As Principal of the Cherra Theological College, Sidney Evans became an influential figure in the CM Foreign Mission. Under his leadership there was a balance between theory and practice. He was also happy with the development of democratic Presbyterianism in the church.[108]

### A new missionary society

The CM work in Mizoram prospered, but there were difficulties. However, good came eventually from the unpleasant division that took place. Peter Frazer and his wife and Watkin R. Roberts worked together in an area where D. E. Jones had laboured for a long time. Peter Frazer was a medical missionary and, by October 1909, was attending to an average of seventy patients a day.[109] The workload did not prevent him from presenting the gospel to the patients, to whom he would give a text from Scripture as well as a bottle of medicine. He and his wife also took a number of children into the compound.[110] The work was making good progress. D. E. Jones was able to report that sixty had been baptised during a period of less than twelve months.[111] The spirit in the meetings was one of revival. Watkin Roberts attended a communion service and felt that the intense feeling was unparalleled even in the Welsh Revival.[112]

The cause of division was Peter Frazer's stand in the Bwai (Boi) controversy.[113] There was a class of people considered as servants or

slaves. Peter Frazer could not regard any group of people in that way
and condemned the social system. Others believed it was for the good
of the group to remain in this position; if they were made completely
free it would not be possible to provide for them. Peter Frazer would
not change his mind, and Watkin Roberts agreed with him. The end
result was that the Frazers left the CM Mission and, with Watkin
Roberts, formed the Thado-Kookie Mission. Watkin Roberts was
honorary Secretary, and others who supported the work were F. Kehl
of Calcutta, D. Lloyd Jones of Aber, Caernarvon, and Arnold Davies
of Wrexham.[114] For a brief time Edwin Rowlands helped the
Mission.[115]

W. R. Dala was appointed field superintendent. He had gained
much experience in working with the Frazers and D. E. Jones, and
was ordained as an elder in 1910. Dala had about seventeen men
under his care, and over twenty young men between the ages of
seventeen and thirty in the Boarding School.[116] Another aspect of the
Mission's work was the distribution of literature, especially portions
of Scripture. Watkin Roberts also translated John's Gospel into the
language of the people. It was quite an achievement to send copies of
religious papers, including *The Life of Faith* and *The Christian*, to
four hundred missionaries and Christian workers.

The *Overcomer*, edited by Mrs Penn-Lewis, was sent to Watkin
Roberts in India. During a visit to Britain he decided to establish an
Indian *Overcomer* magazine.[117] Financial support from the readers of
the *Overcomer* enabled him to be more ambitious. His aim for 1922
was to print and circulate:[118]

1. 4,000 copies of the July *Overcomer* with its invaluable message
   and charts. A copy to every missionary in India.
2. 4,000 copies of each succeeding issue of the *Overcomer*.
3. 1,000 *Overcomer* reprints (monthly) in Bengali.
4. 2,000 copies monthly of 4-page reprints of the 'Logos of the
   Cross', in an important magazine published in India.
5. 3,500 copies of *The Awakening in Wales* [Mrs Penn-Lewis].
6. 3,500 copies of *Face to Face*.
7. A monthly reprint in an important Hill dialect, where there are
   30,000 Christians who need this Message in all its fullness.

Watkin Roberts also received gifts from the Overcomer Conference
at Swanwick and from Sion College, London.

This development in India strengthened the relationships that
already existed between Watkin R. Roberts, F. Kehl (Calcutta), Mrs

Penn-Lewis, the Overcomer Movement and Sion College, London. A further tie was established when J. C. Williams, a friend of Evan Roberts and Mrs Penn-Lewis, was appointed British Secretary. The name of the Mission was changed to the 'North-East India General Mission'.[119] Committee members included the Revs R. Wright Hay, Gordon Watt and R. B. Jones, Rhondda.[120] During 1925 R. B. Jones and Watkin Roberts were travelling the USA on behalf of the Mission.[121]

The activity of Watkin R. Roberts and the Mission led to the formation of the Independent Church of India. The Church is presbyterian in government, reformed in doctrine and baptistic in principle.[122] Some of its present leaders have friends in Wales, and they correspond with each other.[123]

# 15
# Conclusion

A revival is a period of extraordinary manifestation of God's power through the Holy Spirit, bringing about extraordinary results. It has the same main characteristics wherever it happens. These include a profound sense of the presence of God, contrite confession of sin, open worship, and an impact on society in general.

Each of these characteristics was found in the revivals of the first decade of the twentieth century. What is striking is the fact that one country, Wales, should have had such an influence on so many other countries in such a brief period of time. The influence penetrated to all continents of the world. Never before in the history of revivals had such a phenomenon been witnessed.

Furthermore, for the first time in the history of the church in Wales, the Revival produced a worldwide movement, in the Apostolic Church. That same Church also produced some fine preachers. The Apostolics of Scandinavia, for example, regarded Stephen Jeffreys as the greatest preacher that had ever visited their countries. It is easy to lose sight of this aspect and think only of the Apostolics' emphasis on experience and gifts.

Zeal for revival can lead to exaggerated claims concerning a particular awakening. It is right to say that the 1904–05 Revival in Wales profoundly influenced most of the countries that have been considered. It is necessary, though, to distinguish between primary and secondary influence. In India, Madagascar, Patagonia and France, the Revival in Wales was the main influence; but in Korea, Australia and New Zealand the influence was not so direct. In countries where the influence was direct, it varied in degree: the meetings in India and Madagascar were very similar to those in Wales, while the meetings in Russia were quieter.

Missionaries and ministers from Wales played a crucial role in the revivals of the period. The growth in the number of missionaries from Wales was phenomenal. It cannot be said that every single person who went to another country was inspired by the Revival, but there is no doubt that the majority who volunteered for overseas work did so because of its influence. The example may be quoted of an individual being attracted by the fruit of a particular country, but it is difficult to imagine anyone volunteering solely for that reason. Even if that were the case, such a person would be in the minority. Welsh missionaries in Madagascar, India and China, and ministers in the USA and Patagonia, promoted and confirmed the work of revival.

Colleges made a substantial contribution to the spread of revival, and that in two respects. First, they created a spirit of prayer for an awakening. This happened at Spurgeon's and at the Bible School in Germany during the revival, and later in Porth and Swansea, where they continued to pray for revival. Secondly, the colleges provided the personnel for overseas mission. Visitors to Wales from Spurgeon's College and the Tabernacle created revival links with France, Russia and Africa.

A feature of the Revival in Wales was the singing. It is amazing how some of the hymns of that revival were sung throughout the world. The outstanding example is '*Dyma gariad fel y moroedd*' (Here is love vast as the ocean). It was sung in Wales, in Spurgeon's College, in France, Madagascar, India, USA and Patagonia. This hymn, and others too, were sung in the language of the people. The hymns provided a channel for different people to express themselves in their mother tongue. Spiritual vitality led to vigorous use of the native language. It is true that missionaries clashed with the cultures of other countries and would ask the converts to break from habits regarded as pagan. But revival hymns strengthened many languages, including those of minority groups. A friend told Sidney Evans that if he were in Sweden, he would find it like Wales, but for the language. There are characteristics that are common to all revivals, and there are also differences that are bound up with the language.

In Wales, the singing could take up the major part of a service. The same repetition of hymns was found in other countries, especially in India and Madagascar, but there was a better balance between the hymn and the sermon. There were at least two reasons for this. First, the Welsh missionaries were aware of their Welsh background, and of the place of preaching in past revivals. Secondly, the conventions helped in this context, because the programme always included Bible readings and an address on a particular topic.

Wales also interpreted revival to the world. The two prominent examples are Mrs Penn-Lewis and J. Pengwern Jones. Both made an important contribution in this respect, but the latter had a better grasp of theology than the former. Mrs Penn-Lewis tended to assess everything in the light of her doctrine of sanctification. She, Pandita Ramabai and Elisabeth Rowlands championed the place of the woman in Christian service and worship. They argued strongly for giving more responsibility to women in leadership, though they were not so strong in arguing for their ordination. It was the emergence of the Pentecostal churches that strengthened the cause for the ordination of women.

The religious life of Wales was characterised by a stubborn denominationalism. During the Revival of 1904–05 the denominations were brought closer together, only to divide again afterwards. This pattern was repeated in many countries. The Pentecostals believed that the Revival in Wales had prepared the way for the real Pentecost. The Holiness Movement gave central consideration to the work of the Spirit in sanctification, while conservative evangelicals like those in Germany were so anxious to avoid extremes that they were in danger of losing sight of the nature of true revival. Other evangelicals within the denominations were reluctant to align themselves with any of the emerging groups. The same developments are evident in our day, making it imperative that an assessment of revival is Word-centred and not experience-centred.

The children of the revival made many mistakes. There were examples of uncontrolled emotion, unwise counselling, and inadequate response to criticism. On the other hand, the children of the revival safeguarded 'revival' as a spiritual concept, not to be assessed in psychological or sociological terms. Secondary causes can have their place in the preparation of revival, but the source is supernatural. During the revival period, old truths were also rediscovered, especially the Second Coming of the Lord Jesus Christ and the scriptural teaching on demonology.

The Revival in Wales in 1904–05 made a lasting contribution to the revivals of the first decade of the twentieth century. And it was a most valuable contribution. It is not the Welsh male voice choirs or their rugby teams (in the past) that have made the greatest contribution to the world, but the Revival of 1904–05. And that contribution to other countries is something that must be taken into consideration when assessing the Revival in Wales itself.

# References

## Chapter 1: Background

1. Owen Chadwick, *The Secularization of the European Mind in the Nineteenth Century* (CUP, 1975), 226.
2. Willam O. Shanahan, *German Protestants Face the Social Question, 1815–1871* (1963).
3. Chadwick, *The Secularization of the European Mind*, 96, 95.
4. James Moulton Roe, *A History of the British and Foreign Bible Society, 1905–1954* (London, 1965), 71.
5. J. Farquhar, *Modern Religious Movements* (New York, 1915), 28.
6. 'Norway', *The Christian Herald*, 8 June 1905, 498-9; referring to the event in America, Harvey Cox makes the comment, 'It was the most spectacular natural disaster the United States had ever seen, and one can well imagine the apocalyptic sentiments it evoked', *Fire From Heaven* (Cassell, 1996), 59.
7. J. Edwin Orr, *The Flaming Tongue* (Chicago, 1973), 175.
8. 'A Quarter of a Century of Christian Endeavour', *The Sunday Strand,* April 1906.
9. R. Tudur Jones, *Ffydd ac Argyfwng Cenedl*, vol. 2 (Abertawe, 1982), 330.
10. Dana L. Robert, 'Arthur Tappan Pierson, 1837–1911', *Mission Legacies*, eds., Gerald H. Anderson, Robert T. Coote and Norman A. Honer (New York, 1994).
11. John K. Fairbank, ed., *The Missionary Enterprise in China* (Cambridge, Mass., 1974), 98, 95.
12. Dana L. Robert, *Mission Legacies*.
13. Tissington Tatlow, *The Story of the Student Christian Movement of Great Britain and Ireland* (London, 1933), 225, 226, 229.
14. Tatlow, *Student Christian Movement*, 181. Examples of students from Wales attending Student Christian Movement Conferences: 'Cynhadledd y Myfyrwyr yn Edinburgh', *Y Goleuad*, 22 January 1904; CMA, 27, 287 (O. O. Williams), CMA, 27, 305 (J. W. Roberts), both Welsh Presbyterian missionaries.
15. C. Howard Hopkins, '[Andrew Murray] could rightly have been called the patron saint of the South African student movement', *John R. Mott, 1865–1955* (Grand Rapids, 1979), 296.
16. A recent study of Gypsy Smith: David Lazell, *Gypsy from the Forest* (Bryntirion Press, Bridgend, 1997).
17. 'The Circle of Prayer For World-Wide Revival', *The Life of Faith*, 22 November 1905, 988.
18. Dieter Lange, *Eine Bewegung bricht sich Bahn* (Brunnen, 1979): Count Puckler, in their Whitsun Conference, urged those present to pray for revival, which was the answer to Germany's spiritual crisis, 158.
19. Robert Pope, *Building Jerusalem* (Cardiff, 1998), 123, and 8-14 for relevant background.
20. For Keswick: Brynmor Pierce Jones, *The Spiritual History of Keswick in Wales* (Cwmbran, Gwent, 1989).
21. Eifion Evans, *The Welsh Revival of 1904* (Evangelical Movement of Wales, Port Talbot, 1969), 45-8; Jessie Penn-Lewis, *The Awakening in Wales* (Overcomer Publications, Poole, Dorset, n.d.), chapters 1 and 2; R. B. Jones, *Rent Heavens* (Porth, 1930), chapter ii.
22. Eifion Evans, *The Welsh Revival of 1904*, 56-7.
23. Jessie Penn-Lewis, *The Awakening in Wales*, 31, 47.
24. Ibid., 31.

25. Eifion Evans, *The Welsh Revival of 1904*, 56-8.
26. Ibid., 59; Geraint Fielder, *Grace, Grit and Gumption* (Christian Focus/Evangelical Movement of Wales, 2000), 120-1.
27. D. M. Phillips, *Evan Roberts, The Great Welsh Revivalist and his Work* (London, 1906), 122-5; Eifion Evans, *The Welsh Revival of 1904*, 68-71.
28. That happened on 2 November 1904, D. M. Phillips, *Evan Roberts*, 195.
29. Nantlais, *O Gopa Bryn Nebo* (Llandysul, 1967), xvii.
30. W. S. Jones, *Y Diwygiad Crefyddol yn Rhosllanerchrugog* (Rhosllanerchrugog [1905]), 4-9.
31. D. M. Phillips, *Evan Roberts*, 299.
32. Ibid., 285, 295, 296, 305, 326, 327.

## Chapter 2: France

1. W. E . Winks, *History of Bethany Baptist Church, Cardiff* (Cardiff, 1906), 43-8, with a photograph between pages 48 and 49; an account of the funeral, *SWDN*, 9, 14, August 1905, 5, 6; 'The Late Rev. Alfred Tilly', *The Baptist Times*, 18 August 1905, 594. J. Austin Jenkins, R. Edward James, *The History of Nonconformity in Cardiff* (Cardiff and London, 1901), 140-6.
2. Brynmor P. Jones, *Voices from the Welsh Revival* (Evangelical Press of Wales, Bridgend, 1995), 77, taken from *The Baptist Times*, 13 January 1905, 21.
3. The pastor was Charles Davies: J. Williams Hughes, *Charles Davies* (Cardiff, 1937).
4. Richard Cory, JP; for the Cory family: Burke, *The Landed Gentry* (1937).
5. Alfred Thomas (1840–1927), *Dictionary of Welsh Biography (DWB)*.
6. William Edwards (1848–1929), *DWB*.
7. Edward Thomas ('Cochfarf') (1853–1912), *DWB*.
8. Brynmor P. Jones, *Voices*, 78.
9. D. M. Phillips, *Evan Roberts*, 345-6.
10. Ibid., 345.
11. Ibid., 346; 'Incidents of the Welsh Revival', *The British Weekly*, 19 January 1905, 403.
12. Awstin, 'Aberdulais, Friday Jan. 13', *Religious Revival in Wales*, No 3; 'Cerbyd Achubiaeth', *Tarian y Gweithiwr*, 19 January 1905, 1. And R. Tudur Jones mentions a lady praying fervently in French at Llannerchymedd, Anglesey, *Ffydd ac Argyfwng Cenedl*, vol. 2, 197.
13. 'Cardiff', *The British Weekly*, 26 January 1905, 432.
14. Reuben Saillens: he was born 24 June 1855 in Saint-Jean-du-Gard, South France. His father was an evangelist with the Free Churches. Saillens was baptised by Pastor Crétan and later married one of his daughters. He was one of twelve students that left the East London Training Institute in 1875. He worked with the McCall Mission; formed a Baptist church in Paris with the support of the American Baptist Missionary Union. Saillens opened the first faith Bible College in France at Nogent. R. Saillens to Dr Barbour, American Missionary Union, 'Biographical Statement'; Frederick C. Spur, 'Pasteur R. Saillens and His Work', *The Baptist Times*, 15 May 1908, 346; 'Pasteur Reuben Saillens', *The Christian*, 9 November 1905, 17-18, with photograph; Michelle Guinness, *The Guinness Legend* (London, 1988), 121; Klaus Fiedler, *The Story of Faith Missions* (Regnum, Lynx, Oxford, 1994), 179, 201 n.100.
15. The Pioneer Mission: the Mission was started by E. A. Carter; it established new causes and supported existing ones; in 1906 it supported 4 churches in London, 16 in the provinces, 8 in Scotland and 2 in France; in 1908 F. J. Flatt became secretary: 'The Pioneer Mission', *The Baptist Times*, 18 May 1906, 369; 'Baptists and Evangelism', *The Christian*, 5 March 1908.
16. 'Pioneer Mission Work in France', *The Baptist Times*, 1 September 1905, 627; ibid., 5 November 1905, 802.

17. 'Notes from France', *The Christian*, 23 February 1905, 15; Mrs Penn-Lewis, 'The Awakening in Wales', *The Life of Faith*, 22 February 1905, 148.
18. Mme Saillens, *Le Réveil du Pays de Galles* (Valence, 1905), 46-7; Winifred M. Pearce, *Knight in Shining Armour* (London, 1962), 13, 20, 24-5; Caradoc Jones, 'The 1904-05 Revival', *The Evangelical Magazine of Wales*, 7:5, 1968.
19. Saillens, *Le Réveil*, 46-51. One of the company, D. Lortsch, was appointed British and Foreign Bible Society representative in 1901; he became President of the French Free Church Synod; died in 1916: James Moulton Roe, *A History of the BFBS, 1905–1954*, 89. The date of the Ogmore meeting was 10 February 1905: D. M. Phillips, *Evan Roberts*, 358. 'They say that they came especially to see the revival': 'The great Revival in Wales and Elsewhere', *The Christian Herald*, 23 February 1905, 168.
20. Awstin, Sunday 19 March, *Religious Revival in Wales*, No. .5; 'The Work in Wales', *The Christian*, 30 March 1905, Supplement 1; 'The Revival', *SWDN*, 4 May 1905, 6.
21. *SWDN*, 4 May 1905, 6. E. Wyn James deals with the miners' hymn: 'Emyn y Glowyr', *Y Cylchgrawn Efengylaidd*, 19:1, 1980.
22. Paul Passy and M. Sainton were two well-known Protestants belonging to the church at Rue de Lille: American Baptist Missionary Union, *Annual Report*, 1906, 386-7; 1907, 201.
23. 'A Great French Baptist in Edinburgh', *The Baptist Times*, 25 August 1905, 603.
24. Ibid.
25. Ibid.; Lewis Appleton, *Memoirs of Henry Richard* (London, 1889), 100, 133.
26. 'Llydaw a'r Diwygiad', *Yr Herald Gymraeg*, 2 May 1905, 5.
27. *SWDN*, 26 June 1905, 6; ibid., 29 August, 6; *The Baptist Times*, 25 August, op. cit.; 'Ad-drem ar y Diwygiad', *Y Tyst*, 28 Mawrth, 1906, 7; R. Tudur Jones, *Ffydd ac Argyfwng Cenedl*, vol. 2, 197-8.
28. Main works: Bois, *Le Réveil au Pays de Galles* (Toulouse, Introduction 1905); de Fursac, *Un mouvement mystique contemporain: Le réveil religieux du Pays de Galles 1904–5* (Paris, 1907)
29. Bois, *Le Réveil*, 104, 106.
30. Ibid., 598.
31. Ibid., 107 f., 117, 129.
32. The meeting at Briton Ferry was on 20 February 1905, and Dutchmen were also present at Cwmavon the following day. This meeting at Cwmavon was regarded 'as the most terrible meeting of the first Revival journey', D. M. Phillips, *Evan Roberts*, 362; *RRW*, No. 4, 20, 21 February 1905. Johannes de Heer was a member of the Dutch Reformed Church, but endeavoured to unite believers of all denominations. The emphasis on revival was confirmed by establishing a magazine in 1919, *Het Zoeklicht*. Information received from J. J. Pieterman, Holland.
33. Information from J. J. Pieterman.
34. 'The Welsh Revival', 9 March 1905, 544.
35. 'Revival Items', *SWDN*, 22 April 1905, 6.
36. 'Paris', *The British Weekly*, 11 May 1905, 111.
37. 'Newyddiadur Ffrengig a'r Diwygiad', *Y Goleuad*, 10 February 1905, 7.
38. For Paul Passy, see earlier section.
39. 'France and Switzerland', *SWDN*, 4 May 1905, 6.
40. 'Revival Far and Near', *The Christian*, 6 December 1905, 22.
41. 'The Spread of the Revival and its After Mission', *The Methodist Times*, 23 February 1905, 133.
42. School of Oriental and African Studies (SOAS): Methodist Missionary Society (MMS) Correspondence, Fiche 10, letter 24 March 1905; Whelpton worked in France from 1880 to 1906.
43. 'An Awakening at Cannes', *The Christian*, 16 February 1905, 16.
44. 'Revival Items', *SWDN*, 22 April 1905, 6.

45. 'Pioneer Mission Work in France', *The Baptist Times*, 1 September 1905, 627. R. Dubarry: Jack Hoad, *The Baptist* (London, 1986), 164. Dubarry was friendly with B. S. Fidler of the South Wales Bible College, Barry: Noel Gibbard, *Taught to Serve* (Bridgend, Evangelical Press of Wales, 1996), 113.
46. There was a young Methodist minister named Ullern working there: Mrs Penn-Lewis, 'Revival Expectations in France', *The Life of Faith*, 4 October 1905, 829.
47. 'News of the Revival in Wales and Elsewhere', *The Christian Herald*, 15 June 1905, 521.
48. Ibid., 18 May 1905, 433.
49. Ibid., 15 June, op. cit.
50. 'Report Baptist World Congress', *The Baptist Times*, 12 January 1906, 26.
51. 'Revival on the Continent', *The Christian*, 10 August 1905, 18; 'Revival on the Continent', *SWDN*, 17 August 1905, 6; 'Evangelical Wave in France', *The Christian Herald*, 31 August 1905, 190.
52. ABMU, *Annual Report*, 1906, 386.
53. 'News of the Revival in Wales and Elsewhere', *The Christian Herald*, 1 June 1905, 477; Archibald Brown ministered at West Norwood and in 1905 moved to the Tabernacle to share the ministry with Thomas Spurgeon; 'The College Conference', *The Sword and the Trowel*, June 1905.
54. Winifred M. Pearce, *Knight in Shining Armour;* 'What hath God Wrought!', *The Sword and the Trowel*, February 1905; ibid., 'With Pastor Thomas Spurgeon in the Welsh Revival', March 1905.
55. ABMU, *Annual Report*, 1906, 386.
56. 'Revivals', *Baptist Missionary Magazine* (America), 1906, 51.
57. 'The Revival in France', *SWDN*, 26 June 1905, 6.
58. Ibid.
59. 'Preparing for the European Baptist Congress, Berlin', *The Baptist Times*, 10 August 1906, 681.
60. *Ffydd ac Argyfwng Cenedl*, vol. 2, 197-8.
61. 'Revival Expectation in France', *The Life of Faith*, 4 October 1905, 829. Mrs Penn-Lewis and Pastor Saillens: he 'sought her aid against the forces of Satan', Brynmor Pierce Jones, *The Trials and Triumphs of Mrs Jessie Penn-Lewis* (North Brunswick, 1997), 163.
62. 'Paris', 11 May 1905, 111.
63. Bois, *Le Réveil*, 256.
64. *The Life of Faith*, 4 October 1905, 829.
65. 'Prayer and Faith in France', *The Christian Herald*, 26 October 1905, 367.
66. 'France and Revival', *The Christian*, 1 June 1905, Supplement vi.
67. 'France', *Evangelical Alliance Quarterly*, October 1905; 'United Conference in France', *The Christian*, 7 September 1905, 14.
68. Ibid.
69. 'Preparing for Revival in France', *The Christian Herald*, 12 October 1905, 322.
70. 'Revival in France', *The Christian*, 26 October 1905, 36; 'Gospel and Temperance Work in France', *The Welsh Evangelist*, February 1906.
71. J. Edwin Orr, *The Flaming Tongue*, 64; 'Revival in France', *The Christian Herald*, 9 November 1905, 411.
72. J. Edwin Orr, *The Flaming Tongue*, 63.
73. 'Preparing for the European Baptist Congress', *The Baptist Times*, 10 August 1906, 581; two of the leaders, M. Andru and M. Vincent, had been educated at Regent's Park College, London.
74. 'The Work in Wales', *The Life of Faith*, 29 November 1905, 1013.
75. 'Baptist Work on the Continent', *The Baptist Times*, 12 January 1906, 26.
76. 'Some Items', *The Life of Faith*, 2 January 1907, 18.

77. J. Edwin Orr, *The Flaming Tongue*, 62 3.
78. 'Switzerland and Revival', *The Christian*, 23 March 1905, Supplement III.
79. 'Foreign Intelligence', *Evangelical Christendom*, March 1906.
80. H. Elvet Lewis, *With Christ Among the Miners* (London, 1906), 152, and included in *Glory Filled the Land*, ed. Richard Owen Roberts (Illinois, 1989).
81. 'Foreign Intelligence', *Evangelical Christendom*, March 1906.
82. 'The Alliance at Chexbres', *Evangelical Christendom*, Sept–Oct 1907.
83. 'Letter from America', *The Christian*, 25 May 1905, 14.
84. Pasteur R. Saillens, 'Impressions of Algeria', *Missionary Review of the World*, June 1906, 449; taken from *The Sword and the Trowel*. 'Pastor Saillens in Algeria', *The Christian*, 15 February 1906, 24.
85. 'France and Algeria', *Baptist Missionary Magazine*, 1906, 51.
86. 'Pastor Saillens in Algeria', *The Christian*, 15 February 1906, 24.
87. *Annual Report* (BFBS), 1906, 157.
88. 'Baptists on the Continent', *The Baptist Times*, 29 November 1907, 877.
89. 'Baptists and Evangelism', *The Christian*, 5 March 1908.
90. 'Revival in France', *The Christian*, 7 November 1907, 13.
91. J. Edwin Orr, *The Flaming Tongue*, 64.
92. 'Mr Cory' was present at the annual meeting in 1905: 'The Pioneer Mission', *The Baptist Times*, 26 May 1905, 378.
93. 'The late George Soltau', *The Life of Faith*, 20 October 1909, 1183-4; Charlotte Hanbury, *Life of Mrs Head* (1905), 93, 169, 195, 203.
94. 'Emynau y Diwygiad yn y Ffrangeg', *Seren Cymru*, 2 February 1906, 7.
95. Ibid.
96. Jack Hoad, *The Baptist* (Grace Publications, 1986), 172.

## Chapter 3: Germany

1. For a summary of the background: A. P. F. Sell, *Theology in Turmoil* (Michigan, Baker Books, 1986), chapter 2.
2. For Dr Baedeker, see the section on Russia.
3. On her way to Russia: Mary N. Garrard, *Mrs Penn-Lewis, A Memoir* (Bournemouth, 1930), 84.
4. 'Plyg Ni, O Arglwydd', *The Life of Faith*, 15 February 1905, 131.
5. 'Pontycymer', *Y Tyst*, 16 August 1905; *Tarian y Gweithiwr*, 6 February 1905, 1.
6. Jacob Vetter: Dieter Lange, *Eine Bewegung bricht sich Bahn* (A Movement Forges Ahead), 165; Eifion Evans, *The Welsh Revival of 1904*, 150.
7. Ibid.; J. Seitz wrote on the Welsh Revival in *Auf der Warte*, eds., Bernstoff and Lohmann, e.g. February, March 1905; Walter J. Hollenweger, *The Pentecostals* (SCM Press, 1972), 178. For the Hirwaun meeting that Seitz attended: D. M. Phillips, *Evan Roberts*, 348-9.
8. 'Cynhadledd y Forward Movement', *Y Goleuad*, 25 August 1905, 5; 'Revivalist's Activities', *SWDN*, 15 August 1905, 6; 'Lloffion y Mis', *Y Cyfaill*, October 1905.
9. 'Pontycymer', *Y Tyst*, 16 August 1905; 'Y Diwygiad', *Y Gwyliedydd*, 8 June 1905, 5.
10. 'Evan Roberts and the German Penitent', *The Christian Herald*, 24 August 1905, 168. The meeting was at the Ystrad boarding house, Llandrindod. The term 'penitent' refers to a German visitor who was in distress and disturbed the meeting; Evan Roberts and others had to counsel him.
11. 'An Evangelistic Countess', *The Christian Herald*, 12 April 1905, 513; ibid., 'A Countess as Missionary', 11 January 1906, 37. Other ladies mentioned: Mrs Seitz, Saxony (cf. Seitz, reference 7); Mrs Shramm, Leipzig, and Miss Uffrous, Sweden: 'The Great Revival in Wales', ibid., 23 February 1905, 168.
12. Eva von Tiele-Winckler, *Denkstein des lebendigen Gottes* (Signs to the living God)

(*Brunuen Taschen-Buch Nr.* 8, 1970, Giesse M. Basel); details of background and visit to Wales, 34-43.

13. Ibid.
14. Ibid.
15. Dieter Lange, *Eine Bewegung*, 164; 'Plyg ni, O Arglwydd', *The Life of Faith*, 15 February 1905, 131; Eifion Evans, *The Welsh Revival of 1904*, 69.
16. 'German Nobility Visit Welsh Revival', *The Christian Herald*, 7 September 1905, 212-13.
17. Dieter Lange, *Eine Bewegung*, 165.
18. 'The Awakening in Wales and Elsewhere', *The Life of Faith*, 31 May 1905, 436.
19. Martin Girkon (1860–1907): from 1884 he was in Oberfriedrichsdorf; from 1899 in Müllheim: Dieter Lange, *Eine Bewegung*, 164-5. Modersohn is referred to as one who was baptised 'with power from above': Hollenweger, *The Pentecostals*, 63; *The Life of Faith*, 31 May 1905, 436.
20. Mattersey, Donald Gee Centre, Schmidt, 'Divine, Demented or Demonic?', 2.
21. *The Life of Faith*, 31 May 1905, 436.
22. Ibid.
23. Ibid.; NLW, Jessie Penn-Lewis Collection, postcard to Miss Soltau, 27 May 1905.
24. Ibid., letter to 'My darling Granine', 27 May 1905.
25. 'The Revival in Wales and Elsewhere', *The Life of Faith*, 7 June 1905, 455.
26. Ibid., 'Revival Notes', 15 February 1905, 136. Details of Dr Baedeker's visit: 'Dr Baedeker's Continental Tour', *The Evangelical Alliance Quarterly*, April 1905.
27. J. Edwin Orr, *The Flaming Tongue*, 44.
28. 'Wandsbeck Convention', *The Life of Faith*, 24 May 1905, 407; ibid., 'Pentecostal Days in Germany', 28 June 1905, 523.
29. Nora Usher, 'Among the Jews in Hamburg', *The Christian*, 4 October 1905, 16.
30. D. M. Phillips, *Evan Roberts*, 345. F. S. Webster: he was educated at Oxford; was curate of St Aldate's, Oxford, vicar of St Thomas's, Birmingham, and became rector of All Souls, Langham Place, London, in 1898. 'The Rev. F. S. Webster', *The Christian Herald*, 16 March 1905, 234.
31. 'Pentecostal Days in Germany', *The Life of Faith*, 28 June 1905, 455.
32. Ibid.
33. Ibid. The spirit of revival was also experienced at the conference in 1906: 'The Wandsbeck Conference', *The Christian Herald*, 5 July 1906, 14.
34. 'Revival Work in Germany', *The Christian Herald*, 12 April 1906, 345.
35. 'Awakening in Germany', *The Christian*, 20 July 1905, 21.
36. Ibid.; *The Evangelical Alliance Quarterly*, December 1905, 139.
37. Report of Julius Rohrbach, T*he Evangelical Alliance Quarterly*, December 1905. He had written on 'Gospel work in Germany', expressing his commitment to biblical authority: *The Christian*, 26 January 1905, 15.
38. 'The Blankenburg Conference', *The Evangelical Alliance Quarterly*, October 1905, 124-5; the main organisers were Pastor Janssen, B. Kuhn and Karl Mascher.
39. Dieter Lange, *Eine Bewegung*, 166.
40. 'The Blankenburg Conference', *The Evangelical Alliance Quarterly*, October 1905, 124-5.
41. Ibid.
42. 'The Evangelical Alliance and the Present Need of Russia', *The Evangelical Alliance Quarterly*, October 1905, 121-4; Fiedler, *Story of Faith Missions*, 225.
43. Hans Brandenburg, *The Meek and the Mighty* (London and Oxford, 1974), 145.
44. Dieter Lange, *Eine Bewegung*, 187.
45. Newton Marshall, 'Preparing for the European Baptist Congress, Berlin 1908', *The Baptist Times*, 15 June 1906, 430.
46. Eberhard Arnold: Markus Baum, *Against the Wind* (Plough Publishing House, 1998);

Eberhard and Emmy Arnold, *Seeking for the Kingdom of God* (Plough Publishing House, New York, 1974). The invitation to the Bible School: Baum, *Against the Wind*, 53; Arnold also turned down an invitation to be a tutor in the home of Baron von Tiele-Winckler, ibid., 44.

47. *Seeking for the Kingdom of God*, xv; Baum, *Against the Wind*, 9.
48. Baum, *Against the Wind*, 45-6.
49. Ibid., 53.
50. Ibid., 12-15.
51. Ibid., 25-6, 262 n.21; 'Kühn was a simple man, small and physically deformed. He was anything but an intellectual yet he possessed immense charisma', 25; *Seeking for the Kingdom of God*, 61.
52. Ibid., 19.
53. Ibid., 22-5.
54. Ibid., 23.
55. 'Baptist Work on the Continent', *The Baptist Times*, 12 January 1906, 26.
56. Baum, *Against the Wind*, 24.
57. Ibid., 25, 261 n.17.
58. Ibid., 60-1. The change was radical: 'His theology acquired bizarre elements, and he became a Christadelphian', ibid., 256 n.16.
59. Ibid., 41; *Seeking for the Kingdom of God*, 49 n.2; Emmy Hollander, *A Joyful Pilgrimage* (Plough Publishing House, reprint 1976), 11.
60. Ibid., 26.
61. 'Revival Notes', *The Life of Faith*, 13 May 1908, 504.
62. Mattersey, Donald Gee Centre, letter from Redern to Mrs Penn-Lewis, 17 December 1907, in which he refers to the Wasserzug family—one of whom had accompanied Eva von Tiele-Winckler to Wales. Reference to Wasserzug in *The Overcomer* (Mrs Penn-Lewis), 1909, 156. Dr Baedeker was also acquainted with the Tiele-Winckler family: 'Dr Baedeker's Continental Tour', *Evangelical Christendom*, May 1906. The Wincklers and Pastor Lohmann are mentioned in a list of correspondents, NLW, Jessie Penn-Lewis Collection, Nos 30, 35, 36 and 40.
63. Dieter Lange, *Eine Bewegung*, 167, 174.
64. *Seeking for the Kingdom of God*, 44-5.
65. Jonathan Anton Alexander Paul (1853–1931): he began his ministry on Pommeren in 1880; he was an author and his writings include defence of Pentecostalism, hymns and (with others) translation of the New Testament into German. He was the founder of the Müllheim Association, Stanley M. Burgess, Gary B. McGee, eds., *Dictionary of Pentecostal and Charismatic Movements* (Zondervan, Michigan, 1988), 664.
66. Schmidt, 'Divine, Demented or Demonic?', 4. Emil Meyer (1869–1950): he was a prominent preacher and a leading advocate of the tongues movement, Dieter Lange, *Eine Bewegung*, 175, 175 n.409.
67. Ibid., 4; Baum, *Against the Wind*, 263 n.14.
68. Ibid.
69. Baum, *Against the Wind*, 42-3; *Seeking for the Kingdom of God*, 44.
70. Schmidt, 'Divine, Demented or Demonic?', 4-5.
71. Ibid., 6-7; Hollenweger, *The Pentecostals*, 223.
72. It was more divisive than the matter of baptism: Baum, *Against the Wind*, 42.
73. Dieter Lange, *Eine Bewegung*, 186-7. Copies of the Declaration: Mattersey, Donald Gee Centre, 'Translation Copy of Resolutions' and, with variations in the wording, Brynmor Pierce Jones, *Trials and Triumphs*, 175. Mrs Penn-Lewis staunchly supported the anti-tongues movement, e.g. *The Life of Faith*, 'He Stood—and the Lord Wrought', 2 January 1907, 13; 'The Spirit of Truth', 3 June 1907, 585-6; 'The Present Onslaught', 29 May 1907, 469. A. T. Pierson was another supporter, and wrote a series of articles to *The Christian*, 9, 16, 23 May 1907.

74. *Confidence*, April 1908.
75. Emil Humburg (1874–1965): he became the pastor of the largest Pentecostal Assembly in Germany. In 1911 he was the President of the Senior Pastors Conference, *Dictionary of Pentecostal and Charismatic Movements*, 452.
76. Mrs Penn-Lewis continued to fight the tongues movement (see note 73), while A. A. Boddy, Sunderland, crossed to Hamburg to support the movement: 'Remarkable Revival in Scandinavia', *The Life of Faith*, 13 March 1907, 222.
77. 'The Spreading Fire in Europe', *The Life of Faith*, 25 October 1905, 888; report of Pastor Szalay in *The Christian Herald*, 24 August 1905, 169; 'Awakening in Hungary', *The Christian*, 10 August 1905, 26.
78. J. Edwin Orr, *The Flaming Tongue*, 61.
79. *RRW*, No. 3, 10 June 1905; 'Cynhadledd y Forward Movement yn Llandrindod', *Y Goleuad*, 25 August 1905, 5; 'Y Diwygiad a Phapyrau Tramor', *Yr Herald Cymraeg*, 21 February 1905, 6.
80. 'The Revival', *SWDN*, 22 April 1905.

## Chapter 4: Scandinavian Countries

1. J. Edwin Orr, *The Flaming Tongue*, 51.
2. The editorial, *The Missionary Review of the World*, December 1905; 'The Revival in Norway', *SWDN*, 17 August 1905, 6.
3. J. Edwin Orr, *The Flaming Tongue*, 51.
4. 'On Sunday night, 5 October, we opened the City Mission with a meeting in Tivoli theatre', Thomas Ball Barratt, *When the Fire Fell* (Oslo, 1927), 79. Thomas Ball Barratt (1862–1940), *Dictionary of Pentecostal and Charismatic Movements*, 50.
5. Ibid., 87.
6. Ibid., 82.
7. J. Edwin Orr, *The Flaming Tongue*, 52. But Jessie Penn-Lewis says he was converted in 'Armenia': 'Norway', The *Christian Herald*, 8 June 1905, 488-9.
8. 'The "Evan Roberts" of Wales', *The Christian Herald*, 13 July 1905, 36-7; 'Revival Far and Near', *The Life of Faith*, 14 December 1905, 16.
9. 'Y Diwygiad', *Y Goleuad*, 25 August 1905, 9.
10. Barratt, *When the Fire Fell*, 95.
11. Ibid., 96, 97. At the time he was busy arranging prayer meetings for revival. The letter, with slight differences of wording, was included in *The Evening Express*, 11 February 1905, 3.
12. 'The Awakening in Wales and Elsewhere', *The Life of Faith*, 24 May 1905, 416.
13. 'Revival in Norway', *The Life of Faith*, 5 July 1905, 544.
14. 'The Great Revival in Wales and Elsewhere', *The Christian Herald*, 26 January 1905, 83; 'News of the Revival in Wales', 8 June 1905, 498-9.
15. 'A Great Revival in Norway', *The Missionary Review of the World*, April 1906, 310.
16. Nils Bloch-Hoell, *The Pentecostal Movement* (Oslo and London, 1964), 75; Hollenweger, *The Pentecostals*, 63.
17. 'A Note from Sweden', *The Life of Faith*, 19 January 1905, 23.
18. 'Cerbyd yr Iachawdwriaeth', *Tarian y Gweithiwr*, 16 February 1905, 1.
19. 'The Awakening in Wales and Elsewhere', *The Life of Faith*, 24 May 1905, 416.
20. Ibid.
21. J. Edwin Orr, *The Flaming Tongue*, 56.
22. 'The Anglesea Mission', *The British Weekly*, 22 June 1905, 264. A few names are given, including Rev. J. C. Isaksson, Landskrona, Sweden, and Pastor J. H. Ohrn, Christiana: 'The Great Revival in Wales and Elsewhere', *The Christian Herald*, 13 April 1905, 322.
23. 'Y Diwygiad yn Sweden', *Y Goleuad*, 3 November 1905, 5.
24. Ibid.

25. Ibid.
26. Ibid. Mrs Penn-Lewis refers to 'the remarkable conference of October', 'A Long Steady Battle', *The Life of Faith*, 14 March 1906, 230.
27. 'Sweden', *The Christian*, 25 January 1906, 23.
28. 'A Long Steady Battle', *The Life of Faith*, 14 March 1906, 230.
29. In a letter, 12 August 1905, she thanked Mrs Penn-Lewis for the report of Keswick in *The Life of Faith*;.she related how she was helped by God in meetings, but opposed by two clergymen who did not like women addressing meetings: NLW, Jessie Penn-Lewis Collection; cf. Brynmor Pierce Jones, *Trials and Triumphs*, 139.
30. Brynmor Pierce Jones, *Trials and Triumphs*, 163.
31. J. Edwin Orr, *The Flaming Tongue*, 57.
32. 'Finland', *Evangelical Christendom*, March 1906.
33. J. Edwin Orr, *The Flaming Tongue*, 54.
34. Ibid., 55.
35. 'Prayers for Denmark', *SWDN*, 21 April 1905, 6. P. M. S. Jensin wrote the personal letter; signatories of the other letter: S. K. Nielsen, O. H. L. Jensen, C. Mathiasen, N. Edellio, Chr. Andreasen, J. M. Lassen, Vilk. Petersen and J. P. Lursen.
36. Ibid.
37. 'The Awakening in Wales and Elsewhere', *The Life of Faith*, 21 June 1905, 495.
38. 'Y Diwygiad yn Denmark', *Y Goleuad*, 4 August 1905, 6.
39. Hans Peter Mollerup: he was the son of a Lutheran pastor; joined the Midnight Mission in the slums of Copenhagen; from 1896 to 1900 worked with the Mission to Seamen in Hull, England. He returned to Denmark to pastor Freeport Chapel, Copenhagen, and commenced a Danish Cross Church Army: James E. Worsfold, *The Origins of the Apostolic Church in Great Britain* (Wellington, New Zealand, 1991), 232.
40. 'An Alliance Deputation to Copenhagen, Denmark', *Evangelical Christendom*, January 1906; 'Good News from Copenhagen', *The Life of Faith*, 15 November 1905, 963. The two-man deputation from the Alliance—F. S. Webster and W. Fuller Gooch: 'Revival in Denmark', *The Christian*, 16 November 1905, 14. There are interesting references to Fuller Gooch in David G. Fountain, *E. J. Poole-Connor, Contender for the Faith* (Worthing, 1966), 101-2.
41. Ibid.
42. Ibid.
43. Mary N. Garrard, *Mrs Penn-Lewis*, 154; NLW, Jessie Penn-Lewis Collection. Countess Moltke was Baroness Marie Bille. She was the Over-Mistress of the Royal Court of HM Queen of Denmark: Worsfold, *Origins of the Apostolic Church*, 234; T. Tatlow, *The Story of the Student Christian Movement* (London, 1933), 181; J. Edwin Orr, *The Flaming Tongue*, 50.
44. 'Good News from Copenhagen', *The Life of Faith*, 15 November 1905, 963; ibid., 'The Spreading Flame', 25 October 1905, 888. Denmark: Worsfold, *Origins of the Apostolic Church*, 234; T. Tatlow, *The Story of the Student Christian Movement* (London, 1933), 181; J. Edwin Orr, *The Flaming Tongue*, 50.
45. 'Revival Meetings in a Royal Wood', *The Christian Herald*, 5 July 1906, 14.
46. Ibid.
47. 'Revival Times in Denmark', *Evangelical Christendom*, January 1907, 7; ibid., 'Second Alliance Convention in Copenhagen', July 1906.
48. Ibid.
49. J. Edwin Orr, *The Flaming Tongue*, 56.
50. 'Our God is a Consuming Fire', *The Life of Faith*, 6 June 1905, 492-3.
51. Synan, *Holiness–Pentecostal Movements in the USA*, 96.
52. C. F. Parham (1873–1929): 'Parham formulated classical Pentecostal theology in Topeka, Kansas, in 1901, and thus deserves recognition as founder of the Pentecostal

movement', *Dictionary of Pentecostal and Charismatic Movements*, 660.
53. W. J. Seymour (1870–1922): he was 'the leading figure' in the Azusa Street Mission; detailed article by Synan, *Dictionary of Pentecostal and Charismatic Movements*, 778-81, with photograph; Harvey Cox, *Fire From Heaven*, chs. 2 and 3.
54. Synan: *Holiness–Pentecostal Movements in the USA*, 53, 54.
55. Joseph Smale (1867–1926): he ministered as a Baptist before setting up the New Testament Church early in 1906; before the end of his life he was pastor of Grace Baptist Church: *Dictionary of Pentecostal and Charismatic Movements*, 791.
56. Dayton, ed., *How Pentecost Came to Los Angeles*, 18.
57. Ibid., 22.
58. 'Los Angeles', *The Christian*, 27 July 1905, Supplement vi; ibid., 'California', 17 May 1906, 4. The date given is 28 May, but cf. Dayton, ed., *How Pentecost came to Los Angeles*, 16, giving 17 June; Hollenweger, *Pentecostals*, 27 n.10, says July, and Nils Bloch-Hoell mentions July, 'on his return from Wales', 33.
59. Ibid.
60. Dayton, ed., *How Pentecost Came to Los Angeles*, 62.
61. Synan in the introduction to Frank Bartleman, *Azusa Street* (1925), xii.
62. Dayton, ed., *How Pentecost Came to Los Angeles*, 11.
63. Ibid., 18.
64. Ibid., 64.
65. Ibid., 65; letter 14 November 1905.
66. Barratt, *When the Fire Fell*, 100.
67. Ibid., 103.
68. Ibid., 100, 103, 105, 123, 127. Strangely, Donald Gee does not refer to the November meeting: *Wind and Flame*, 16.
69. Ibid., 142.
70. Donald Gee, *Wind and Flame*, 20.
71. Nils Bloch-Hoell, *The Pentecostal Movement*, 68.
72. Donald Gee, *Wind and Flame*, 26. Petrus Lewi Pethrus (1884–1974): an international Pentecostal leader and prolific writer. A Baptist, but became a Pentecostal in 1907 under the influence of T. B. Barratt. Pethrus was expelled from the Swedish Baptist Convention in 1913; he remained in Philadelphia, Stockholm, until 1958: *Dictionary of Pentecostal and Charismatic Movements*, 711-12, with photograph. Barratt and Pethrus: David Bundy, 'Swedish Pentecostal Mission Theory And Practice To 1930: Foundational Values In Conflict', *25th Meeting of the Society for Pentecostal Studies and the European Pentecostal and Charismatic Research Association, 10-14 July 1905* (Mattersey, Doncaster).
73. Barratt, *When the Fire Fell*, 146; ibid., chapter xiv for later developments.
74. Donald Gee, *Wind and Flame*, 26. It was from Denmark that Barratt crossed to be with A. A. Boddy in Sunderland, England, to share in Pentecostal work in that place: Barratt, *When the Fire Fell*, 149.
75. Worsfold, *The Origins of the Apostolic Church in Great Britain*, 233.

## Chapter 5: Russia

1. Hans Brandenburg, *The Meek and the Mighty*, 46; Hollenweger, *The Pentecostals*, 269-70.
2. Brandenburg, *The Meek and the Mighty*, 47.
3. Ibid., 100.
4. Ibid., 102; Pavlov's sufferings: J. H. Rushbrooke, *Baptists in the USSR* (London, 1943), 4; Michael Bourdeaux, *Faith on Trial in Russia* (London, 1971), 32-6.
5. David Fountain, *Lord Radstock* (Southampton, Mayflower Books, 1988).
6. R. S. Latimer, *Dr Baedeker and His Apostolic Work in Russia* (London, 1907).

7. Latimer, *Dr Baedeker*, ch. XIII especially.
8. Ibid. Photograph of the Lieven family opposite page 80: Princess Lieven, Princess Mary (killed in an accident), Princess Alicia, Princess Sophie, Prince Paul and Prince Anatol. Prince Anatol was elected President of the Russian Evangelical Alliance in 1909: 'The Evangelical Alliance Annual Meeting', *The Life of Faith*, 5 May, 1909.
9. Princess Sophie Lieven, 'A Seed That Brought Forth Much Fruit', Typescript, Oxford Centre for Mission Studies, Keston, Oxford.
10. Brandenburg, *The Meek and the Mighty*, 105.
11. Lieven, 'A Seed', 8.
12. Ibid., 18.
13. Was active in Bible distribution: 'large supplies of Scriptures have been purchased for the sick and the wounded by Colonel Paschkoff', *Annual Report*, BFBS, 1879, 95.
14. Fountain, *Lord Radstock*, 28, 39.
15. Latimer, *Dr Baedeker*, 78.
16. Johann Kargel: he came from Bulgaria and had a Turkish passport which protected him from the police for some time, but was banished from St. Petersburg (Petrograd), with Count Korff. Wielded wide influence on young and old, peasants and academics: Brandenburg, *The Meek and the Mighty*, 131-2; R. S. Latimer, 'Russia's Opportunity', *The Christian*, 16 July 1905, 19.
17. Latimer, *Dr Baedeker*, 113, 129, 143; also, a photograph of von Wrede, opposite page 164; W. T. Stunt, et al., *Turning the World Upside Down: A Century of Missionary Endeavour* (Bath, Echoes of Service, 1972), 353-5.
18. Baron Paul Nicolay (died 1919): a Finnish nobleman; settled in a large estate in Monrepos, Finland; studied law in St. Petersburg, and while there was introduced by Count Pahlen, a close friend, to the Lieven circle. He was influenced by Keswick pietism; committed to student and social work: Brandenburg, *The Meek and the Mighty*, 136-8; C. Howard Hopkins, *John R. Mott*, 250. Mrs Penn-Lewis corresponded with Nicolay's biographer, Hedwig von Redern, named in the list of correspondents: NLW, Jessie Penn-Lewis Collection, and Mattersey, Donald Gee Centre, letter from von Redern, 17:12:07.
19. Hopkins, *John R. Mott*, 250-1.
20. Lieven, 'A Seed', 50, 86.
21. Brandenburg, *The Meek and the Mighty*, 139.
22. Baron Uixküll: he was a rich landowner; became a Christian in 1890 and was baptised in 1892 by one of the believing peasants. The Baron preached regularly and became treasurer of the Baptist Union of Russia. Had a significant role in establishing the Berlin College and personally collected money for a theological school at Lodz, Poland. 'A Russian Baptist Nobleman', *The British Weekly*, 20 July 1905, 363; 'Signs of the Times', *The Missionary Review of the World*, 1908, 407; 'Byd-gynghres y Bedyddwyr', *Seren Cymru*, 21 July 1905.
23. 'A Vast Change in Russia', *The Life of Faith*, 2 January 1907, 13.
24. Visits of Mrs Penn-Lewis to Russia: Mary N. Garrard, *Mrs Penn-Lewis*, chapter V, 174-6; Brynmor Pierce Jones, *Trials and Triumphs*, chapter 8.
25. Garrard, *Mrs Penn-Lewis*, 117, 134; Brynmor Pierce Jones, *Trials and Triumphs*, 67.
26. Garrard, *Mrs Penn-Lewis*, 92.
27. Princess Lieven, 'A Seed', 47.
28. Garrard, *Mrs Penn-Lewis*, 97.
29. NLW, Jessie Penn-Lewis Collection, letter from Mrs Penn-Lewis to 'My precious Granine & beloved Co', 7 May 1905.
30. Ibid., to 'Dear Brethren and Sisters in Christ', 17 October 1905.
31. Ibid., letter dated 17 August 1905.
32. 'The Awakening in Wales', *The Life of Faith*, 3 May 1905, 357; 'Neath'; *SWDN*, 24 April 1905, 6.

33. Other sources: Awstin, *Religious Revival in Wales*, No 2; D. M. Phillips, *Evan Roberts*, 326, 351.

34. William Fetler, *The Leading of God* (Russian Missionary Society, 3rd edn.), 3-5; Howard B. Grose, 'Wilhelm Fetler, Revival Evangelist', *Missions*, 1911, 664-8; A. McCaig, *Wonders of Grace in Russia* (Latvia, 1926), ch. 17.

35. Winifred M. Pierce, *Knight in Royal Service*, 14, with photograph of students; Allan Titley, 'Land Aflame', *The Evangelical Magazine of Wales*, 13:5, 1974.

36. Caradoc Jones, 'The 1904–5 Revival', *The Evangelical Magazine of Wales*, 7:5, 1968.

37. John Wood, *Born in the Fire* (n.d.), 3, and reference made to other visits to the Rhondda. Another author comments on Fetler's visit to Wales, 'He was never the same afterwards, his great burden being that God would send revival to Latvia and Russia': T. Omri Jenkins, *Five Minutes to Midnight* (Evangelical Press, 1989), 17.

38. Winifred M. Pierce, *Knight in Royal Service*, 15-16; 'Revival at the Tabernacle', *The Baptist Times*, 7 April 1905, 262, 14 April, 279; and reports in *The Christian Herald*, 6 April 1905, 300, 18 May, 14-15, 1 June, 477.

39. W. Fetler, 'Glad Tidings from Russia', *The Life of Faith*, 2 May 1906, 384.

40. Ibid., 'The Spreading Joy in Russia', 29 August 1906, 792.

41. Ibid.

42. Ibid.

43. 'Siberia', *The Life of Faith*, 31 October 1906, 977.

44. Ibid., 'Week of Prayer for Russia', 3 October 1906, 883; 'Echoes of the Week of Prayer', 31 October 1906, 977.

45. Ibid., 'Russia', 2 January 1907, 13.

46. Ibid., 'Keswick in Russia', 14 November 1906, 1025.

47. Ibid., 'The Spreading Joy', 5 September 1906, 806.

48. Ibid., 'Russia Won't Perish', 19 December 1906, 1237.

49. Ibid., 'Glad Tidings from Russia', 16 May 1906, 423.

50. Caradoc Jones, *The Evangelical Magazine of Wales*, 7:5, 1968. J. Edwin Orr, *The Flaming Tongue*, 62, gives 1909 as Fetler's return to Russia, but it was 1907.

51. J. W. Ewing, 'Baptist Opportunity in Russia', *The Baptist Times*, 18 December 1908, 881.

52. Howard B. Grose, *Missions*, 1911, 666.

53. Michael Rowe, *Russian Resurrection* (London, 1994), 49.

54. D. R. Owen, 'Llwyddiant y Gwirionedd yn Rwsia', *Seren Cymru*, 8 November 1907, 7.

55. Had 'just started Sunday school' in November 1907: 'Baptists on the Continent', *Baptist Times*, 29 November 1907, 877. For further development, 'Russia's Opportunity', *The Christian*, 18 June 1908, 16; A. McCaig, *Wonders of Grace*, chs. 3, 4 and 8; Robert Sloan Latimer, *With Christ in Russia* (London, 1910), chs. 3, 4 and 5.

56. 'Foreign Correspondence', *Evangelical Christendom*, December 1906; ibid., 'Liberty and Love in Russia', January 1907.

57 Howard B. Grose, *Mission*, 668.

58. Could have been established during his college days, because Fetler refers to it in 1908, when he returned to England for a brief period. Madam Tchertkoff was also present at the centre, 'Pray for Russia', *The Life of Faith*, 4 November 1908, 1154. Later, the Welshman John Thomas was one of the speakers with William Fetler at Slavanka; notice of the convention in *The Overcomer*, July 1922.

## Chapter 6: United States of America

1. There is a detailed study by Iain Murray, *Revival and Revivalism* (Banner of Truth, Edinburgh, 1994).

2. 'Topeka Revival', *Dictionary of Pentecostal and Holiness Movements*, 850-2; Vinson Synan, *Holiness–Pentecostal Movements in the USA*, 81; also refers to earlier

examples of speaking in tongues, and traces the fragmentation of the Holiness Movement in chapters II, III and IV.

3. Vinson Synan, 55-7.
4. 'Anglesey Mission', *SWDN*, 17 June 1905, 6.
5. J. Edwin Orr, *The Flaming Tongue*, 65.
6. Ibid., 75, 76, 77.
7. *Michigan Christian Herald*, 9 February 1905.
8. Ibid., leading article, 1 June 1905.
9. Ibid., 9 February 1905.
10. Ibid.
11. Ibid; 'The Great Welsh Revival', *The Examiner*, 19 January 1905.
12. *The Examiner*, 19 January 1905.
13. Ibid.
14. *Lessons on the Welsh Revival* (London, 1904) and published in *Revival*, vol. 37, 1931; as 'The Source and Power of the Welsh Revival' in *The Christian Commonwealth* (London); reprinted in *The Congregationalist* (Boston, Pilgrim Press, n.d.), and as 'The Revival' in *Glory Filled The Land*, ed. Richard Owen Roberts. In 1907, *With Christ Among the Miners* by Elvet Lewis was published in New York and Cincinnati.
15. Chicago, New York and Toronto, 1905. Contributors: Arthur Goodrich, Campbell Morgan, W. T. Stead, W. W. Moore and Evan Hopkins.
16. Details in 'Publisher's Note'.
17. Robert F. Coyle, *The Great Revival in Wales* (New York, 1905), 17f. D. M. Phillips, one of the biographers of Evan Roberts, contributed to the volume: 'The Progress of the Great Welsh Revival', taken from *The British Weekly*, 15 December 1904.
18. 'Cynadledd Fawr y Diwygiad', *Y Tyst*, 8 March 1905, 9; Griffith John, Swansea, of the London Missionary Society, received a copy of Pierson's *Acts of the Apostles* when the author was preparing to go to Wales to help with the revival: Noel Gibbard, *Griffith John* (Bryntirion Press, Bridgend, 1998), 179.
19. 'The Awakening in Wales', *The Life of Faith*, 22 March 1905, 231-2.
20. Arthur Goodrich, *The Story*, 59.
21. J. Edwin Orr, *The Flaming Tongue*, 179.
22. George T. B. Davies, *When The Fire Fell* (Philadelphia, 1945), 77. The Swansea meetings were held 1-4 January 1905: D. M. Phillips, *Evan Roberts*, 331-40.
23. Davies, *When The Fire Fell*, 76-8.
24. Ibid., 76, 79.
25. 'Cenadwri at Eglwys Dduw', *Yr Herald Cymraeg*, 18 July 1905, 1-3.
26. *The Christian Herald*, 15 February 1906, 152.
27. *The Missionary Review of the World*, 1905, 300.
28. 'American Revivals', *The Christian Herald*, 16 March 1905, 231.
29. Ibid.; J. Edwin Orr, *The Flaming Tongue*, 73.
30. J. Edwin Orr, *The Flaming Tongue*, 73.
31. Ibid.
32. Ibid., 79.
33. 'Revival in the United States', *The Christian Herald*, 2 February 1905, 99.
34. Ibid.; 'Great Awakening in Denver USA', *The Life of Faith*, 22 February 1905, 157.
35. J. Edwin Orr, *The Flaming Tongue*, 80; Brynmor Pierce Jones, *Instrument of Revival*, 275.
36. 'British Columbia', *The Missionary Review of the World*, October 1905, 786.

## Chapter 7: The Welsh Communities

1. Gwilym R. Roberts, *New Lives in the Valley* (New Hampshire, 1998), 227. Even in Hyde Park, regarded as the 'Welsh town' of Scranton, colliers were leaving the pit for

the office: Bill Jones, 'Y Gymuned Wir Gymreig Fwyaf yn y Byd', *Cof Cenedl*, ed. Geraint H. Jenkins (Llandysul, 1993), VIII, 173.

2. Jay G. Williams, *Memory Stones* (New York, 1993), 108.
3. Ibid., 39; idem; *Songs of Praises* (New York, 1996).
4. Emrys Jones, 'Some Aspects of Cultural Change in an American Welsh Community', *Transactions Honourable Society of Cymmrodorion*, 1952.
5. David Jones, *Memorial Volume of Welsh Congregationalists in Pennsylvania* (Utica, 1934), 51.
6. Jay G. Williams, *Memory Stones*, 39.
7. L. Ton Evans (Junius): T. M. Bassett and S. H. Olsen, 'Lewis Ton Evans (Junius)', *Trafodion Cymdeithas Hanes y Bedyddwyr*, 1993; 'Nodion o Dalaethau Dwyreiniol America', *Seren Cymru*, 17 February 1905.
8. T. Gwernogle Evans: he was born in Merthyr Tydfil and was educated in the Bala Congregational College. Ministered in Wales; moved to Taylor, Pa., and Granville, New York. Returned to minister in Wales and turned Presbyterian: David Jones, *Memorial Volume*, 232; T. D. Gwernogle Evans, *Bras Hanes Ei Hunan* (Aberteifi, n.d.). Other examples: Morien Môn Hughes and R. Sirhowy Jones.
9. 'Newcastle', *Seren Cymru*, 21 July 1905, 11.
10. Ibid., '*Diwygiad Disymwth*', 3 March 1905, 9.
11. Ibid. R. Tudur Jones refers to H. P. Roberts, *Ffydd ac Argyfwng Cenedl*, vol. 2, 195, 224 n.65, and cites J. Edwin Orr as his source; but Orr refers to J. D. Roberts: *The Flaming Tongue*, 70. J. D. Roberts ministered at Johnstown, Pennsylvania.
12. 'Diwygiad Disymwth', *Seren Cymru*, 3 March 1905, 9.
13. John Thomas Griffith (1845–1917): he was born in Pen-marc, South Wales; the first Welshman to be educated in Crozer Seminary, Pennsylvania; spent his last years in Maesteg, South Wales: *Reminiscences* (Morriston, 1913), 118; B. G. Owens, 'Casgliad Coleg y Bedyddwyr, Bangor', *TCHB*, 1973.
14. Letter to Spinther, 27 April 1905, NLW, 'Casgliad Spinther'.
15. *Reminiscences*, 119.
16. 'Fair Haven', *Y Cyfaill*, March 1905, 126.
17. Ibid., 127.
18. Ibid., April 1905, 162.
19. 'Cwrs y Byd', *Y Lladmerydd*, March 1905.
20. 'Lloffion y Mis', *Y Cyfaill*, June 1906, 245, 'Nid oes genyf [*sic*] oleuni oddiwrth yr Arglwydd wneuthur unrhyw addewid i ddyfod trosodd' [I have no light from the Lord to make any promise to come to you].
21. Ibid., 'Granville', March 1905, 126.
22. Ibid., 'Adgofion am Flwyddyn y Diwygiad yn Middle Granville', March 1906, 124-5.
23. Ibid.
24. 'Rev. Maurice Griffith at Home', *The Llanelly Mercury*, 28 September 1905, 7.
25. T. Solomon Griffiths: he was an elder in Moriah, Utica, editor of *Y Cyfaill*: Daniel Jenkins Willams, *A Hundred Years of Welsh Calvinistic Methodism in America* (Philadelphia, 1937), 65, with a photograph opposite 66. The author of the history was preaching in Wales during the Revival, and preached every night for five weeks in Anglesey: 'Y Parch Daniel Jenkins Williams', *Y Cyfaill*, September 1906.
26. *Y Cyfaill*, March 1906.
27. Joseph Roberts: received by the Vermont Presbytery from Wales in 1870; he was home missionary and pastor; retired 1916; died 1921: Daniel Jenkins Williams, *Hundred Years*, 362, 436.
28. Ibid., 435: received by transfer from Wales, 1905.
29. Ibid., 432: received by the South Pennsylvania Presbytery, 1887.
30. Ibid., 426: transfer from Wales to Minnesota, 1883. His wife was in Wales during the

early part of the Revival; a special meeting was arranged to welcome her back: *Y Cyfaill*, 1905, 29.

31. *Y Cyfaill*, March 1906.
32. David Jones: preacher, poet, historian and hymn-writer. Born in Brecon, Wales; educated Bala Congregational College; ordained Newquay, 5 December 1883. In America, pastor at Scranton; died 8 September 1933; his wife was Hannah Jane Humphries, Towyn, North Wales: biography by J. Twyson Jones in David Jones, *Memorial Volume*, 281-5.
33. T. C. Edwards (1848–1927), *DWB*.
34. 'Amrywion o Scranton', *Y Tyst*, 24 May 1905, 6. J. Twyson Jones: was born in Sirhowy, Tredegar; educated Spring Hill; brother of R. Sirhowy Jones. He ministered in many places in America: Jermyn, Pennsylvania; 5th Avenue, Pittsburg; Ebensburg; Ioana City; Council Buffs; East Laming, Michigan and Kalamazo: David Jones, *Memorial Volume*, 268-70.
35. J. Vinson Stephens: preacher and poet; he was born in Llangadog, Carmarthenshire; educated at Brecon Memorial College; ministered at Beaufort, Gwent, and Buckley, Flint, before going to America in 1891. David Jones, *Memorial Volume*, 321-2.
36. 'Scranton, PA.', *Y Tyst*, 12 April 1905.
37. 'Llythyr o America', *Y Tyst*, 13 June 1905, 6; the date was 6 May, David Jones, *Memorial Volume*, 40. L. Ton Evans (Junius) believed that the attackers had made a mistake and that they had hoped to destroy the Baptist chapel when he was present: *TCHB*, 1993. The Baptists, Congregationalists and Calvinistic Methodists had magnificent chapels almost next door to each other: *Cof Cenedl*, VIII, 173.
38. There was a case in Wales where the villagers arranged a procession and prayer meeting to prevent a local innkeeper from winning a local election: 'Ad-drem', *Y Tyst*, 20 December 1905.
39. 'At Olygydd y Seren', *Seren Cymru*, 23 February 1905, 10. J. Cromwell Hughes: he was born in Blaenau Ffestiniog in 1876; educated at Bangor; ordained at Bethesda, Swansea, 1903. Account of the welcome meeting at Hyde Park: 'America', *Seren Cymru*, 20 October 1905, 9.
40. 'Y Diwygiad yn Ymledu', *Tarian y Gweithiwr*, 5 October 1905, 6.
41. 'Y Diwygiad', *Y Cyfaill*, April 1905, 166.
42. Ibid., 'Chicago'.
43. Ibid., 165.
44. Ibid., 162, 166.
45. 'Notes from Wales', *The Methodist Recorder*, 1 February 1906, 77. Morgan was a native of Pont-rhyd-y-groes, Ceredigion; pastored English and Welsh churches in America: *The Cambrian* (Utica), August 1906.
46. Ibid.
47. The letter appeared in *The Christian Herald*, 15 February 1906, 152.
48. Ibid.
49. Articles in *Seren Cymru*: 'Gohebiaeth o America', 21 July 1905, 11; 'O Youngstown i Denver', 25 August 1905, 1-2. During the tour, T. Teifion Richards received a call to minister at Chatham Street, Pittsburgh, which he accepted. T. Teifion Richards: he was from Calfaria, Raven Hill, Swansea; ministered at the First Baptist Church, Scranton. Jay G. Williams, referring to the ministers of the First Baptist Church, includes 'T. Teifion Roberts'; should be Richards. Williams says of the chapel, 'At the height of the coal era the Welsh Baptist church was known as the church of the coal bosses', *Songs of Praises*, 158.
50. The minister was 'Mr Davies from Ffestiniog, North Wales', *Seren Cymru*, 25 August 1905, 1-2.
51. 'Welsh Revival', *British Weekly*, 9 March 1905, 571. She was the sister of David Williams, minister of Castle Street, Llangollen, North Wales. R. Tudur Jones gives

the name as Robert Williams: *Ffydd ac Argyfwng Cenedl*, vol. 2, 224 n.67.

52. 'O'r America', *London Welshman*, 28 January 1905, 7.
53. 'Welsh Revival', *British Weekly*, 9 March 1905, 571.
54. 'Y Diwygiad yn America', *Seren Cymru*, 19 May 1905, 7. D. Rhoslyn Davies minis-
    tered at Providence, Plymouth.
55. Ibid., 'Brynferch' composed revival hymns: *Seren Cymru*, 25 August 1905, 14.
56. Ibid.
57. Ibid.; Daniel Jenkins Williams, *Hundred Years*, 427. Other revivalist ministers are
    mentioned by Ellinor Williams: Rowland Jones, Middle Granville, 'Llith Miss Elinor
    Williams', *Y Drych*, 8 February 1906, 21, Daniel Jenkins Williams, *Hundred Years*,
    428; D. Ivor Evans, Shenandoah, formerly minister at Cowbridge, South Wales, 'Y
    Diwygiad yn America', *Seren Cymru*, 19 May 1905, 7, 'Yma ac Acw yn yr Unol
    Dalaethau', *Seren Cymru*, 27 July 1906, 6, Jay G. Williams, *Songs of Praises*, 120-1;
    Morien Môn Hughes, Morrisville, 'Morrisville', *Y Drych*, 8 March 1906, 5, 'Am
    Gymry ar Wasgar', *Yr Herald Cymraeg*, 11 July 1905, 7, David Jones, *Memorial
    Volume*, 246.
58. 'Yn New York ac Albany', *Y Drych*, 25 January 1906, 1.
59. Ibid., 'Ardaloedd y Chwareli', 18 January 1906, 1.
60. Ibid., 'Lloffion o Granville', 25 January 1906, 5.
61. Ibid., 'Llith Miss Elinor Williams', 8 February 1906, 2; 'Adgofion Am Flwyddyn y
    Diwygiad yn Middle Granville a'r Cylch', *Y Cyfaill*, March 1906, 124-5.
62. Ibid.
63. Ibid., 'New York a Vermont', 23 August 1906, 5.
64. Ibid., 'New York a Vermont', 8 March 1906, 5; J. Edwin Orr, *The Flaming Tongue*, 83.
65. Ibid., 'Ymweliad â Columba Ohio', 21 March 1907, 2; 'Johnstown, Pittsburg,
    Canonbury', 25 April 1907, 5.
66. Ibid., 'Pigion o Pittsburg', 17 May 1906, 3.
67. J. Tudor Rees: he was the author of *Evan Roberts, His Life and Work* (London, 1905).
    Dewi Michael: he was from Cilgerran, Ceredigion. His popular choice at Tabernacle,
    Cardiff, 'last Sunday' was 'Bendithiaist goed y meysydd' (You blessed the trees of
    the field), *Cardigan and Tivyside Advertizer*, 3 February 1905; reference and photo-
    graph in *The Christian Herald*, 2 March 1905, 190.
68. 'Pigion o Pittsburg', *Y Drych*, 17 May 1906, 3.
69. Ibid., 'Yr Efengylydd Gypsy Smith', 24 January 1907, 1. Howell Davies: he was born
    of Welsh parents in Oshkosh; studied at Princeton and was highly commended as a
    student by B. B. Warfield: ibidem, article and photograph, 30 May 1907, 1.
70. Seth Joshua (1858–1925), *DWB, 1951–1970*; Geraint Fielder, *Grace, Grit and
    Gumption*. Sam Jenkins: Gomer Morgan Roberts, *Hanes Eglwys Trinity Llanelli*
    (Llanelli, 1958), 22.
71. Geraint Fielder, *Grace, Grit and Gumption*, 147; Howell Williams, *The Romance of
    the Forward Movement* (Denbigh, 1946), 176.
72. T. Mardy Rees*, Seth Joshua and Frank Joshua, the renowned evangelists* (1926), 86.
73. T. C. Thomas: he was from Loughor, the home of Evan Roberts. Was a school-
    master and pastored the church at Bedlinog without accepting any payment. Led one
    of the revival meetings at Trecynon, Tuesday, 15 November 1904, which was the
    first week of Evan Roberts' first journey: *Y Diwygiad a'r Diwygiwr* (Dolgellau,
    1906), 67; 'Bedlinog', *Y Goleuad*, 27 January 1905, 6. A full description of the
    Tuesday meeting is found in D. M. Phillips, *Evan Roberts*, but the author does not
    mention T. C. Thomas.
74. 'Yr Efengylwyr yn Racine', *Y Drych*, 14 March 1907, 8.
75. Ibid., 'Cyfarfodydd Diwygiadol', 21 March 1907, 5. Another Welsh person who
    supported Wilbur Chapman in song was Mrs James Rees, Minnesota. She had visited
    Wales, where she met Evan Roberts and attended revival meetings; one of her

favourite hymns was 'Dyma gariad' (Here is love): 'Mrs James Rees, Minneapolis', *Y Cyfaill*, March 1906.

76.  Ibid., 'New York a Vermont', 28 March 1907, 5.
77.  Brynmor Pierce Jones, unpublished thesis, 'A Biographical Study of the Rev. R. B. Jones (1869–1933), First Principal of South Wales Bible Institute, with A Critical Survey of Welsh Fundamentalism in the first post-war era', 116.
78.  *RRW*, No. 6, Tuesday, 13 April 1905; Brynmor Pierce Jones, unpublished thesis, 116; 'Home Coming of the Rev. R. B. Jones', *Rhondda Leader*, 8 June 1907, 2.
79.  NLW, R. B. Jones Collection, No. 1, letter from E. E. Thomas to R. B. Jones, 9 February 1904.
80.  Ibid., No. 4, Evan Roberts to R. B. Jones, 29 January 1907.
81.  'Yma ac Acw o'r Unol Daleithiau', *Seren Cymru*, 22 March 1907.
82.  'The Rev. R. B. Jones in America', *Rhondda Leader*, 13 April 1907, 8.
83.  'Yma ac Acw o'r Unol Daleithiau', *Seren Cymru*, 26 April 1907.
84.  Ibid., 2 August 1907, 12. One of the ministers in Parsons was R. E. Williams, 'formerly of Carnege' [Carn Ingli, Pembrokeshire?]: 'Y Diwygiad yn America', *Seren Cymru*, 19 May 1905, 7.
85.  'O Ddinas Scranton', *Y Drych*, 11 April 1907, 4; Brynmor Pierce Jones, unpublished thesis, 11-18.
86.  Ibid.
87.  *The King's Champions* (Cwmbran, Gwent, reprint 1986), 76.
88.  'Efengylydd Cymreig yn Scranton', *Y Drych*, 18 April 1907, 3.
89.  'Home Coming of the Rev. R. B. Jones', *Rhondda Leader*, 8 June 1907, 2.
90.  NLW, R. B. Jones Collection, letter from W. J. Nicholas to R. B. Jones, 7 August 1907.
91.  'Nodion o Hyde Park', *Seren Cymru*, 19 July 1907, 15.
92.  'Efengylydd Cymreig yn Scranton', *Y Drych*, 18 April 1907, 3; 'Cenadaeth y Parch. R. B. Jones yn Nyffryn Wyoming', *Seren Cymru*, 6 September 1907, 11; 'PA America', *Y Tyst*, 15 May 1907, 7.
93.  Brynmor Pierce Jones, *The King's Champions*, 78. R. B. Jones was followed by W. S. Jones, Llwynypia, Rhondda, and W. T. Francis, Aberduar, Carmarthenshire: 'Gohebiaeth o America', *Seren Cymru*, 3 July 1907.

## Chapter 8: Patagonia

1.  NLW, 'Dyddiadur Gutyn Ebrill', NLW 18217D (Diary); 'O'r Wladfa Gymraeg', *Yr Herald Cymraeg*, 25 July 1905, 3.
2.  Griffith Griffith (Gutyn Ebrill): born in Cross Foxes, near Dolgellau, Merionethshire; died at Llwyn Ebrill, Gaiman, 9 September 1909, aged 80: NLW, 18217D.
3.  Eluned Morgan's debt to the Revival: Dafydd Ifans, ed., *Tyred Drosodd* (Evangelical Press of Wales, Bridgend, 1977), 12-13; Guto Roberts and Marian Elias, *Byw ym Mhatagonia* (Gwasg Gwynedd, 1993), 114. On the other hand she owed R. B. Jones a great debt for leading her 'into a completely new life in Christ': NLW, R. B. Jones Collection, No. 4, letter dated 8 June [1933]. Probable solution is that after her experiences in the Revival, Eluned Morgan was led into a holiness experience as taught by R. B. Jones.
4.  Author of *Ar Lannau'r Gamwy* (Liverpool, 1927).
5.  Ibid., 244-7.
6.  'Dyddiadur Gutyn Ebrill' [Diary]. Translation: 'Heard that the Awakening meetings in Bryngwyn are as lively as the meetings in the Gaiman. May God prosper the honest and the pure.'
7.  'O'r Wladfa Gymreig', *Yr Herald Cymraeg*, 25 July 1905, 3. Account by Eluned Morgan of the meetings in March, 'Yr adfywiad gwladfaol', *Y Drych*, 10 March 1905.
8.  'Dyddiadur Gutyn Ebrill.' Reading letters from Wales in public in Cwm Hyfryd: 'O'r

Cwm', *Y Drafod*, 25 August 1905. Other meetings in April: 'Y Diwygiad', 7 April 1905, 'Y Gaiman', 21 April 1905.

9. e.g., 'La Fe Religiosa En Gales', 14 April 1905.

10. e.g., 'Y diwygiad crefyddol YN NGHYMRU', 20, 27 January 1905; 'Lloffion o Gymru', 3 February; 'Y diwygiad yn Nghymru', 10 March; 'Colofn y Cymry', 31 March. The pamphlets published by *The Western Mail* were sent to Patagonia by D. R. Daniel, 'Barry Dock', *Y Drafod*, 7 April 1905.

11. Evan Roberts: 'P. Price ac Evan Roberts', *Y Drafod*, 14 April 1905; idem, 'Mr Evan Roberts yn Merthyr', 12 May 1905, 'Cenhadaeth Evan Roberts', 16 June 1905.

12. Hymns included in *Y Drafod*: 'Y Gŵr wrth ffynon Jacob' (The man at Jacob's well); 'Tyred, Arglwydd, i'r cyfarfod' (Come, Lord, to the meeting), 10 March; 'A glywaist ti sôn am Iachawdwr y byd?' (Have you heard of the Saviour of the world?), 31 March; 'Galw Finau' (Call me), 16 June 1905.

13. *Ar Lannau'r Gamwy*, 245-6.

14. Robert Owen Jones, *Yr Efengyl yn y Wladfa* (Bridgend, 1987), 24.

15. 'Y Diwygiad Gwladfaol', *Y Drafod*, 19 May 1905.

16. *Yr Efengyl yn y Wladfa*, 25, 26.

17. 'Dyddiadur Gutyn Ebrill.' Translation: 'Young People's prayer meeting in the Gaiman —numerous gatherings throughout the day. Many enlisted for the army—including Morgan Rhenwlad, Harry Garfield and Willie Jones Caerfyrddin and others. It is hoped that under the influence of the spirit the effects will follow and that they will be lasting. Mr Humphreys (returned from the Andes) with them in the Gaiman during the services of the two days.'

18. 'Y Diwygiad Gwladfaol', *Y Drafod*, 26 May 1905.

19. Ibid.

20. *Yr Efengyl yn y Wladfa*, 26-8.

21. Ibid., 28-9. 'Mae yn ein meddiant enwau cynifer a 53 o ddychweledigion mewn oedfa y dydd hwnnw' [We possess the names of as many as 53 converts in one meeting on that day]: 'Hanes Bethel Gaiman', NLW, 19100B.

22. 'Y Dwygiad Gwladfaol', *Y Drafod*, 26 May 1905; reference, most probably, to the meeting mentioned by Sarah Morgans de Roberts, and she also gives the names of a number of people, *Yr Efengyl yn y Wladfa*, 28.

23. Ibid.

24. Janet Owen, interviewed by Dr Phil Ellis, Cardiff, during his stay in Patagonia.

25. Ibid.

26. 'Dyddiadur Gutyn Ebrill', 1 July 1905. Reminiscences of Tudur Evans: R. Bryn Williams, ed., *Atgofion o Batagonia* (Llandysul, 1980), 111, 113. His father, J. C. Evans, from Cwmaman, Aberdare, had emigrated to Patagonia in 1874. There are brief details in E. Pan Jones, *Oriel Coleg Caerfyrddin* (Merthyr Tydfil, 1909), 108.

27. Lewis Humphreys: he was in the first group that went to Patagonia; returned to Wales but went back to Patagonia in 1886; died 22 January 1910, 72 years of age: NLW, 18217D.

28. 'O'r Wladfa Gymreig', *Yr Herald Cymraeg*, 25 July 1905, 3.

29. 'Llythyr oddiwrth Evan Roberts', *Y Drafod*, 25 August 1905.

30. Ibid., 'Cyfarfod gweddi yr wythnos', 21 July 1905.

31. Ibid., 'Trelew', 28 July 1905.

32. 'O'r Dyffryn Uchaf', 25 August 1905.

33. Ibid., 'O'r Dyffryn Uchaf', 17 November 1905; 'Undeb Eglwysi'r Wladfa', 22 December 1905. Reports from Wales continued to appear in *Y Drafod*, e.g. 'Yn Nghyfarfod Evan Roberts', 3 November 1905; 'Nodiadau Cyffredinol', 8 December 1905.

34. Mrs Owen Jones MSS, received from Tegai Roberts, Gaiman Archives. Translation: 'Many of the young men came forward to take part spontaneously, some of them had not taken part in public before. There were no ministers or church officers at that

time, the population was sparse and they lived far apart from each other. The roads were bad; natural ditches, full of water, often frozen and dangerous for the horses as they could fall into them. Such was the will that there was no turning back in spite of the difficulties. It meant going on the back of the thin *sgribliad* during the night—a league and a half to two leagues to hold a prayer meeting.'

35. Ibid.; 'Gwladfa Sarmiento', *Y Drafod*, 18 August 1905. Translation: 'We had no chapel at that time but the Welsh people came together and a few belonging to other nationalities as well. We would sing in three languages, English and spanish. We went to a home by permission and sometimes we were ridiculed. It was like the Tower of Babel.'

36. Ibid.

37. The *DWB* is misleading regarding Eluned Morgan's movements between 1903 and 1909. The article stated that Eluned Morgan travelled Wales during the period from 1903 until 1909. She was in Wales in 1902; returned to Patagonia and was there during revival meetings in May 1905. She was in Wales again during 1905 to 1906, accompanied by Griffith Pugh. She returned to Patagonia but visited Wales again in 1908. Letters to J. C. Evans, 1905, 1906, Gaiman Archives, copies sent by Tegai Roberts; W. R. P. George, *Fy Nghyfaill Hoff* (Llandysul, 1972), 113, 128, 77, 102, 107, 116, 126, 149; 'Llongau', *Y Drafod*, 16 June 1905.

38. Another Patagonian in Cardiff was Ivor J. Pugh, and he reported on the revival in Wales, 'Y Diwygiad', *Y Drafod*, 12, 18 August 1905; could be related to the Griffith Pugh who travelled to Wales with Eluned Morgan.

39. Letter written from 51 Hamilton Street, Cardiff, 1 December 1905, *Fy Nghyfaill Hoff*, 113; D. M. Phillips, *Evan Roberts*, 451, 535.

40. Letter to J. C. Evans, from 'Alavon's study in North Wales', *Fy Nghyfaill Hoff*, 124. Alafon was Owen Griffith Owen (1847–1916), *DWB*.

41. *Y Cyfaill* (America) drew attention to the meetings: 'Lloffion y Mis', May 1906. Eluned Morgan had completed the lecture in November 1905, *Fy Nghyfaill Hoff*, 116.

42. D. D. Walters: he was educated at Carmarthen Presbyterian College; left for Patagonia in 1906 and ministered there for seventeen years. He returned to Wales and ministered at Brynsiencyn, Anglesey: T. M. Thomas, *Hanes Eglwys Annibynol Ebeneser, Crwbin* (Llanelli, n.d.), 15-16, with a photograph: *Oriel Coleg Caerfyrddin*, 245. Tudur Evans married a sister of D. D. Walters, *Atgofion am Batagonia*, 59.

43. *Fy Nghyfaill Hoff*, letter 5 October 1905, 113.

44. Ibid., letter June 1906, 128.

45. Ibid., letter March 1908, 149.

46. 'Trwy y Rhidyll', *Y Drafod*, 16 June 1905.

47. Ibid., 'Y Rhidyllydd a'r Diwygiad', 14 July 1905, and some correspondence during September 1905.

48. Ibid., 'P. Price ac Evan Roberts', 14 April 1905.

49. Ibid., 21 April, 18 August 1905.

# Chapter 9: The West Indies

1. 'Revival Notes', *The Life of Faith*, 29 March 1905, 259.

2. Ibid.

3. Ibid., 'Jamaica', 30 November 1905, 16.

4. *The Christian*, 19 April 1906, 25.

5. Ibid., 6, 13 September 1906, 6, 25; 'Jamaica', *The Missionary Review of the World*, September 1906, 643.

6. 'We Stood—and the Lord Wrought', *The Life of Faith*, 2 January 1907, 13.

7. Letter H. E. Turner, 16 December 1906, *Revival News* (Kingston), March 1907.

8. *The Life of Faith*, 2 January 1907.

9.   'A Baptismal Scene', *The Christian*, 23 May 1907, 25.
10.  Ibid., 'St Kitts, West Indies', 12 April 1906, 24.
11.  'Cenadon Newydd', *Yr Eurgrawn*, January 1906; he left for Trinidad, 9 December 1905: 'To and from the field', *The Foreign Field*, February 1906.
12.  Ibid., Reports April 1906.
13.  The editorial, *Revival News*, March 1907.
14.  Ibid., 'The Revival in Clarendon', March 1907.
15.  Miss Lettice King to 'My dear sister in Christ', 5 March 1907, NLW, Mrs Penn-Lewis Collection.
16.  Ibid.
17.  'After the Earthquake', *Revival News*, March 1907.
18.  Ibid.
19.  Ibid.
20.  Ibid.; 'Come, O Breath, and Breathe', *The Life of Faith*, 20 February 1907, 170.
21.  'The Revival in Jamaica', *The Christian*, 7 January 1909.

## Chapter 10: South Africa

1.   J. Edwin Orr, *Evangelical Awakenings in Africa* (Minneapolis, 1975), 125.
2.   Ibid., 129.
3.   'The Throne Life of Victory', *The Life of Faith*, 4 April 1906, 287.
4.   Reported on revival in Johannesburg, *The Life of Faith*, 19 April 1905, 322. Bessie Porter (1850–1936): born in Belfast; from 1894 to 1897 worked with YWCA in Swansea; married Alfred Head in Swansea, 7 December 1907; is author of the hymn, 'O Breath of Life, come sweeping through us'; was a close friend of Mrs Penn-Lewis: 'More on Bessie and Mary', *The Evangelical Library Bulletin*, Autumn 2001; Garrard, *Mrs Penn-Lewis*, 131.
5.   Fiedler, *Story of Faith Missions*, 218-19; J. Edwin Orr refers to Walton as 'beloved by Briton, Boer and Bantu', *The Flaming Tongue*, 117.
6.   Charlotte Hanbury, *Life of Mrs Head* (1905), 169.
7.   Brynmor Pierce Jones, *The Spiritual History of Keswick*, 7, 9-10.
8.   He was present at the Hirwaun revival meetings, *Tarian y Gweithiwr*, 30 November 1905, 1.
9.   Albert A. Head, 'Jottings of my Journey to South Africa', *The Life of Faith*, 25 October 1905, 932.
10.  Ibid. Fiedler says that the Wellington convention was established in 1906: *Story of Faith Missions*, 248.
11.  Ibid.
12.  J. Edwin Orr, *The Flaming Tongue*, 120.
13.  J. Edwin Orr, *Evangelical Awakenings in Africa*, 131; has details of W. M. Douglas.
14.  Ibid., 129.
15.  Charles Inwood was one of the group involved in establishing Keswick in Wales: Brynmor Pierce Jones, *The Spiritual History of Keswick*, 7.
16.  Charles Inwood, 'In South Africa', *The Life of Faith*, 3 October 1906, 884.
17.  *The Baptist Times*, 11 May 1906, Supplement, i.
18.  J. Edwin Orr, *Evangelical Awakenings in Africa*, 130-1.
19.  'South Africa', *The Monthly Treasury*, January 1906.
20.  *Missionary Review of the World*, 1906, 645. Full account of Mott's visit: C. Howard Hopkins, *John R. Mott*, 296-300.
21.  'Llandrindod Convention', *The Life of Faith*, 8 August 1907, 12.
22.  NLW, Mrs Jessie Penn-Lewis Collection, letter 1908; no specific date.
23.  E. Lewis Evans, *CGG*, 103.
24.  'Kuruman', *LMS Annual Report*, 1906, 227.

25. 'The Revival in the Mission Field', *The British Congregationalist*, 16 August 1906.
26. 'The Revival in Central Africa', *The Chronicle*, September 1906; 'Y Genhadaeth', *Y Dysgedydd*, October 1906.
27. Ibid.
28. David John Rees: he was educated at Durham University; went to East Africa in 1897 and became Principal of the Theological College, Kongwa; died 24 March 1924; his wife was Agnes Anna Barnett Mackenzie Cooper. Elizabeth Knox, *Signal on the Mountains* (Canberra, 1991), 218.
29. Ibid., 168.
30. Ibid., 169, 176.
31. Henry Richards: he was born in Somerset, 16 May 1851; baptised at Tredegarville Baptist Church, Cardiff; attended Harley House/East London Training Institute (Grattan Guinness), and went to Africa in 1879. Married: (1) Mary Richards, (2) ? (3) Mary Eliza Cole. Biography sent by the Archivist, ABMU, Valley Forge, Pennsylvania; T. M. Bassett, *The Baptists of Wales and the BMS*, 68.
32. See the section on France.
33. 'Livingstone Inland Mission', *Cardiff Times*, 6 July, 5; 9 November, 5; 30 November, 7; 12 October, 5, 1878; 26 January, 3; 26 April, 3, 1879; David Lagergen, *Mission and State in the Congo* (Uppsala, 1970), 35-6, 41; Michelle Guinness, *The Guinness Legend* (London, 1988), 120-3 (Alfred Tilly not mentioned); *Jubilee Tredegarville Baptist Church, 1861–1911* (Cardiff, 1911), 7, 24-5. Early executive: John Cory, Esq., JP; Richard Cory, Jun., Esq.; Rev. Alfred Tilly, Tredegarville, Cardiff; Mr and Mrs H. Grattan Guinness, London; James Irvine, Esq., Liverpool, and John Carver, Esq., Brighton: Mrs H. Grattan Guinness, *The First Christian Mission in the Congo* (London, n.d.), 27.
34. He wrote an account of the Revival: *The Pentecost on the Congo* (Boston, revised edition, 1906).
35. David Lagergen, *Mission and State*, 36.
36. 'A Revival on the Congo', *The Christian Herald*, 24 August 1905, 169.
37. Ibid.
38. Thomas Lewis, *These Seventy Years, An Autobiography* (London, n.d.), 226-7; Hope Morgan was from Bryn-mawr, Powys.
39. 'Yma ac Acw o'r Unol Dalaethau', *Seren Cymru*, 11 January 1907, 3.

# Chapter 11: Madagascar

1. Richard Lovett, *The History of the London Missionary Society* (London, 1899), vol. 1; Noel Gibbard, *Cymwynaswyr Madagascar* (Bryntirion Press, Bridgend, 1999), chapters 1 and 2.
2. CWM, Madagascar Correspondence, 10 March, 18, 21, 31 May 1892; report of Henry E. Clark in *Antananarivo Annual*, 1893.
3. CWM, 25 March 1905.
4. Ibid., 1 March 1905.
5. E. Lewis Evans, *CGG*, 83-4, 85, 78-9, and a biography of Thomas Rowlands: Edward and Emrys Rowlands, *Thomas Rowlands of Madagascar* (London, n.d.).
6. Noel Gibbard, *Cymwynaswyr Madagascar*, 140-1.
7. Ibid., 141.
8. Rowlands, *Thomas Rowlands*, 66. Other sources give similar accounts: 'When news of Revival in Wales reached him [Thomas Rowlands], a longing and expectation in the hearts of many Christians was created, and they began to pray earnestly for revival': 'Ambohimandroso', *LMS Report*, 1906, 285; 'As each mail brought fresh news from Wales, expectancy and longing were intensified': Mrs Rowlands, 'Revival in Madagascar' *The Chronicle*, September 1905; 'A Revival in Madagascar', *The*

*Missionary Review of the World*, November 1905, 878.

9. Mrs Rowlands, 'The Revival in Madagascar', *The Chronicle*, September 1905. In her report to *The Life of Faith*, Mrs Rowlands gives the date as 5 May: 20 July 1905, 609.
10. Ibid.
11. Ibid.
12. 'Good News From Madagascar', *The Life of Faith*, 26 July 1905, 609.
13. 'Revival in Madagascar', *The Chronicle*, November 1905.
14. Rowlands, *Thomas Rowlands*, 67-8.
15. CWM, Madagascar Correspondence, 25 September 1905.
16. Ibid.
17. Ibid.; the report gives 141, but the total was 142.
18. Ibid., 23 December 1905.
19. *LMS Report*, 1906, 286.
20. 'Y Genhadaeth', *Y Dysgedydd*, May 1906; 'Four Wonderful Days', *The Chronicle*, March 1906.
21. Ibid.
22. Ibid.
23. 'Madagascar', *The Chronicle*, March 1906.
24. *In Five Fields, Report of the Friends Foreign Mission Union*, 1906, 54.
25. Ibid., 41-2.
26. 'Revival in Madagascar', *The Life of Faith*, 10 October 1906.
27. 'An All-Night Prayer and its Results', *The Chronicle*, November 1906.
28. 'Y Genhadaeth', *Y Dysgedydd*, March 1906.
29. Rowlands, *Thomas Rowlands*, 68-9.
30. CWM, Madagascar Correspondence, 10 July 1906.
31. 'Ambalavao', *LMS Report*, 1906, 279.
32. Ibid., 286.
33. Ibid., 287.
34. CWM, Madagascar Correspondence, 10 July 1906.
35. Ibid.
36. *Report BFBS*, 1906, 181.
37. *LMS Report*, 1906, 277.
38. Ibid., 'Betsileo Mission', 1907.
39. 'Report From Madagascar', *The Missionary Review of the World*, January 1908, 6-7.
40. J. Edwin Orr, *The Flaming Tongue*, 115.
41. 'An All-Night Prayer and its Results', *The Chronicle*, November 1906.
42. Ibid.
43. Noel Gibbard, *Cymwynaswyr Madagascar*, 151-2.

## Chapter 12: India (1)

1. Ednyfed Thomas, *Bryniau'r Glaw* (Gwasg Pantycelyn, 1988), 147.
2. Ibid., 148-9.
3. Jonathan Goforth, *By My Spirit* (London, *c.* 1928), 184.
4. 'Llythyr o Khasia at Evan Roberts', *Y Goleuad*, 24 March 1905, 5-6; 'Days of Grace on the Khassi Hills', *The Life of Faith*, 25 August 1909, 959.
5. Ibid. Sidney Evans refers to Evan Roberts receiving the letter, but does not name the missionary: Sidney Evans, Gomer M. Roberts, eds., *Cyfrol Goffa Diwygiad 1904–1905* (Caernarfon, 1954), 96-7.
6. CMA, 27, 243, 20 May 1905.
7. *Y Goleuad*, 24 March 1905, 5-6.
8. CMA, 27, 281, letter of E. H. Williams, Mawphlang, 5 April 1905.
9. CMA, 27, 163, 8 February 1905.

References

245

10. 'Revival Reaches India', Awstin, *RRW*, No. 6 (Western Mail pamphlets); included in *The Llangollen Advertizer*, 28 April 1905. Many authors have claimed incorrectly that John Roberts was in Wales when the revival broke out: for example, J. Meirion Lloyd, *Ar Bob Bryn Uchel* (Liverpool, n.d.), 54; J. Edwin Orr, *Evangelical Awakenings in India* (New Delhi, 1970), 50; J. Fortis Jyrwa, *The Wondrous Works of God* (Meghalaya, 1980), 45, and C. L. Hminga, *The Life and Witness of the Church in Mizoram* (Mizoram, 1987), 69. For John Roberts' visit to Wales, 1906–07: R. J. Willams, *Y Parchedig John Roberts, DD* (Liverpool, 1923), 256-8.
11. 'Rev. Maurice Griffiths at Home', *Llanelly Mercury*, 28 September 1905, 7. The missionary O. O. Williams refers to the visit: 'Their deep interest in the Revival makes them regret in many ways their absence from Wales in these wonderful days, but their visit to the mission field and a tour round the world may combine for them the Revival & missionary work in a way that will bring a rich blessing to the Churches': CMA, 27, 287, 20 February 1905.
12. CMA, 27, 281, 5 April 1905.
13. J. Pengwern Jones, *India Awake* (Calcutta, 1905), 22.
14. CMA, 27, 281, 5 April 1905.
15. Ibid.
16. Ibid.
17. Ibid., 30 May 1905.
18. J. Pengwern Jones, *India Awake*, 22.
19. CMA, 27, 243, 30 August 1905.
20. 'The Revival in Khasia'; D. M. Phillips received report from J. Pengwern Jones, *SWDN*, 3 May 1905, 6. Phillips received at least one letter a week from Jones, writing with his heart 'on fire for revival', 'Cwrs y Byd', *Y Lladmerydd*, July 1905.
21. Mrs John Roberts, *The Revival on the Khassi Hills* (Caernarvon, 1907), 12.
22. Ibid., 13.
23. Idem, *Y Diwygiad ar Fryniau Khasia* (Newport, 1907), chapter 2.
24. CMA, 27, 243; 'Y Cronicl Cenhadol', *Y Drysorfa*, July 1905, 20 May 1905.
25. CMA, HZ1/41/1, 24 June 1905.
26. Ibid.
27. Ibid.; Mrs John Roberts, *Y Diwygiad ar Fryniau Khasia*, 40-4; CMA, 27, 239, 21, 27 June 1905.
28. J. Pengwern Jones, *India Awake*, 28.
29. Ibid.
30. Ibid., 29; 'Y Cronicl Cenhadol', *Y Drysorfa*, August 1905, 6 June 1905.
31. CMA, 27, 281, 30 May 1905.
32. J. Pengwern Jones, *India Awake*, 27.
33. 'The Shillong Presbytery', CMA, 27, 260.
34. Ibid.
35. Ibid.; Mrs John Roberts, *Y Diwygiad ar Fryniau Khasia*, 66-70, based on J. C. Evans' report, CMA, 27, 260.
36. CMA, 27, 256, 31 August 1905; Mrs John Roberts, *Y Diwygiad ar Fryniau Khasia*, 59-63.
37. Ibid.
38. 'Mawphlang District', CMA, 27, 281.
39. Ibid.; other presbyteries mentioned by Mrs John Roberts, 'Y Cronicl Cenhadol', *Y Drysorfa*, January 1906, letter 15 November 1905.
40. Ibid.
41. 'Sylhet', *The Friend of Sylhet*, March 1906, 48.
42. Ibid., front page.
43. CMA, 27, 256, 30 March 1906. For Pengwern Jones: D. G. Merfyn Jones, 'Rev. Pengwern Jones (1859–1927)', *Nine Missionary Pioneers*, ed. J. Meirion Lloyd

(Caernarfon, 1989).

44. Ibid.; also 24 May 1906; CMA, 27, 243, 20 April 1906; Mrs John Roberts, *Y Diwygiad ar Fryniau Khasia*, 75-8.
45. Ibid. A letter was also received from Miss Davies, Tre-borth, Wales, who was in India at the time: letter of Robert Evans, 'Y Cronicl Cenhadol', *Y Drysorfa*, July 1906.
46. CMA, 27, 256, 30 March 1906.
47. Ibid.
48. Ibid.; letter E. M. Lloyd, 13 April 1906, 'Y Cronicl Cenhadol', *Y Drysorfa*, June 1906; ibid., letter Robert Evans, 20 April 1906, July 1906; two letters in *The Monthly Treasury*, June 1906, taken from The *Friend of Sylhet*, April 1906.
49. CMA, 27, 256, 22 June 1906, and included in *The Harvest Field*, 1906, 194-7, with the editor's note that Rev. J. Pengwern Jones 'continues to send out his cyclostyled sheets giving information of the progress and results of the Revival'.
50. Ibid., 30 May 1906.
51. Letter 7 August 1906, 'Y Cronicl Cenhadol', *Y Drysorfa*, October 1906.
52. Ibid., letters: 18 August, 28 September, November and December respectively.
53. CMA, 27, 256, 10 February 1907.
54. Ibid.
55. Ibid.
56. Ibid.
57. Ibid.
58. Ibid. The scriptural reference: Revelation 2, verse 4.
59. Ibid.
60. Ibid. For the 'rice collection': Ednyfed Thomas, *Bryniau'r Glaw*, 159-60.
61. William Williams (1859–1892): J. Meirion Lloyd, *Y Bannau Pell* (Caernarfon, 1989), 22-6.
62. D. E. Jones (1870–1947), his wife Katherine Ellen (1868–1950), Edwin Rowlands (1867–1939): J. Meirion Lloyd, *Y Bannau Pell*, 267, 269-70.
63. Arthington Trust: Brian Stanley, *The History of the Baptist Missionary Society* (Edinburgh, 1992), 381-3, and photograph of Robert Arthington, 129.
64. Brian Stanley, *History BMS*, 271-2; J. Meirion Lloyd, *Y Bannau Pell*, chapter 2.
65. Ibid., 272.
66. 'We are holding prayer meetings nightly for a still greater blessing and we know too that our weak hands are being held up by the praying church at home': letter Katie Jones, n.d., *The Monthly Treasury*, February 1906.
67. J. Meirion Lloyd, *Y Bannau Pell*, 84. It is difficult to decide on the exact number that went to Mairang; probably it was ten, seven from the north and three from the south: J. Meirion Lloyd, *Ar Bob Bryn Uchel*, 54; ibid., *History of the Church in Mizoram* (Mizoram, 1991), 90. Note also, with differences, J. M. Lloyd, *Arloesydd Lushai, D. E. Jones* (Westminster, 1958), 20; J. Pengwern Jones, 'The Revival in the Lushai Hills', CMA, 27, 256; 'Y Diwygiad yn Torri allan yn Lushai', *Y Cenhadwr*, September 1951; C. L. Hminga, *The Life and Witness*, 70.
68. *Y Cenhadwr*, 1951.
69. Ibid.; cf. J. Meirion Lloyd, *Y Bannau Pell*, 85.
70. J. Meirion Lloyd, *Y Bannau Pell*, 86; D. E. Jones, 'Hunangofiant Cenhadwr', *Y Seren* (Bala), 26 August 1950, 2.
71. Ibid., 87; *Y Cenhadwr*, September 1951; CMA, 27, 256.
72. CMA, 27, 256, 5 May 1906; Mrs John Roberts, *Hanes y Diwygiad ar Fryniau Khasia*, 80.
73. *Y Cenhadwr*, September 1951; letter D. E. Jones, 21 July 1906, *Y Drysorfa*, October 1906.
74. Oxford, Angus Library, BMS, Lushai Log Book, 1N/113, Report 1906.
75. J. H. Lorraine, 'Revival Fire in Lushailand', *The Missionary Herald*, November 1907.
76. Ibid.; Lushai: Log Book, 1N/113; Hminga, *Life and Witness*, 84-5.

77. CMA, 27, 256.
78. J. Meirion Lloyd believes that Edwin Rowlands was wrongly accused of immorality, *Y Bannau Pell*, 94-6.
79. Letter Robert Evans, 30 April 1908, *Y Drysorfa*, 1908.

## Chapter 13: India (2)

1. 'Latter Rain Falling in the East: Early Twentieth Century Pentecostalism in India and the Debate over Speaking in Tongues', *Church History*, September 1999.
2. Ibid.
3. J. Edwin Orr, *Evangelical Awakenings in Southern Asia* (Minneapolis, 1975), 108; Helen Dyer, *Revival in India* (London, 1907), 28-9; W. B. Boggs, *The Revival in India* (Boston, 1907), 3-4.
4. Mary Garrard, *A Memoir*, chapter IX; Brynmor Pierce Jones has 'Rudeshill' instead of Rudisill, *Trials and Triumphs*, 108-12; NLW, Jessie Penn-Lewis Collection.
5. Pandita Ramabai (*c.* 1858–1922): *Dictionary of Pentecostal and Charismatic Movements*, 755-6.
6. 'General Missionary Intelligencer', *Missionary Review of the World*, May 1906, 394.
7. Based on: Edward E. Hayward, 'Pandita Ramabai', *The Missionary Herald*, July 1907.
8. Helen Dyer, *Revival in India*, 43.
9. Ibid.
10. Ibid., 43-5.
11. Ibid., 48.
12. Mrs Penn-Lewis, 'What Shall We Say to all This?', *The Life of Faith*, 20 September 1905, 794; idem, 'India Awakening', 27 September 1905, 813; 'Y Diwygiad yn Ymledu', *Tarian y Gweithiwr*, 5 October 1905, 6, drawing attention to Mrs Penn-Lewis's reports.
13. Helen Dyer, *Revival in India*, 49-53.
14. Ibid., 50; Nicol MacNicol, *Pandita Ramabai* (Calcutta, 1926), 117-18.
15. 'A Revival at Ratnagiri', *The Harvest Field*, January 1906.
16. Ibid.
17. Ibid.
18. Report by A. L. Wiley, dated 29 January 1906, in *The Friend of Sylhet*, February 1906, continued March and May; reports received by Mrs Penn-Lewis from missionaries, *The Life of Faith*, June 1906, 44.
19. Walter B. Sloan, 'Introduction', *The Revival in Manchuria*, James Webster (London, 1910), 3. Howard Agnew Johnston (1860–1936): he was sent out by the Evangelistic Committee of the Presbyterian Church in the USA; was minister of Madison Avenue, New York: *Report 1907, Board of Foreign Missions of the Presbyterian Church in the USA* (New York, 1907), 3, 17; E. W. Burt, 'A Pentecostal Experience', *The Missionary Herald*, August 1906.
20. *The Harvest Field*, January 1906.
21. Report 1907, *Board of Foreign Missions of the Presbyterian Church in the USA*, 203, 217.
22. Helen Dyer, *Revival in India*, 62; SOAS, MMS, Bombay Correspondence, Fiche 9, 7 February, 21 June 1906.
23. 'The Awakening in Wales and Elsewhere', *The Life of Faith*, 12 July 1905, 555.
24. 'Present Religious Awakenings in India', *The Harvest Field*, January 1907; Eugene Stock, *The History of the Church Missionary Society*, vol. 4, 172. Thomas Walker (1859–1912): he was born in Matlock, Derby, and educated at St John's, Cambridge; known for evangelism and Bible teaching in Tamil; a prominent convention speaker and closely associated with Amy Carmichael of Dohnavur, who wrote his biography: J. D. Douglas, ed., *New International Dictionary of the Christian Church* (Exeter, 1974).

Dohnavur experienced revival and, according to one of the girls, 'Jesus came to Dohnavur': Frank Houghton, *Amy Carmichael of Dohnavur* (London, 1953), 146.

25.  Helen Dyer, *Revival in India*, 64, 95.

26.  *The Chronicle*, November 1905, 317. Wills wrote a paper to stimulate interest in revival: CWM, Travancore, Box 22, 26 March 1905. It was in Kachiwa, Benares, and then in Neyoor that E. E. Evans, LMS, worked; E. Lewis Evans says that he had Welsh connections: *Cymru a'r Gymdeithas Genhadol* (London, 1945), 129-30.

27.  CWM, Travancore, 7 December 1905; 'Travancore', *The Friend of Sylhet*, November, December 1905.

28.  'Shall We Pass on the Torch?', *The Life of Faith*, 8 November 1905, 931; 'Travancore', *The Friend of Sylhet*, November 1905.

29.  J. Edwin Orr, *Evangelical Awakenings in Southern Asia*, 136.

30.  Ibid., 137.

31.  CWM, South India, Canarese, Box 13, 23 February 1905; 'India', *The Chronicle*, April 1905.

32.  'Musoorie', *The Friend of Sylhet*, June 1905; WMMS Report 1906–08, xxx, 81; 'Shall We Pass on the Torch?', *The Life of Faith*, 8 November 1905, 931.

33.  Helen Dyer, *Revival in India*, 136.

34.  *Baptist Missionary Magazine*, 1906, 47.

35.  Ibid., 1907, 268.

36.  'The Revival at Ongole', *The Missionary Review of the World*, November 1906; 'Revival Far and Near', *The Christian*, 4 October 1906, 25; Helen Dyer, *Revival in India*, 134-5; J. Edwin Orr, *Evangelical Awakenings in Southern Asia*, 120-3; 'Ongole', *The Friend of Sylhet*, January 1906.

37.  'The Awakening in Wales', *The Life of Faith*, 8 March 1905, 193; Awstin [Revival], 'Its Position and Progress', *RRW*, No. 5.

38.  Mrs Penn-Lewis did not name the author, but comparison with other accounts shows he must have been J. A. Baker: 'Arm Ye Yourselves', *The Life of Faith*, 17 October, 1906, 941.

39.  Ibid.

40.  William Powell: he was born in Llangorse, Powys, 1860; home church was Abercarn; educated at Pontypool Baptist College. He emigrated to Canada; moved to Florida and worked with the Strict Baptists in South India. Powell retired in 1926 and died in Cardiff, 1938: T. M. Bassett, *The Baptists of Wales and the Baptist Missionary Society*, 51. 'The Work in Bapatra was the particular interest of a Welsh Baptist named Powell': 'Unpublished Memoir of Wilfred Kuhrt', 10; reference sent by Chris Richards, Grace Baptist Mission, Abingdon.

41.  John Dare Thomas: he was educated at Pontypool Baptist College and ministered at Ferndale, Rhondda, before going to India. His wife was from Laxfield, Suffolk. Welcome meetings were held for them in India, 22 December 1904: *Report 1904*, South India Strict Baptist Missionary Society, 41-4, 84-5; *Rays From The East*, April 1905, 9-10, 13. They left for India in 1904 and not 1905/6 as suggested by T. M. Bassett, *The Baptists of Wales and Baptist Missionary Society*, 54. J. Dare Thomas had baptised a number of converts before the end of 1905: 'Bedydd Crediniol yn St. Thomas Mount, Deheudir India', *Seren Cymru*, 15 December 1905, 1; with a photograph of a baptismal service.

42.  Letter, 9 February 1906, *Rays From The East*, April 1906.

43.  J. D. Thomas, 'The news of revival has now bursted out in India', 'Colofn Gymreig y Rhondda', *The Rhondda Leader*, 4 February 1905, 8, letter dated Madras, 4 January 1905.

44.  *The Baptist Missionary Magazine* (America), 1906, 334.

45.  ABMU, *Annual Report 1907*, 111.

46.  *The Baptist Missionary Magazine*, 1908, 410.

47. ABMU, *Annual Report 1908*, 110-11.
48. John Craig, *Forty Years Among the Telugus, A History Of The Mission Of The Baptists Of Ontario And Quebec, Canada, To The Telugus, South India, 1867–1907*, 150; J. Edwin Orr, *The Flaming Tongue*, 150.
49. *Fortieth Report of the Foreign Mission of the Baptist Convention of Ontario and Quebec* (Orillia, 1906), 33, 20, 29; W. Gordon Gardner, *Hand to the Indian Plow*, 147.
50. John Craig, *Fifty Years*, 152; J. Edwin Orr, *The Flaming Tongue*, 139.
51. Ibid.
52. *Among the Telugus, Report Canadian Baptist Telugu Mission 1906* (Madras, 1907), 17; *Fortieth Report*, 30-1.
53. *Forty First Report Foreign Mission Board* (Orillia, 1907), 11; *Among the Telugus*, 7.
54. Ibid., 21.
55. Ibid., 20.
56. *The Baptist Missionary Magazine*, 1907, 266-7.
57. 'The Re-kindling of the Fire in Wales', *The Life of Faith*, 18 October 1905, 869.
58. CMA, 27, 256, letter, n.d., from 19 Cubborn Rd., Bangalore; *Y Tyst*, 25 April, 12.
59. Ibid.
60. 'From Our Brethren in India', *The Life of Faith*, 31 January 1906, 95.
61. CMA, 27, 256, letter dated 4 July 1905.
62. 'The Awakening in Wales', *The Life of Faith*, 15 February 1906, 129.
63. Helen Dyer informed Mrs Penn-Lewis that Dr Rudisill had visited Mukti: Mattersey, Donald Gee Centre, letter 24 October 1907.
64. N. Wiseman, *Elizabeth Baxter* (London, 1928), chapter VIII; Mrs Baxter had accompanied Mrs Penn-Lewis to revival meetings in Wales. Helen Dyer, *Revival in India*, 66.
65. Albert Norton (died 1923): native of Chicago; collaborated with Pandita Ramabai in famine relief in 1899. His Home for Boys witnessed Pentecostal phenomena: *Dictionary of Pentecostal and Charismatic Movements*, 641.
66. Wiseman, *Elizabeth Baxter*, chapter VIII. Another Roberts (F. D. O. Roberts) left the Mission to join the CMS: Stock, *The History CMS*, IV, 220. Continuing Roberts links: 'O'r Maes Cenhadol', *Yr Efengylydd*, October 1924.
67. 'Asansol, Bengal', *The Friend of Sylhet*, December 1905.
68. 'From Our Brethren in India', *The Life of Faith*, 31 January 1906, 96.
69. *The Friend of Sylhet*, February 1906, 24; *The Harvest Field*, 115f.
70. Ibid., 26.
71. Ibid., 27.
72. Ibid.
73. Emlyn H. Davies, E. Lewis Evans, *CGG*, 129.
74. CWM, Bengal, Box 21, 12 June 1906.
75. Ibid.
76. 'Sylhet', *Y Drysorfa*, November 1906.
77. 'Y Genhadaeth yn India', *Y Tyst*, 22 August 1906, 6.
78. Ibid., 'Wythnos Fawr yn Berhanpore', 12 September 1906.
79. Ibid.
80. The Jabalpur Convention', *The Harvest Field*, December 1906.
81. CMA, 27, 256, 4 August 1908; she was the niece of the Rev. Hugh Roberts, Rhyd-y-main, Merioneth. References to the Hensleys: Stock, *The History CMS*, vol. 4, 222, 182, 186, 232, 61.
82. 'The Seventh All-India Christian Endeavour Society Convention', *The Harvest Field*, January 1906.
83. Letter, 29 January 1906, *Y Drysorfa*, April 1906. This meeting of Welshmen is interesting: J. Pengwern Jones, J. Peter Jones and Sam Higginbottom. For J. Peter Jones

and Sam Higginbottom: D. Ben Rees, ed., *Llestri Gras a Gobaith* (Cyhoeddiadau Modern Cymraeg, 2001); for J. Peter Jones, *DNB*.

84. 'Darjeeling Convention', *The Christian Herald*, 1 November 1906, 18; 'Darjeeling', *The Friend of Sylhet*, September 1906.
85. Helen Dyer, *Revival in India*, 123; J. Edwin Orr, *Evangelical Awakenings in India*, 153; *Y Blwyddiadur* (CM), 1928, 233.
86. Mattersey, Donald Gee Centre, 'Special News Sheet Pelibhit', 15 September 1906, from the Industrial Evangelistic Mission.
87. Ibid.; J. Edwin Orr, *Evangelical Awakenings in India*, 151, 152.
88. CWM, North India, Box 21, letter J. A. Joyce, 11 April 1905.
89. Daniel Jones: T. M. Bassett, *The Baptists of Wales and the BMS*, 48.
90. J. Edwin Orr, *Evangelical Awakenings in India*, 153.
91. 'The Revival, Meerut', *The Friend of Sylhet*, January, May 1906.
92. 'Ludhiana', *The Friend of Sylhet*, August 1906.
93. 'Ajmera, Rajputana', *The Christian*, Supplement vii, 25 May 1905.
94. Basil Miller, *Praying Hyde* (Zondervan, 1964), 49; J. Pengwern Jones was present at these meetings, ibid. 57-8; Frederick and Margaret Stock, *People Movements in the Punjab* (Bombay, 1975), 132.
95. Stock, *People Movements in the Punjab*, 133.
96. Miller, *Praying Hyde*, 85; ibid., 123-6 for Praying Hyde's visit to Llangollen, North Wales, when J. Pengwern Jones was home on furlough; idem, 1943 edn., 57-9. David Smithers, 'John Hyde', A Revival Resource Centre, Internet.
97. CMA, 27, 256, 15 October 1906.
98. Mattersey, Donald Gee Centre, writing to F. Kehl, 18 February 1908.
99. 'News of the Revival in Wales and Elsewhere', *The Christian Herald*, 28 September 1905, 279; 12 October 1905, 323.
100. J. Edwin Orr, *Evangelical Awakenings in India*, 149; 'Sialkot', *The Friend of Sylhet*, October 1905. J. Pengwern Jones spoke on 'Can God Trust You?' and Miller says, 'The audience was swayed by the power of the Spirit working through him': *Praying Hyde*, 63.
101. 'Revival in India', *The Life of Faith*, 11 October 1905, 846.
102. CMA, 27, 256, 24 July 1906.
103. Ibid.
104. Ibid., 28 August 1906. For later Sialkot meetings: Miller, *Praying Hyde* (1943 edn.), chapter VII.
105. Frederick and Margaret Stock, *People Movements in the Punjab*, 135.
106. Helen Dyer, *Revival in India*, 101, 102.
107. 'Delhi', *The Friend of Sylhet*, August 1905.
108. CMA, 27, 256, 2 October 1907; for the continuing influence, J. Edwin Orr, *The Flaming Tongue*, 154.
109. Alfred Goodrich Garr (1874–1944): he was born in Danville, Kentucky, and educated at Danville, Asbury College, Woolmore, Kentucky. Ministered in India, Japan and China. He returned to the USA in 1911; was an itinerant preacher and then pastor of Garr Auditorium, *Dictionary of Pentecostal and Charismatic Movements*, 328-9.
110. Mattersey, Donald Gee Centre, Miscellaneous File, letter F. Kehl to George Wilson, 25 February 1907, and also, letter (n.d.) George Wilson to Kehl.
111. Ibid., Box File, containing extracts from letters.
112. Ibid., loose bundle, letter to Mrs Penn-Lewis, 4 July 1907.
113. Ibid., Indian file, letter to Kehl, 24 December 1907.
114. The Christian Missionary Alliance was founded by A. B. Simpson (1843–1919). Articles of Faith: baptism of the Spirit after regeneration, and healing as part of the redemptive work of Christ; did not insist on speaking with tongues as the sign of baptism with the Spirit: *Dictionary of Pentecostal and Charismatic Movements*.

115. Mattersey, Donald Gee Centre, Indian File, Longbucot Heard writing to Mrs Penn-Lewis, 17 July 1907.

116. Ibid., Loose Bundle, letter to Kehl, 18 April 1908.

117. Ibid.

118. A. T. Pierson contributed a series of articles to *The Christian* during 1907. Typical of Mrs Penn-Lewis's contribution was an article entitled 'The Present Onslaught', *The Life of Faith*, 29 May 1907, 469.

119. Mattersey, Donald Gee Centre, letter from Ward to Mrs Penn-Lewis, 30 March 1907, and in July of the same year he was urging believers to test the spirits: 'The Revival in India', *The Life of Faith*, 21 August 1907, 780.

120. T. B. Barratt, *When The Fire Fell*, 157-8.

121. Ibid., 160.

122. Brynmor Pierce Jones, *Trial and Triumphs of Mrs Penn-Lewis*, 143, but cf. 186, 189, 192-3.

123. Mattersey, Donald Gee Centre, Box File, 9 April 1907, 28 February 1907; Brynmor Pierce Jones, *Trials and Triumphs of Mrs Penn-Lewis*, 141.

124. Ibid.

125. Ibid., letter 6 April 1908; first meeting 3 April.

# Chapter 14: China, Korea and Manchuria

1. Detailed account of the period by A. J. Broomhall, *Hudson Taylor and China's Open Country*, Book Seven, Part Four. Archibald E. Glover, *A Thousand Miles of Miracles in China* (London and Glasgow, 1931 edn.).

2. Kenneth Scott Latourette, *A History of the Expansion of Christianity* (Exeter, 1971 edn.), vol. VI, 340.

3. J. Edwin Orr, *Evangelical Awakenings in Eastern Asia* (Minneapolis, 1975), 34, 35.

4. For Samuel Pollard: W. A. Grist, *Samuel Pollard, Pioneer Missionary in China* (Taipei, 1971 reprint), chapter III; 'S. Pollard West China Hwa Mio', *The Life of Faith*, 10 October 1906, 911.

5. Benjamin Williams: he had spent nine years in China but had to return because of ill health; died at Swansea 12 December 1905: 'Cwmbwrla', *Y Tyst*, 11 October 1905; idem, 'Cyfarfod Coffa'r Parch. Benjamin Williams', 29 December 1905.

6. The minister was David Jones, a native of New Tredegar; ministered at Cwmbwrla from 1870 until 1910: *Llawlyfr Undeb Abertawe a'r Cylch*, May 1960, 57.

7. SOAS, CIM/PP, Box 24, Fiche 485.

8. 'China', *The Chronicle*, September 1905.

9. The CMS missionary was William Müller, 'Y Diwygiad', *Tarian y Gweithiwr*, 8 June 1905.

10. *Y Diwygiad a'r Diwygiwr* (Dolgellau, 1906), 337.

11. 'News of Revival in Wales and Elsewhere', *The Christian Herald*, 21 December 1905, 542-3.

12. 'Shantung', *The Chinese Recorder*, June 1906.

13. Ibid.

14. Ibid.

15. Ibid.

16. E. W. Burt, 'A Pentecostal Experience', *The Missionary Herald*, August 1906; references to Burt in Brian Stanley, *History BMS*, 303, 305, 316. *Report Board Foreign Missions of the Presbyterian Church USA*, 1906, 49, 58.

17. Ibid.; Kenneth Scott Latourette, *A History of Christian Missions in China* (London, 1929), 619-20.

18. P. D. Bergen, 'Good News From Shantung', *The Chinese Recorder*, July 1906.

19. *Report Board Foreign Missions of the Presbyterian Church USA*, 1907, 124, 126.

20. Burt, *The Missionary Herald*, August 1906.
21. *Report Board Foreign Missions Presbyterian Church USA*, 1907, 100.
22. 'A Revival Still Continues', *The Chinese Recorder*, November 1906. At Union College 196 students out of 200 professed faith: J. Edwin Orr, *Campus Aflame*, 135.
23. Ibid., 'Chefoo', July 1906.
24. *Report Board Foreign Missions of the Presbyterian Church USA*, 1907, 110.
25. 'Spiritual Awakening in Yang-chow', *China's Millions*, September 1906.
26. *Report Board Foreign Missions of the Presbyterian Church USA*, 1907.
27. W. B. Sloane, 'A Survey of Revival Movements in China', *China's Millions*, January 1909, 5; Arthur Peill, 'The Spiritual Awakening in T'sang Chou', July 1906, 156-7.
28. Arthur Peill, *The Beloved Physician* (LMS, 1922), 112.
29. Ibid., 117.
30. Ibid., 123.
31. Frederick Charles Roberts (1862–94), Mary Roberts (1858–1933), E. Lewis Evans, *CGG*, 154-5.
32. Peill, *Beloved Physician*, 125; also, 'News of Revival', *The Christian Herald*, 5 July 1906, 15.
33. Ibid., 126.
34. Clark had suggested a collection to celebrate the Jubilee of the missionary Griffith John, and went to China to see the missionary personally: Noel Gibbard, *Griffith John, Apostle to China* (Bryntirion Press, Bridgend, 1998), 175. D. Wynne Evans: he was from Briton Ferry, South Wales; ministered at Llanrwst, North Wales, Llanelli, Chester and London: *Coflyfr y Dathliad, 1875–1925* (Llanelly, 1925), 19; Brynmor Pierce Jones, *The Spiritual History of Keswick in Wales*, 126, 127.
35. Peill, *Beloved Physician*, 126, 127.
36. Noel Gibbard, *Griffith John*, 185.
37. 'Missionary News', *The Chinese Recorder*, September 1907.
38. 'Awakening in Wu-Cheng', *The Life of Faith*, 10 July 1907.
39. Ibid.
40. 'Revival at Hou-Kou, Kiang-si', *China's Millions*, October 1906.
41. Ibid.
42. 'Missionary News', *The Chinese Recorder*, September 1909.
43. Martha Huntley, *To Start a Work: The Foundation of Protestant Mission in Korea* (Seoul, 1987), 408.
44. Henry Appenzeller: he was educated at Franklin and Marshall College, Pennsylvania, and entered Drew College to be prepared for overseas work; arrived in Korea in 1885: W. E. Griffis, *A Modern Pioneer in Korea* (New York, 1912) and Kwang Shun Chin, 'A Historical and Theological Assessment of the Korean Revival', Ph.D., University of Wales, 2000 ('Assessment'). A fellow Methodist was G. H. Jones: he arrived in Korea in 1887 and worked in the Chemulpo area; he started *The Korean Repository*, 1892, and *The Korean Review*, 1906: Kwang Shun Chin, 'Assessment', 122.
45. e.g. Horace G. Underwood, who was born in London, 1859; the family moved to America, and Horace attended the Dutch Reformed Church; he went to Korea with the Northern Presbyterian Church USA: Kwang Shun Chin, 'Assessment', 28-9; Lilliash Underwood, *Underwood of Korea* (New York, 1918). Dr Samuel Moffet: he arrived in Korea in 1890; set up the Pyeng Yang Seminary, and one of the first graduates was Sun-Ju Kil, a prominent revival leader: Kwang Shun Chin, 'Assessment', 33.
46. R. A. Hardie: he was born in Caledonia, Ontario. From 1892 to 1898 worked with the Canadian Colleges Mission Board; joined the Southern Methodist Board and became Principal of Hyeub-Sung Seminary: Kwang Shun Chin, 'Assessment', 111 n.4, 66.
47. George Paik, *The History of Protestant Mission in Korea* (Seoul, 1970 edn.), 367, 368.
48. Kwang Shun Chin, 'Assessment', 67.
49. Ibid., 72.

50. J. Edwin Orr, *Evangelical Awakenings in Eastern Asia*, 27.
51. William Blair and Bruce Hunt, *The Korean Pentecost* (Banner of Truth, 1977), 25. Kenneth Scott Latourette suggests other considerations: readiness to accept Western education and the need for the security the church could provide: *The History of the Expansion of Christianity*, vol. VI, 426.
52. 'More Messengers of the Cross', *The Life of Faith*, 11 July 1906, 592; 'Revival in Korea', *Missionary Review of the World*, May 1906, 395.
53. Huntley, *To Start a Work*, 410; *Report BFBS*, 1906, 282-3; George Thompson Brown, *Mission To Korea* (Board of World Mission Presbyterian Church USA, 1962), 59.
54. J. Edwin Orr, *Evangelical Awakenings in Eastern Asia*, 27.
55. Blair and Hunt, *The Korean Pentecost*, 66-7. Another missionary, Jean Perry, mentions the change that came over the lives of the missionaries, and that this led to a change in the lives of others: *Twenty Years A Korean Missionary* (London, n.d.), 42-3.
56. Kwang Shun Chin, 'Assessment', 77.
57. Paik, *Protestant Missions in Korea*, 368, quoting Graham Lee, 'How the Spirit Came to Pyeng Yang', *The Korean Mission Field*, vol. 3, no. 3, March 1907, 33-7. A report from North China referred to Johnston's visit to Britain and India. He was 'greatly impressed' with what he saw in these two countries: 'More Messengers of the Cross', *The Life of Faith*, 1 July 1906, 591; Henry A. Rhodes, ed., *History of the Korean Mission* (Seoul, n.d.), 281.
58. *Report Board of Foreign Missions of the Presbyterian Church USA*, 1907, 282.
59. Blair and Hunt, *The Korean Pentecost*, 61.
60. Graham Lee, 'A Mighty Work of the Spirit in Korea', *The Life of Faith*, 10 April 1907, 306; Kil was baptised by Graham Lee.
61. Early morning prayer: Paik, *Protestant Missions in Korea*, 377.
62. Blair and Hunt, *The Korean Pentecost*, 70; Graham Lee, 'A Mighty Work of the Spirit in Korea', *The Life of Faith*, 10 April 1907, 306.
63. Ibid., 72.
64. Ibid., 73; Samuel Hugh Moffett, *The Christians of Korea* (New York, 1962), 53; J. Edwin Orr, *Evangelical Awakenings in Eastern Asia*, 28-9.
65. Kwang Shun Chin, 'Assessment', 88, 80, 131.
66. Rhodes, *History of the Korean Mission*, 284.
67. Kwang Shun Chin, 'Assessment'.
68. Paik, *Protestant Missions in Korea*, 373.
69. Huntley, *To Start a Work*, 414.
70. Blair and Hunt, *The Korean Pentecost*, 76.
71. C. Howard Hopkins, *John R. Mott*, 307.
72. 'Revival News', *The Life of Faith*, 29 April 1908, 454.
73. Kenneth Scott Latourette, *A History of Christian Missions in China*, 574.
74. Duncan Maclaren, 'Outpouring of the Spirit in Manchuria', *The Life of Faith*, 18 March 1908, 284; 'An Awakening in Manchuria', *Missionary Review of the World*, June 1908, 284; *China's Millions*, July 1908, 113; Kenneth Scott Latourette, *History of Christian Missions in China*, 574-5; G. Thompson Brown, *Earthen Vessels* (New York, 997), wrongly gives 1908 as the year in which Goforth visited Korea, 486.
75. Jonathan Goforth: biography, Rosalind Goforth, *Goforth of China* (Grand Rapids, Michigan 1937).
76. Jonathan Goforth, *By My Spirit* (London and Edinburgh, *c*.1928)
77. Rosalind Goforth, *Goforth of China*, 177-8.
78. Ibid.
79. Mattersey, Donald Gee Centre, Box File, Jonathan Goforth, 'Prayer and Revival', from *The Life of Faith*, 4 December 1912.
80. See note 74.
81. Austin Fulton, *Through Earthquake, Wind and Fire* (Edinburgh, 1967), 48.

82. Rosalind Goforth, *Goforth of China*, 183.
83. Walter Phillips, 'The Revival in Manchuria', *The Chinese Recorder*, September 1908, 523.
84. James Webster, *Revival in Manchuria*, with introduction by Walter B. Sloan (London, 1909, 1910), 15-16.
85. Ibid., 17.
86. Ibid., 10.
87. Walter Phillips, 'The Revival in Manchuria', *The Chinese Recorder*, September 1908, 523.
88. Webster, Revival in Manchuria, 19.
89. Ibid., 77.
90. Ibid., 30.
91. Ibid., 35; *China's Millions*, July 1908, 114.
92. Jonathan Goforth, 'The God Who Can Move London', *The Life of Faith*, 5 May 1909, 460. He worked with students: J. Edwin Orr, *Campus Aflame*, 135, 254 n.15. Altogether he preached in twenty-eight cities: G. Thompson Brown, *Earthen Vessels*, 486.
93. CWM, North China, 2 March 1908; also 4 August, 2 November 1908.
94. J. F. Hoskyn, 'The Revival at Taning, Shansi', *China's Millions*, February 1909; also 'The Revival in Shansi', *The Chinese Recorder*, December 1908; Marshall Broomhall, *The Jubilee Story of the China Inland Mission* (London, 1915), 269.
95. 'The Revival in Shansi', *The Chinese Recorder*, December 1908.
96. Rosalind Goforth, *Goforth of China*, 194.
97. Ibid., 195.
98. Ibid., 198; Jonathan Goforth, *By My Spirit*, chapter VI.
99. Ibid.; Brynmor Pierce Jones, *The Spiritual History of the Keswick in Wales*, 21.
100. Orr-Ewing, 'The Revival in Kiangsi', *China's Millions*, October 1909.

## Chapter 15: Japan

1. J. Edwin Orr, *Evangelical Awakenings in Eastern Asia*, 21-2.
2. Ibid., 22.
3. Hopkins, *John R. Mott*, 255; J. Edwin Orr, *Evangelical Awakenings in Eastern Asia*, 24.
4. 'Our Teachers' Home in Llandrindod Wells', *The Life of Faith*, 15 August 1906, 748; J. Edwin Orr, *The Flaming Tongue*, 175.
5. J. Edwin Orr, *The Flaming Tongue*, 175. More detail on Kanamori in the section 'Leaves and Fruit'.
6. 'Revival Among Japanese', *The Christian Herald*, 18 May 1905, 433.
7. 'A Cheering Letter From Japan', *The Life of Faith*, 28 March 1906, 271.
8. J. Edwin Orr, *Evangelical Awakenings in Eastern Asia*, 24.
9. 'Christianity in Japan', *Evangelical Christendom*, May–June 1907, 77.
10. Hopkins, *John R. Mott*, 314.
11. Ibid.

## Chapter 16: Australia and New Zealand

1. J. Edwin Orr, *The Flaming Tongue*, 108-9.
2. Ibid., 109.
3. 'Gair o Queensland', *Y Goleuad*, 15 September 1905, 13.
4. Ibid.
5. Ibid.
6. 'Australian Sheaves', *The Christian*, 25 January 1906.
7. J. Edwin Orr, *The Flaming Tongue*, 111.

8. 'At Olygydd Seren Cymru', *Seren Cymru*, 30 March 1906, 11.
9. 'The Rev. Maurice Griffiths at Home', *The Llanelly Mercury*, 28 September 1905, 7.
10. 'New Zealand', *The Christian*, 23 November 1905, 23; J. Edwin Orr, *The Flaming Tongue*, 110.
11. 'New Zealand', *The Christian*, 7 December 1905, 14.
12. Ibid., 4 January 1906.
13. Ibid., 'A Note from the Antipodes', 16 August 1906, 25.
14. 'The Waihi Revival', *The Life of Faith*, 22 November 1905, 988.
15. Ibid.
16. Ibid.

## Chapter 17: Continuing Impact

1. *The Soul of France*, 211.
2. *Report BFBS*, 1913, 20. R. Tudur Jones has some helpful insights: *Ffydd ac Argyfwng Cenedl*, vol. 2, 203-6.
3. *The Overcomer*, 1909, 39.
4. Ibid. 118-19; 1910, 54; 1911, 168.
5. Ibid., 'The Bible Booklet in Russia', 1909, 55.
6. Neprash was the author of 'The Spirituality of the Welsh Revival'; it is included in *Glory Filled the Land*, ed. Richard Owen Roberts. More detail on developments in Russia: T. Omri Jenkins, *Five Minutes to Midnight*.
7. Nicholas Hope, *German and Scandinavian Protestantism, 1700–1918* (Oxford, 1995), 584, 585.
8. Ednyfed Thomas, *Bryniau'r Glaw*, 248-9; J. Meirion Lloyd, *Y Bannau Pell*, 117, 127, 197.
9. Moffett, *The Christians in Korea*, 52.
10. Ibid., 50; Geo. Heber Jones, 'The Growth of the Church in the Mission Field', *International Review of Mission*, vol. 1, 1912.
11. 'The Revival Fruit in Khasia', *The Overcomer*, 1911, 127.
12. Creech, 'Visions of Glory', *Church History*, 1996, 410. Hollenweger maintains that the 'Pentecostal theory about women and the actual roles which women play in the Pentecostal movement are not so easy to reconcile': *The Pentecostals*, 486, and his classification of Pentecostal women leaders, 486-8.
13. Bois, *Le Réveil au Pays de Galles*, 121-2.
14. R. Saillens, compiler, *Sur Les Ailes De La Foi* (1905; the thirteenth edition 2000, Nogent Sur Marne). 'Emynau y Diwygiad', *Seren Cymru*, 2 February 1906, 7, refers to a collection of hymns in French, translated from English versions used in Wales. The volume contained about forty tunes and about fifty hymns. The tunes included Tôn y botel, Caersalem and Bryn Calfaria. The translations of 'Dyma Geidwad' (Here's a Saviour) and 'Dyma gariad' (Here is love) were 'near the mark'. Could this volume be the first edition of *Sur Les Ailes de La Foi*? Other collections influenced by the Revival: the Khasi Hymn Book, 1922; the Peniel Hymn Book that was used by Peniel Independent Pentecostal Church, London. See next chapter for Ben Griffiths, the pastor.
15. De Fursac, 'La Musique Religieuse', *Un mouvement mystique contemporain*.
16. Ibid., 57, 58-9. The Saillens hymn book *Sur les Ailes de la Foi* is still used and has seen eight editions; information from M. Blocher, Nogent Sur Marne; Jack Hoad, *The Baptist*, 163. Welsh hymns and tunes also influenced collections in Germany and Khasia. In Britain, influence on *The Peniel Hymn Book* used by Peniel Independent Pentecostal Church; information from Mrs Jose and Mrs Dyer, Kenfig Hill.
17. D. G. Merfyn Jones, *Y Popty Poeth*, 79.
18. J. Meirion Lloyd, *Y Bannau Pell*, 78.
19. J. M. Lloyd, *Arloesydd Lushai*, 9, 14.

20.  R. J. Williams, *Y Parchedig John Roberts, DD*, 298, 278, 285.
21.  J. Meirion Lloyd, *Ar Bob Bryn Uchel*, 73-4.
22.  'Edwin Rowlands', *Glad Tidings*, February 1968; CMA, 27, 300.
23.  J. Meirion Lloyd, *Y Bannau Pell*, 96.
24.  E. Wyn James, 'Emynau Indiaidd J. Pengwern Jones', *Bwletin Emynau Cymru*, 1995–96.
25.  *India Awake*, 21, 28, 35.
26.  *The Friend of Sylhet*, 1906, 47.
27.  'A Visit to the Khassee Hills', *The Monthly Treasury*, June 1906; the Welsh version in *Trysorfa y Plant*, June, September 1906.
28.  'Wondrous Cross', *The Overcomer*, August 1910, 127.
29.  W. B. Boggs, *The Revival in India*, 8.
30.  *The Friend of Sylhet*, 1906, 27.
31.  'The Great Revival in Wales', *The Christian Herald*, 19 January 1905, 61.
32.  The poet and hymn-writer Evan Rees (Dyfed) wrote a hymn based on the revivalist's message to Anglesey, 'Cofiwch y gwaed' (Remember the blood): Ap Nathan, ed., *Emynau Dyfed* (Tonyrefail, 1924), 49.
33.  Kwang Shun Chin, 'Assessment,' 352-3; *The Friend of Sylhet*, 47.
34.  CMA, 27, 257; Brynmor Pierce Jones, *Trials and Triumphs*, 135-6.
35.  *India Awake*, 1905, 35.
36.  Robert Owen Jones, *Yr Efengyl yn y Wladfa*, 27, 28, 29.
37.  Ibid.
38.  'Pigion o Pittsburgh', *Y Drych*, 17 May 1906, 3; 18 January 1906, 5.
39.  *Evening Express*, 5 January 1905, 2.
40.  There are two versions of the collection: NLW, R. B. Jones Collection, Nos. 9 and 23.
41.  *Clychau Seion*, 43, 78, 79.
42.  Torrey's letter to Evan Roberts: D. M. Philips, *Evan Roberts*, beginning of Part 1.
43.  'Dr Torrey on Revival', *The Sunday Strand*, 1905. Norman Grubb could use the phrase 'continuous revival' and say that 'revival is really just obeying the Holy Ghost': *Continuous Revival* (London, 1952), 45.
44.  J. Kennedy Maclean, *Torrey and Alexander* (London, n.d.), 32.
45.  William Fetler, *The Fundamentals of Revival* (1929), 64-5.
46.  Ibid., 31.
47.  Ibid., 42, 45.
48.  Stephen Neill, *A History of Christian Missions*, 421.
49.  Mattersey, Donald Gee Centre, 'An Open Letter', Box File. For the different opinions within Pentecostalism: Hollenweger, section 4 in ch. 24 of *The Pentecostals*.
50.  See the section on Germany.
51.  'Pentecost and the Gift of Tongues', *The Life of Faith*, 10 November 1909, 1259, which includes the manifesto.
52.  Ibid.
53.  Ibid. An example of a criticism of the Berlin Declaration, 'This Movement is from Below', *Confidence*, August 1910; cf. J. I. Packer's discussion of the similarities and differences between 'evangelicals' and 'Pentecostals-charismatics': *Keep In Step With The Spirit* (Leicester, Inter-Varsity Press, 1984), chs. 5 and 6.
54.  'The Outpouring Spirit and Service', *The Overcomer*, July 1926.
55.  Ibid., 'Tarrying', 1911, 14; Hollenweger, *The Pentecostals*, 233.
56.  Ibid., 'An Autobiographical Sketch', December 1914; letter from von Redern to Mrs Penn-Lewis, 17 December 1907, Mattersey, Donald Gee Centre.
57.  Ibid. On the other hand, some believed that there was 'something of the occult' in Evan Roberts' methods: R. Tudur Jones, *Ffydd ac Argyfwng Cenedl*, vol. 2, 213.
58.  'Bilom-Bora', *The Chronicle*, April 1911.
59.  Mattersey, Donald Gee Centre, letter of J. Pengwern Jones, 2 February 1906.

60. Ibid.
61. 'The Swadeshi Movement', *Missionary Herald*, September 1907.
62. H. K. Synrem, *Revivalism in Khasi Society* (New Delhi, 1992), 12-13.

## Chapter 18: Revival, Doctrine and Society

1. Creech, 'Visions of Glory', *Church History*, 1996, 411.
2. Ibid., 421. 'The Pentecostal Movement', *Confidence*, August 1910. One of the Welsh leaders, William Andrews, Swansea, acknowledged the 'mighty work' that had been accomplished in South Wales, but 'we want something far greater than the Welsh Revival was', ibid., April 1910.
3. Brynmor Pierce Jones, *The King's Champions*, 160-1, 101, 227, 142.
4. Anderson, et al., *Mission Legacies*, 32.
5. Kwang Shun Chin, 'Assessment', 129.
6. Ibid.
7. Ibid. Iain Murray tends to overemphasise the negative aspects of premillennialism, e.g. *The Puritan Hope*, 203-6. It was a creative force in the lives of many individuals, groups and churches.
8. The Hutterian Society of Brothers and John Howard Yoder, eds., *God's Revolution* (New York, English translation 1983), 85, 61.
9. Eberhard and Emmy Arnold, *Seeking for the Kingdom of God*, 241-3.
10. *God's Revolution*, 51.
11. Ibid., 50. 'We say, the Holy Spirit is a harbinger of God's future', 31.
12. Ibid., 52.
13. Emmy Arnold, *A Joyful Pilgrimage*, 80-2; Markus Baum, *Against the Wind*, 219-21.
14. Markus Baum, *Against the Wind*, 101.
15. Ibid., 106-8.
16. Ibid., 107.
17. Ibid., 108.
18. Ibid., 65, 101; *God's Revolution*, 35-9; Emmy Arnold, *A Joyful Pilgrimage*, 31, 101, 113, 150-1.
19. Markus Baum, *Against the Wind*, 125, 141; Emmy Arnold, *A Joyful Pilgrimage*, chapters 4 and 7.
20. Markus Baum, *Against the Wind*, 147; Emmy Arnold, *A Joyful Pilgrimage*, 53. A number of the Blumhardts works have been translated into English. Karl Barth recommended their works. A recent study: Frank D. Macchia, *Spirituality and Spiritual Liberation: The Message of the Blumhardts in the Light of Württemburg Pietism* (Mettuchen, NJ, 1993); ibid., 'Waiting and Hurrying for the Healing of Creation: Implications in the Message of the Blumhardts for a Pentecostal Theology of Healing', *25th Meeting Pentecostal Studies*.
21. Markus Baum, *Against the Wind*, 19.
22. Ibid., 14, 72, 102, 119, 180.
23. Ibid.: for the development of his thinking on war, chapters 6 and 7. For Arnold's part in the later resistance movement in Germany: Marjorie Hindley, '"Unerwünscht": One of the Lesser Known Confrontations with the National Socialist State, 1933–37', *German History*, vol. II, No. 2, 1993.
24. D. W. Bebbington, 'Baptists and Fundamentalism in Inter-war Britain', *Protestant Evangelicalism*, ed. Keith Robbins (Oxford, 1990), 319. The trustees included R. Wright Hay (Bible League); idem, there were divisions within Methodism and Anglicanism as well, 201-2. 'The Bible Missionary Trust', *The Bible Call*, March 1923.
25. Cover of *The Overcomer*, July 1922. John Thomas was brought up in Maesteg, South Wales. Reminiscences of his early days: 'Incidents of My Youthful Days', *The Sunday Companion*, 2 January 1904; 'John Thomas, Lerpwl', *Seren Cymru*, 7 April 1905.

26. Brian Stanley, *The History of the BMS*, 378-80.
27. Watkin R. Roberts, 'Brwydr y Beibl' (The Bible Battle), *Yr Efengylydd*, February, May 1923; ibid. John Thomas, 'Y Feirniadaeth Ddinystriol' (The Destructive Criticism), April to December 1924.
28. Notice of meetings, *The Bible Call*, May, July 1924; May, June 1925; May–June, 1926.
29. 'Rev. J. Macdonald's Journal of a Visit to Wales', *The Bible Call*, June 1923.
30. D. W. Bebbington, 'Baptists and Fundamentalism in Inter-war Britain', 319.
31. 'The North East General Mission', *The Bible Call*, January 1926.
32. Brian Stanley, *The History of the BMS*, 379.
33. George Howells, *The Soul of India* (London, 1913), 407, 404, 413-14.
34. *The Bible Call*, September 1924, 138.
35. 'Modernism in India', *The Bible Call*, April–June, 1927.
36. Paul Kanamori, *Paul Kanamori's Life Story* (London and Glasgow, n.d.), 63.
37. Ibid., 93.
38. *How I Discovered Modernism Among American Baptists* (Baptist Bible Union of North America, 1924), 6-7. Introduction by T. T. Shields, Canada, who was closely associated with Baptists in Britain, and visited Porth, Rhondda. A few years later, there was a bitter dispute between Fetler and Shields. The American accused the Russian of exaggeration, ambition and dishonesty; he also believed that Fetler's teaching tended towards perfectionism: 'Pastor William Fetler', *The Gospel Witness*, 9 April 1931, ed. T. T. Shields. Fetler was also accused of changing his mind on the 'Pentecost' issue. He declared for 'pentecostalism', but then declared that he was a Baptist. Pentecostals, especially in America, thought that he was misleading them: C.W.S., 'A Statement Concerning Pastor William Fetler's Work in Eastern Europe', *The Gospel Call of Russia*, September 1930. Evangelical Baptists and Pentecostals in Wales continued to support Fetler. He was present at the opening of the Apostolic Church's old building at Pen-y-groes and his name can still be seen on one of the stones in the front wall. The Hall was raised in commemoration of the Revival of 1904–05.
39. Ibid., 12, 16, 17.
40. 'Editorial Notes', *The Bible Call*, Jan.–March, 1928.
41. 'The Prayer Outlook', *The Overcomer*, April 1925.
42. Mrs Henry M. Woods, *Revival in Romance and Realism* (London, n.d.), 25.
43. Ibid., chapter: 'A Momentous Occasion'.
44. Ibid., 123.
45. Ibid., 135-6.
46. Kwang Shun Chin, 'Assessment', 138-9.
47. Goforth, *Goforth of China*, 232-3.
48. Tatlow, *The Story of the Student Christian Movement*, 273. On the Continent, Arnold Eberhard deplored the emergence of a sceptical approach to Scripture in the SCM: Baum, *Against the Wind*, 44, 109-10. Later in life he became more subjective in his approach to Christian doctrine.
49. Ruth Rouse and Stephen Charles Neill, eds., *A History of the Ecumenical Movement* (Geneva, 1986 edn.), 360.
50. Robert E. Speer, 'Foreign Missions Or World-Wide Evangelism', *The Fundamentals*, vol. XII: a clear presentation of the uniqueness of Christianity.
51. Rouse and Neill, *A History of the Ecumenical Movement*, 603, 650; Tatlow, *The Story of the Student Christian Movement*, 489; Hopkins, *John R. Mott*, 332-5, 409-10.
52. Douglas Johnson, ed., *A Brief History of the International Fellowship of Evangelical Students* (Lausanne, 1964), 13, 14, 60, 68; idem, *Contending for the Faith* (IVP, 1979), 71-8.
53. *The Missionary Enterprise in China and America* (Cambridge, Mass., 1974), 128.
54. Brynmor Pierce Jones, *The King's Champions*, 142.

55. The popular lecture was 'The Higher Criticism the Greatest Crime of Modern Times', delivered at New College, Edinburgh. His article to *The Contemporary Review* was 'The Bankruptcy of the Higher Criticism'; criticised in *The Expository Times*, vols. XVI and XVII.

## Chapter 19: To the Ends of the Earth

1. E. Cynolwyn Pugh, 'Siloam Gyfeillon a'r Diwygiad', *Y Traethodydd*, May 1951; idem, 'The Welsh Revival of 1904/5', *Theology Today*, July 1955.
2. 'Reminiscences', *The Treasury*, 1978. Geraint Fielder, *Grace, Grit and Gumption*, 184-7.
3. He ministered in Cwm-bach, Aberdare; he was the author of *What is Revival?* (Ambassador, 1995), with an introduction by John Thomas (Liverpool, Bible College, Swansea, itinerant preacher).
4. Author of *I Saw the Welsh Revival* (Chicago, 1957). There are a number of different editions.
5. The brothers were from Cefn-mawr, Wrexham. Emlyn Davies was a vocalist and an ARCM; author of a hymn tune, 'Bryn Howel'. Arthur Davies was a baritone solo winner at the National Eisteddfod and had an outstanding ministry in Gilgal, Porthcawl. Both brothers helped R. B. Jones in revival meetings. NLW, Minor Lists, E. K. Jones, 'History of Gilgal Baptist Church, Porthcawl'; 'Revival Edition', *The Evening Express*, 18 February 1905, 3; article and photograph in *Y Tyst*, 23 May 1996, 3; information from Gethin Davies, Llangollen, one of the Davies family.
6. E. K Jones, 'History of Gilgal'; John McNeill (1854–1933): Alexander Gammie, *John McNeill* (London, Glasgow, Edinburgh, n.d.), with photograph of Arthur Davies and John McNeill, 80.
7. The Mission Hall was Bryn Seion, Cross Hands; the original group was from Bethania Welsh Congregational Church: Noel Gibbard, *Hanes Plwyf Llan-non* (Llandysul, 1984), 57.
8. NLW 19993, 'Autobiography of Edward Wilkins'.
9. Account of the journey: *Profiad Yn Nghyd A Hanes Taith Edward Wilkins o Gross Hands, Llanelli i Cape Town Deheudir Affrica* (Llanelli, 1910).
10. NLW, 19993D.
11. Ibid. Others that went 'by faith': Noah Evans to France, *Riches of Grace,* November 1927, 209; John Evans: David Matthews, *I Saw the Welsh Revival*, 109; Brynmor Pierce Jones, *How Lovely Are Thy Dwellings*, 20.
12. David Matthews, *I Saw The Welsh Revival*, 109; NLW, 19993D.
13. 'South Africa', *Confidence*, January 1911.
14. Eliazer Jenkins' sister was the mother of Sally (Evans), who married D. T. Griffiths: see the section on missionaries in this chapter. A brother had three sons who entered the Congregational ministry: Howell, Idris, and Emlyn Jenkins (who became President of the Welsh Union of Independents). Another brother gave the land to build the Mission Hall. Two descendants are still living in Cathays, Cardiff, the two sisters Betsy and Olwen; information from them. Noel Gibbard, *Hanes Plwyf Llan-non*, 57.
15. Mentioned in the previous chapter. 'The Pentecostal Movement', *Confidence*, August 1910; William Kay, *The Inside Story* (1990), 58-9.
16. T. M. Jeffreys kept up the revival prayer meeting, 'Ever since the Welsh Revival, our little Church nursed the Fire; our meetings have been kept open': 'News from Monmouthshire', *Confidence*, April 1908. By 1910 there were eighteen groups in Wales: Waun-lwyd (T. M. Jeffreys), Ton-y-pandy, Pen-y-groes, Pontarddulais, Pen-y-graig, Clydach Vale, Aberkenfig, Maes-teg, Cross Hands, Llandeilo, Mountain Ash, Grovesend, Ammanford, Cwm-twrch, Dowlais, Llwynhendy, Port Talbot and

Aberaeron: list in Desmond Cartwright, 'From The Valleys They Came', Appendix 1 (MA Thesis, Mattersey, in conjunction with Sheffield University).

17.  'Pastor Jeffreys' Departure to Armenia', *Confidence*, July 1910.
18.  Ibid., 'Pastor Jeffreys' Visit to Armenia', September 1910.
19.  Ibid. 'The Pentecostal Meetings in London', May 1912. Pastor Hill and D. S. Jones were friends, and both friendly with R. B. Jones, Porth: David Ollerton, *The Revival's Children* (1980), 6-8, 18-19, 23; photographs of Pastor Hill, 5, 23. T. Mercy, 18 Islwyn Road, Wattsville, Cross Keys, was a member of the PMU Home Reference Council: 'Index of Missionaries', Pentecostal Missionary Union (PMU). I thank Pastor Desmond Cartwright, Cardiff, for the opportunity to see this volume.
20.  Desmond Cartwright, 'From The Valleys They Came', 8. By 1912 the centres were: Aberkenfig, Aberaeron, Ammanford, Llwynhendy, Pen-y-groes/Bryn-teg/Gors-goch, Cross Hands, Llanelli, Glanaman, Trecynon, Pontardawe, Mountain Ash, Seven Sisters and Llandybie: *Showers of Blessing*, No. 8, 1912.
21.  'Index of Missionaries', PMU. The Union, a missionary organisation, was formed by A. A. Boddy and Cecil Polhill (one of the Cambridge Seven): William Kay, *Inside Story*, 57-9. The following had left before 1924: Blodwen Terrel, Cross Keys to India; Dan Wilkins, Kenfig Hill to South America; Dick Williams, South Wales: 'Wales', *Redemption Tidings*, June 1927; idem, 'Welsh Notes', June 1925.
22.  Ibid., Reports in *Redemption Tidings*, July, October 1924; May, September 1929. W. F. P. Burton, *God Working With Them* (London, 1933), 191, 195-7 and 259. Margaret Gittings is included; photograph of Mr and Mrs Gittings and baby opposite 260. Garfield Vale was from Gorseinon and his wife from Newport, Gwent; Leonard Gittings and his wife were from Pen-y-waun, Hirwaun: 'Index of Missionaries', PMU; Brynmor Pierce Jones, *How Lovely Are Thy Dwellings*, 109.
23.  Cyril Taylor: selection of references from *The Elim Evangel*, 'News From Our Congo Evangelist', December 1921; 'Itinerating in the Congo', November 1922; 'Reports from the Belgian Congo', September and November 1924; 'Itinerating in the Congo', April 1925; E. C. W. Bolton, *George Jeffreys*, ed. Chris Cartwright (Sovereign World, 1999), 52. George Thomas and his wife: selections from *The Elim Evangel:* 'Elim Missionaries for Mexico', January 1925; 'Items of Interest', February 1926; 'News From our Mexican Missionaries', May 1926; 'The Mexican Border', 1 August 1927; 'Preaching Christ Across the Seas', 1 September 1928. A number were 'anointed' for service in 1924, including Mr and Mrs George Thomas, Dowlais, for Mexico; Annie Jones, Ystrad; Garfield Owen, Ystrad; May Rensley, and Bernard Fox, Newport, for Africa; Dan and Gwennie Walters, Aberaman; E. J. North, Cric, for India: 'Port Talbot Convention', *Redemption Tidings*, October 1924. It was the first annual convention of the Assemblies of God in Wales and Monmouth.
24.  Brynmor Pierce Jones, *How Lovely Are Thy Dwellings*, Appendix A. Malcom R. Hathway, 'The Role of William Oliver Hutchinson and the Apostolic Faith Church in the Formation of the British Pentecostal Churches', unpublished lecture. List of centres and leaders: Pen-y-groes, Pastor D. Williams; Swansea, Pastor W. Boulton; Ammanford, Bro. W. J. Thomas; Cross Hands, Bro. D. C. Morgan; Glanaman, Bro. D. J. Davies; Llandybie, Bro. S. Bowen; Llwynhendy, Bro. Thos. Jones; Mountain Ash, Bro. T. Thomas; Pontardawe, Bro. W. James; Trecynon, Bro. J. Forward, and Tumble, Bro. D. J. Morgan: Worsfold, *The Origins of the Apostolic Church in Great Britain*, 72.
25.  'Penygroes Agog', *South Wales Press*, 15 January 1913, 8. Worsfold rightly says that the date 1917 is wrong, Rees Evans, *Precious Jewels* (Llandeilo, 1962), 8; but Worsfold himself gives the date as 5 March, *The Origins of the Apostolic Church in Great Britain*, 26.
26.  Worsfold, *The Origins of the Apostolic Church in Great Britain*, 54-5.
27.  Ibid., 64-5. Numerous references in *Showers of Blessing*, e.g. 'Editorial', April 1915;

'The Eternal Word', June 1915; 'Missionary Notes', August 1915; 'Missionary Notes', March–April, 1917.

28. Ibid., 28, 68, 72. 'Ffarwelio â Swift a Mrs Swift a'r Holl o honynt. A llawer o'r Saint ar y Station y boreu hwn am wyth o'r gloch fy gawsom gyfle i ganu moliant Iesu ar y Station, God be with you till we meet again': 'Dyddiadur' D. P. Williams, 13 December 1913, Swansea, Apostolic Office. [Entry from Diary of D. P. Williams, 13 December 1913, referring to the farewell for Mr and Mrs Swift at Swansea Station.] References to Swift at Siddall Hall, Swansea: *Confidence*, April 1912, 90; May 1912, 112.

29. 'To South America for Christ', *Riches of Grace*, July 1922, 25; Worsfold, *The Origins of the Apostolic Church in Great Britain*, 187, 228, 229, 230.

30. D. T. Morris: he was born in the Swansea Valley. The father was converted in the 1904 Revival but was a backslider. When restored, his baptism, and that of his wife, led to the son's conversion, *Riches of Grace*, July 1922, 28-9.

31. Worsfold, *The Origins of the Apostolic Church in Great Britain*, 230; letters from 'Jim' and 'George', *The Apostolic Missionary Herald*, October 1925; report of the farewell meeting for Myfanwy Williams, 'Departure of Welsh Lady Missionary for Argentina', *The Amman Valley Chronicle*, 3 June 1926, 4.

32. Letter from George Evans, 29 July 1925, *The Apostolic Church Missionary Herald*, October 1925.

33. Worsfold, *The Origins of the Apostolic Church in Great Britain*, 231.

34. Bath, Echoes of Service, D. T. Morris, Personal File; 'Departures', *Echoes of Service*, October 1930.

35. Thomas Napier Turnbull, *Brothers in Arms* (Puritan Press, 1963), 57. A word from God came to D. P. Williams in the Bournemouth Conference, 1913, 'Carmania, Carmania'. The prophet interpreted it as a ship on the sea with people going to another land. In 1922, three Apostolics left Liverpool in the ship *Carmania* for the USA: 'Cyfarchiad Ymadawol', *Riches of His Grace*, November 1922.

36. Ibid., 28.

37. Ibid., 61, 63, 67, 73-4; Worsfold, *The Origins of the Apostolic Church in Great Britain*, 221f, 232f. In 1926 the Apostolic Church had 4 churches in Argentina, 6 in Ireland and 2 in France; the Danish wing had missionaries in China, Russia and France: 'Departure of a Welsh Lady Missionary for Argentina', *The Amman Valley Chronicle*, 3 June 1926, 4.

38. Worsfold, *The Origins of the Apostolic Church in Great Britain*, 233-4, 236, 239-40. Letters from Bjorner to Pen-y-groes, *Riches of Grace*, December 1923.

39. Thomas Roberts and Dr Naeser: 'Reports–France', *The Apostolic Church Missionary Herald*, Convention Number 1926, 38-41; *Riches of Grace*, November 1927, 209. Roberts was staying in Dr Naeser's home. In 1928 Roberts was considered too young to be called a pastor: Minutes, Missionary Council Meetings, August 1928 (Swansea Office). The two missionaries were in France in 1925, and the date 1930 given by Frank Orna-Ornstein is too late: *France—Forgotten Mission Field* (Watford, EMF, n.d.), 129.

40. 'Great Convention at Caersalem', *Llanelly Mercury*, 27 October 1921, 3; Bath, Echoes of Service, D. T. Griffiths, Personal File; Fredk. A. Tatford, *Red Glow Over Eastern Europe* (Bath, Echoes of Service, 1986), 131-2; W. T. Stunt, Pulling, Pickering, Simmons, Boak and Warren, eds., *Turning the World Upside Down* (Bath, Echoes of Service, 2nd edn., 1972), 355. Another Welsh link: William Fetler and John Thomas, missionary and pastor in Korea. John Thomas was from Carmarthenshire and left for Korea in 1910 under the auspices of the Oriental Missionary Society; he was the main speaker at Fetler's Missionary Conference early in the 1920s: Gweneth Thomas Zarfon, *Faith as a Grain of Mustard Seed* (Cae'r Nant, 1995); reference to Thomas and Fetler, 175-6.

41. Stuart K. Hine, *Not You, But God* (Stuart K. Hine, 1973), 322.
42. Brynmor Pierce Jones, *Trials and Triumphs*, 166.
43. 'News From Poland', *The Overcomer*, January 1923; McCaig, *Wonders of Grace*, ch. 28.
44. 'A Message From Poland', *Yr Efengylydd*, July 1926; Reports, 'Poland', *Echoes of Service*, June 1926, May 1931, April 1933.
45. Arianwen Jones was with R. B. Jones in the Training School: Brynmor Pierce Jones, *The King's Champions*, 290.
46. Hine, *Not You, But God*, 35.
47. Ibid., 45; Stunt, et al., *Turning the World Upside Down*, 355. They were regarded as Open Brethren from 1921. Nantlais mentions a Davies from Llandeilo who went with the Open Brethren to India. He was the brother of W. H. Davies (BMS); the first name is not given: Nantlais, *Gogledd Myrddin a'r Genhadaeth Dramor* (Ammanford, 1926), 20. There is no Davies from Wales listed in W. T. Stunt, et al., *Turning The World Upside Down*.
48. Hine, *Not You, But God*, 35.
49. 'Poland', *Echoes of Service*, March 1926.
50. Hine, *Not You, But God*, 50; Stunt, et al., *Turning The World Upside Down*, 615; Bath, Echoes of Service, Personal File. Hine has a photograph of Mr and Mrs Griffiths, Mr and Mrs Hine, Mr and Mrs Shneidrook and Mr and Mrs McCregor: *Not You, But God*, 58.
51. Norman Grubb, *Rees Howells Intercessor* (London, 1969), chapters 2–4 for the background; 36, 149. Evan was a farmer's son, from Bronwydd, near Carmarthen: J. D. Williams, *Cynhadledd y Sulgwyn Rhydaman*, 18.
52. Fiedler, *The Story of Faith Missions*, 220.
53. Norman Grubb, *Rees Howells*, 158.
54. Ibid., 166.
55. Ibid., 167; Rees Howells, 'Diwygiad Affricanaidd', *Yr Efengylydd*, February 1916.
56. Ibid., March 1916.
57. Ibid., 'Diwygiad Rusitu', January 1917.
58. Norman Grubb, *Rees Howells*, 173, 174.
59. Ibid., 179.
60. 'Gair o Ddwyrain Affrica', *Yr Efengylydd*, November 1923. He was present at the Llanelli Convention, 1921: *Llanelly Mercury*, 27 October 1921, 3.
61. Ibid., 'Dros Dir a Môr', August, September 1923; Bassett, *The Baptists of Wales and the BMS*, 28, 70; The Howellses sailed from Liverpool, 5 November; farewell meetings for Watkin Edwards 5 and 12 November: entries from the Diary of Mr Perkins, sent by his son Ronnie Perkins, Carmarthen.
62. Norman Grubb, *C. T. Studd* (London, 1978 edn.), 162; Brynmor Pierce Jones, *The Spiritual History of Keswick in Wales*, 27. Albert Davies was the son of the Rev. Trefor Davies, Llanelli; minister of Soar Congregational Church. An uncle was Thomas Davies, well-known Apostolic in Pen-y-groes and further afield. Two of Thomas Davies's sons are Gaius Davies, Kent, former co-editor of the Welsh Evangelical Magazine, and Dr Albert Davies, Cardiff. A sister of Albert Davies married Anthony Davies ('Llygad Llwchwr'), correspondent of the *News Chronicle*. There were eight children altogether; two died when young. 'Death of Rev. W. Trefor Davies', *Llanelly Mercury*, 4 January 1934, 3; information received from Gaius and Albert Davies, and Michael Brogden, WEC.
63. Alfred B. Buxton, *The First Ten Years of the Heart of Africa Mission* (London, 1920, 4th edn.), 33; more information, 51-3; photographs, 53, 121, 123. William Edwards, Principal of the Baptist College, Cardiff, was one of the Mission's referees, ibid., 73; Norman Grubb, *Alfred Buxton of Abyssinia and Congo* (London, 1942), 46.
64. Emily Davies was at Porth with R. B. Jones, 1920–2: Brynmor Pierce Jones, *The*

*King's Champions*, Appendix C. Emily Davies married Ronald Swift of Leicester in 1929; he was another Heart of Africa missionary. After her husband's death in 1943, Emily and her three children returned home to join her fourth child; information received from Michael Brogden, WEC.

65. Edward Evans: *The Lightbearer*, references from 1908 to 1917. Letter from the SUM archivist: 'Edward Evans seems to have left Nigeria in 1925 when the Freed Slaves Home closed.' Welsh letters from Edward Evans in *Y Goleuad*, 25 August, 5; 1 September, 10, 1909; 20 July, 8-9, 3 August, 1910. Other Welsh persons working in Africa were: Mrs. Fallows with the Africa Inland Mission (AIM); she was on fur-lough in 1921 and speaking at the Ammanford Convention, 'Cynhadledd Ammanford 1921', *Yr Efengylydd*, July–August 1921; E. Owen was on furlough in 1925, but returning to Africa: 'From An Outgoing Missionary', *Yr Efengylydd*, July 1925.

66. 'Gwaith ar Linellau Ffydd', *Yr Efengylydd*, March 1912. For the societies working in South America: Stephen Neill, John Goodwin, Gerald H. Anderson, *Concise Dictionary of Christian World Mission* (London, 1970, 1971); W. Mann, *An Unquenchable Flame* (London, 1968). Willis Collins Hoover, the 'Father of Pentecostalism' in Chile, monitored the work of Evan Roberts and A. B. Simpson and was also influenced by Mukti, India, 'Willis Collins Hoover (1856–1936)', *Dictionary of Pentecostal and Charismatic Movements*.

67. In 1911 the family lived in 1 Millwood Street, Notting Hill: husband and wife, Elis and John, Edith and Gladys, Thomas included in italics: *Annual Report*, Charing Cross Welsh Presbyterian Church, 1911, sent by Merfyn Thomas, National Library of Wales, Aberystwyth; Charles Edwin Jones, *A Guide to the Study of the Pentecostal Movement* (New Jersey and London, 1983), 600; Donald Gee, ed., *Pentecost*, March 1956, 10. The church was situated in Kensington Park Road, on the corner of Elgin Crescent.

68. Reminiscences of Mrs Jose and her daughter, Mrs Dyer, Kenfig Hill.

69. Brynmor Pierce Jones, *Spiritual History of Keswick in Wales*, 34-5; J. D.Williams, *Cynhadledd y Sulgwyn*, 17-18.

70. 'The Bible School for Christian Workers', *Yr Efengylydd*, Nov–Dec., 1919; Brynmor Pierce Jones, *The King's Champions*, 235-6. A valedictory service for a missionary in 1916 confirmed the conviction that there should be suitable training for missionaries: Noel Gibbard, *Taught to Serve*, 20-2.

71. Brynmor Pierce Jones, *The King's Champions*, Appendix C. For some reason Lilian Jones is not included, and Bronwen Hale is included under 'Students Eventually Placed In Pastorates'; 'O'r Maes Cenhadol', *Yr Efengylydd*, June 1924, August 1926.

72. Ibid., Michael Rowe, *Russian Resurrection*, 79-80.

73. R. B. Jones, 'I Riga ac yn Ôl', *Yr Efengylydd*, February 1927; Brynmor Pierce Jones, *The King's Champions*, 210.

74. Noel Gibbard, *Taught to Serve*, 23-32. Biographies of Ieuan and Sarah Jones, Ioan Wyn Griffith, *Draw Draw yn China* (Abertawe, 1997), 243-5.

75. 'The Testimony of a Geneva Evangelist', *The Overcomer*, 1914, 142-3; *Geneva Bible Society Jubilee Year* (Geneva Bible Society, 1993); Noel Gibbard, *Taught to Serve*, 66-8, 101.

76. Phoebe Joyce Evans (née Hall), 1890–1987: SOAS, biographical detail, PP MS 63, Box 14, File 67. She said that the missionary call would be coming and going but 'would return stronger than ever', File 68, volume 1. File 67 includes tributes to 'Mrs Madagascar Evans' paid at her funeral in Swansea, 30 June 1987, by Miss Gwyneth Evans, retired Madagascar missionary, and the Rev. F. M. Jones, minister of the deceased.

77. Details of her work in Madagascar and her return to Britain, File 68 and volumes 2 and 3. E. Lewis Evans should have included her with her husband, *CGG*, 133. Another Welshwoman, Mary Roberts, felt the influence 'deriving directly from Welsh revival-ist tradition': Rosemary Seton, 'Welsh Woman Missionaries of the London

Missionary Society' in 'Wales, Women and Religion', *Journal of Welsh Religious History*, vol. 7, 1999, 116.

78. SOAS, CWM, Candidates' Papers, Box 14; 'Ordeinio Cenhadwr', *Yr Efengylydd*, August, 1926.

79. Ibid. It was with the LMS that he went to Madagascar and not with a Faith Mission as stated by Brynmor Pierce Jones, *The King's Champions*, 240. He pastored in Mission Halls after returning.

80. SOAS, CWM, Candidates' Papers, Box 39; NLW, 13716C; E. Lewis Evans, *CGG*, 89; T. Lloyd Roberts, 'Y Gŵr o'r Blaenau', *Y Cylchgrawn Efengylaidd*, Winter, 1960.

81. NLW, 13716C.

82. 'Gweithwyr i'r Cynhaeaf', *Yr Efengylydd*, August 1909, and reports 'Africa', 1909–18; Bassett, *The Baptists of Wales and the BMS*, 67.

83. See the section on France. J. W. Hughes, *A Brief Memoir* (London, 1962), 19; Bassett, *The Baptists of Wales and the BMS*, 66-7; Oxford, The Angus Library CP/362, A 42; his wife, Margaret, died 5.4.58.

84. Brian Stanley, *The History of the Baptist Missionary Society*, 138, 350. Another Welsh person, W. H. Davies, Llandeilo, left for India in 1924 but returned in 1927 because of ill health. His wife, Eunice (Thomas), was the daughter of the Rev. T. Thomas, Carmel, Llandybie: 'Dros Dir a Môr', *Yr Efengylydd*, January 1925, March 1926; Bassett, *The Baptists of Wales and the BMS*, 56.

85. Bassett, *The Baptists of Wales and the BMS*, 53; 'Cwrdd Ymadawol Miss Beatrice James', *Seren Cymru*, 22 November 1907; Brynmor Pierce Jones, *Sowing Beside All Waters* (Gwent Baptist Association, 1985), 132-3.

86. Ibid., 56; Brynmor Pierce Jones, *The King's Champions*, 236-7, Appendix C.

87. Ibid., 53-4; Lilian M. Edwards, *A Welshwoman's Work in India*, 4-6; Oxford, The Angus Library, India, Box 1N/68. A moving account of her dedication is given by T. W. Chance, ed., *The Life of Principal Edwards* (Cardiff, 1934), 132-3.

88. Ernest Garfield Evans, another Baptist, spent some time in Lushai; he became an army chaplain and ministered at home: Brynmor Pierce Jones, *The King's Champions*, Appendix C. Bassett has a Garfield Ernest Evan entering Cardiff Baptist College in 1932. He went to Lahore in 1936, *The Baptists of Wales and the BMS*, 57.

89. See sections on France and Russia. D. T. Morgan was another Baptist who left the BMS and with Watkin R. Roberts joined the Baptist Missionary Trust. See section on 'Continuing Impact'.

90. Pearce, *Knight in Shining Armour*, 24-5, 29, 33; *Report*, American Baptist Missionary Union, 1906, 388; *Report*, American Baptist Foreign Mission, 1912, 133.

91. Pearce, *Knight in Shining Armour*, 31.

92. Ibid., 42.

93. Ibid., 43.

94. CMA, Register of Missionaries.

95. CMA, 27, 314; D. E. Jones, 'Hunangofiant Cenhadwr', *Y Seren* (Y Bala), 17 June 1950, 2; J. Meirion Lloyd, *Y Bannau Pell*, 105, 158, 266.

96. CMA.

97. Ibid., 27, 338.

98. Ibid., 27, 363.

99. Ibid., 27, 319; 'Y Golofn Genadol', *Y Goleuad*, 14 September 1910, 10.

100. Ibid., 27, 337.

101. Ibid., 27, 330. He was a cousin of Fred and Mary Roberts, Tientsin, China.

102. Eifion Evans, *The Welsh Revival 1904*, 58.

103. 'Outward Bound from Doric Lodge', *The Regions Beyond*, July 1908; CMA, 27, 311; D. G. Merfyn Jones, *Y Popty Poeth*, 114-15.

104. CMA, 27, 341. Helen Rowlands was an outstanding missionary, combining academic

ability and godliness; some of her letters were published in Welsh: *Pwy a'n Gwahana?*, ed. Evelyn Roberts (Porthmadog, n.d.); G. Wynne Griffith, *Cofiant Cenhades* (1961).

105. Hetty Evans, Nurse Hopkins, CMA, 27, 338, 363.
106. Ednyfed Thomas, *Bryniau'r Glaw*, 174, 184, 199-200, 225, 250; CMA, 27, 347; 'Yr Oriel Genhadol', *Y Cenhadwr*, vol. III, 6. Sidney Evans (1883–1960) was born in Morriston, and not in Gorseinon as stated in *Llestri Gras a Gobaith*, 61.
107. *Annual Reports*, Primitive Methodist Mission, 1913–19; photograph, 1914–15, xlix.
108. Ednyfed Thomas, *Bryniau'r Glaw*, 184, 220. Other CM missionaries that could be mentioned are Frederick Joseph and Margaret Sandy. They were influenced by J. M. Saunders and his wife, both prominent in the 1904–05 Revival: J. Meirion Lloyd, *Y Bannau Pell*, 159. Sandy welcomed the revival in Lushai in 1919, *Y Drysorfa*, 1920, 36-7.
109. 'Lushai', *Y Drysorfa*, January 1910.
110. J. Meirion Lloyd, *Y Bannau Pell*, 101,103-4.
111. 'Llythyr o Lushai', *Y Goleuad*, 8 September 1909, 6.
112. Ibid., 'Detholion o Lythyrau', 1910, 10.
113. CMA, 27, 314, 315, 316.
114. 'Llef o Macedonia', *Yr Efengylydd*, 1915, 168; *Y Drysorfa*, August, December 1915.
115. J. Meirion Lloyd, *Y Bannau Pell*, 96.
116. Ibid., 102, 106; 'Cenhadaeth y Thado-Kukie', *Yr Efengylydd*, April 1916, and further information May 1912, May 1918, December 1920, February, May 1923; a number of articles during 1925.
117. 'Overcomer Reprints in India', *The Overcomer*, December 1914.
118. Back cover of *The Overcomer*, July 1922.
119. J. C. Williams: he was a friend of Evan Roberts and Mrs Penn-Lewis; worked with the Russian Missionary Society: 'The Editor's Personal Letter', *The Overcomer*, July 1926.
120. Ibid., back page, January 1924.
121. Ibid., July 1923.
122. *Independent Church of India* (Brochure, 1986).
123. 'The Independent Church of India', *The Evangelical Magazine of Wales*, 22:4, 1983. The article does not refer to the Frazers and says that Watkin R. Roberts went out from Canada. He went out from Wales and went to Canada later. Also: 'Cenhadon Cymreig Bryniau Manipur', *Y Cylchgrawn Efengylaidd*, 21:2, 1983; 'Un o Wyrthiau'r Ugeinfed Ganrif', XVI:2, 1977.

# Index